A FIFTH LAKELAND SKETCHBOOK

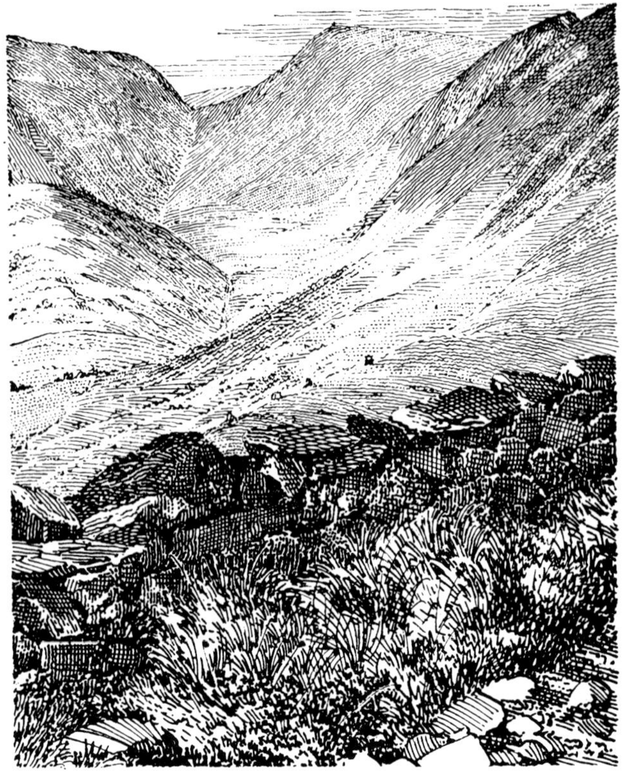

The upper Troutbeck valley

PUBLISHED
by
FRANCES LINCOLN
LONDON

A FIFTH
LAKELAND SKETCHBOOK

A Wainwright

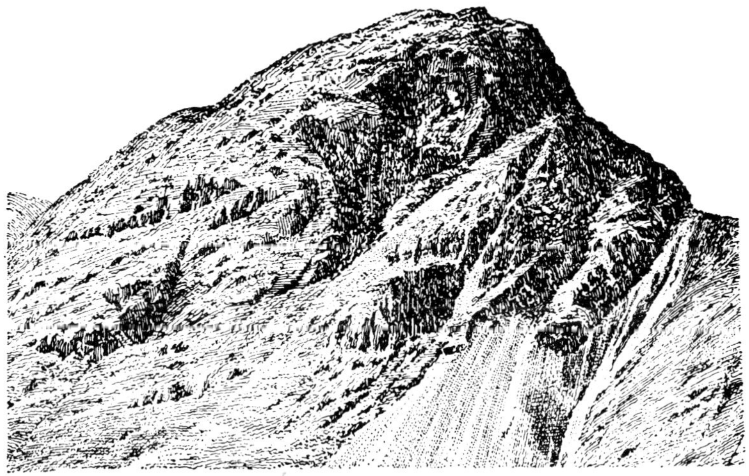

Stirrup Crag, Yewbarrow

FRANCES LINCOLN LIMITED
4 Torriano Mews
Torriano Avenue
London NW5 2RZ
www.franceslincoln.com

First published by Frances Lincoln 2004
Originally published by the Westmorland Gazette, Kendal, 1973

Printed and bound in Singapore

A CIP catalogue record is available for this book from the British Library.

ISBN 0 7112 2337 8

THE MAPS IN THIS BOOK

Each drawing is accompanied by a simple map designed to identify the location of the viewpoint in relation to its surroundings.

Conventional symbols are used, and additionally, where necessary, the viewpoint is indicated thus: ⓥ and, in the case of a distant view, the limits of the range of view are indicated by dotted lines, thus:

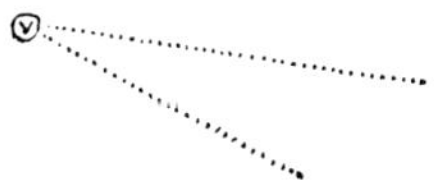

All these maps are on the scale of two miles to an inch, and the top of each is north.

THE DRAWINGS IN THIS BOOK *in the order of their appearance:*

Brockhole, built privately as a country house, is now owned by the Lake District Planning Board and used as a National Park Centre with the object of assisting visitors to appreciate the district more fully by means of educational and information services, a purpose it serves admirably.

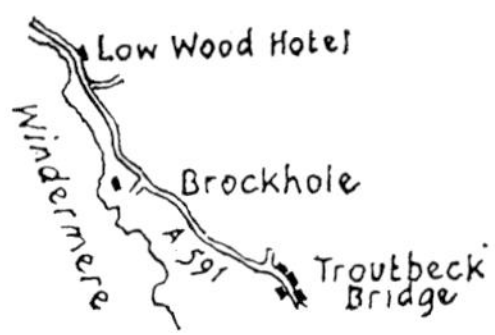

321 Brockhole, Windermere

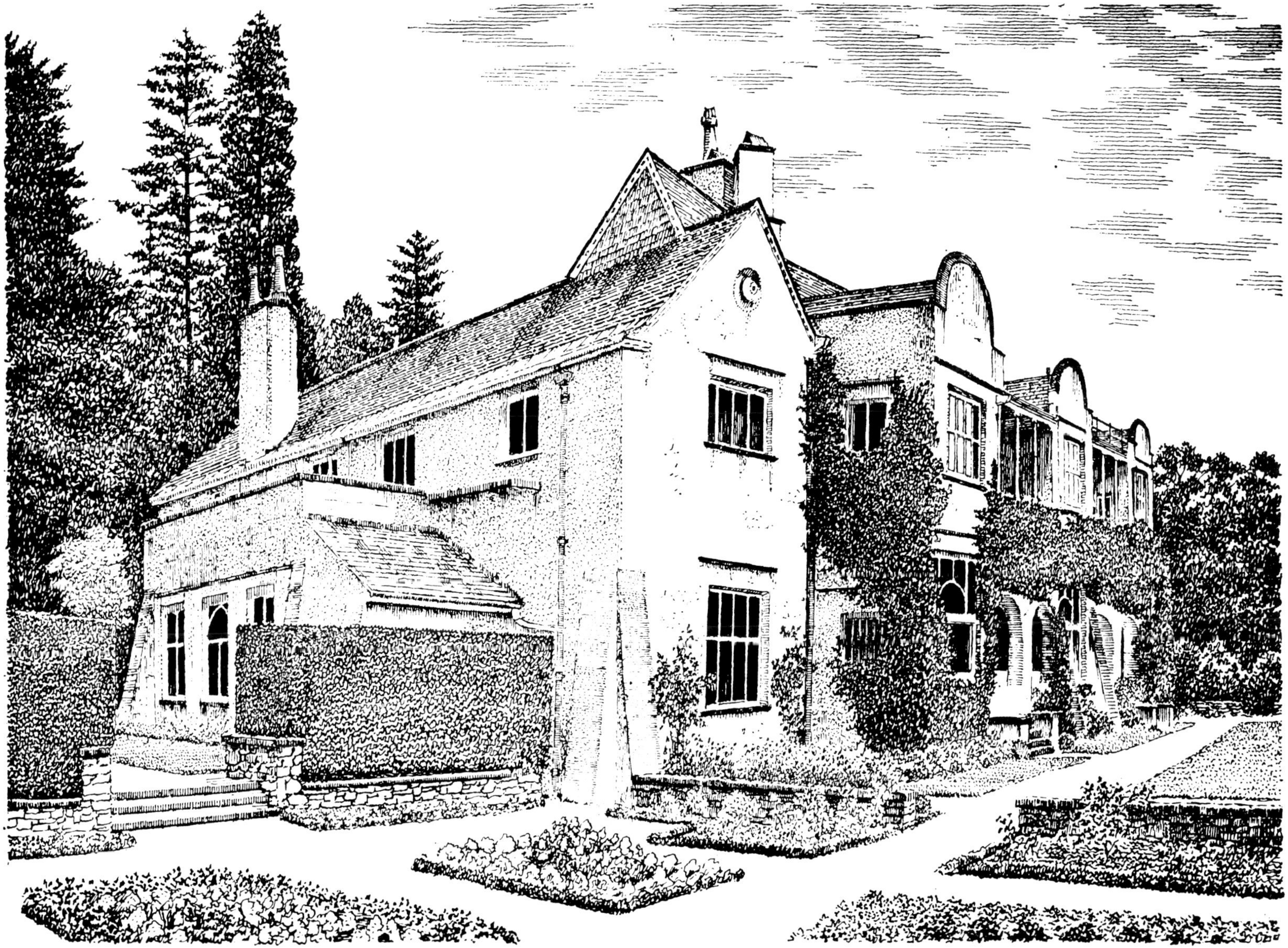

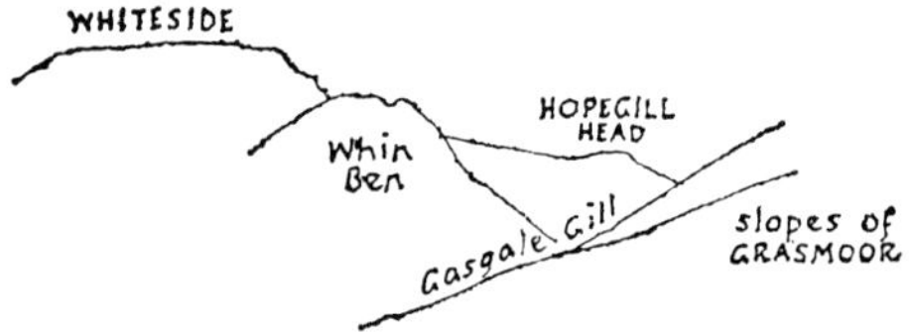
WHITESIDE
HOPEGILL HEAD
Whin Ben
Gasgale Gill
slopes of GRASMOOR

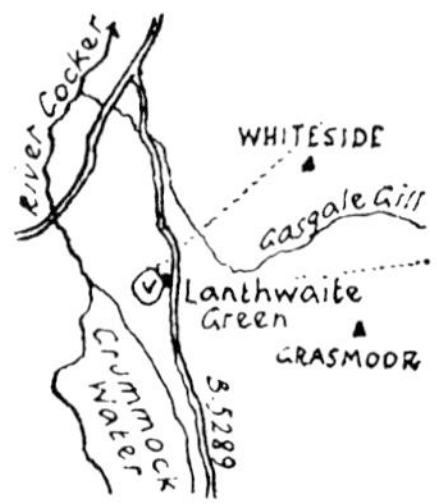
River Cocker
WHITESIDE
Gasgale Gill
Lanthwaite Green
GRASMOOR
Crummock Water
B.5289

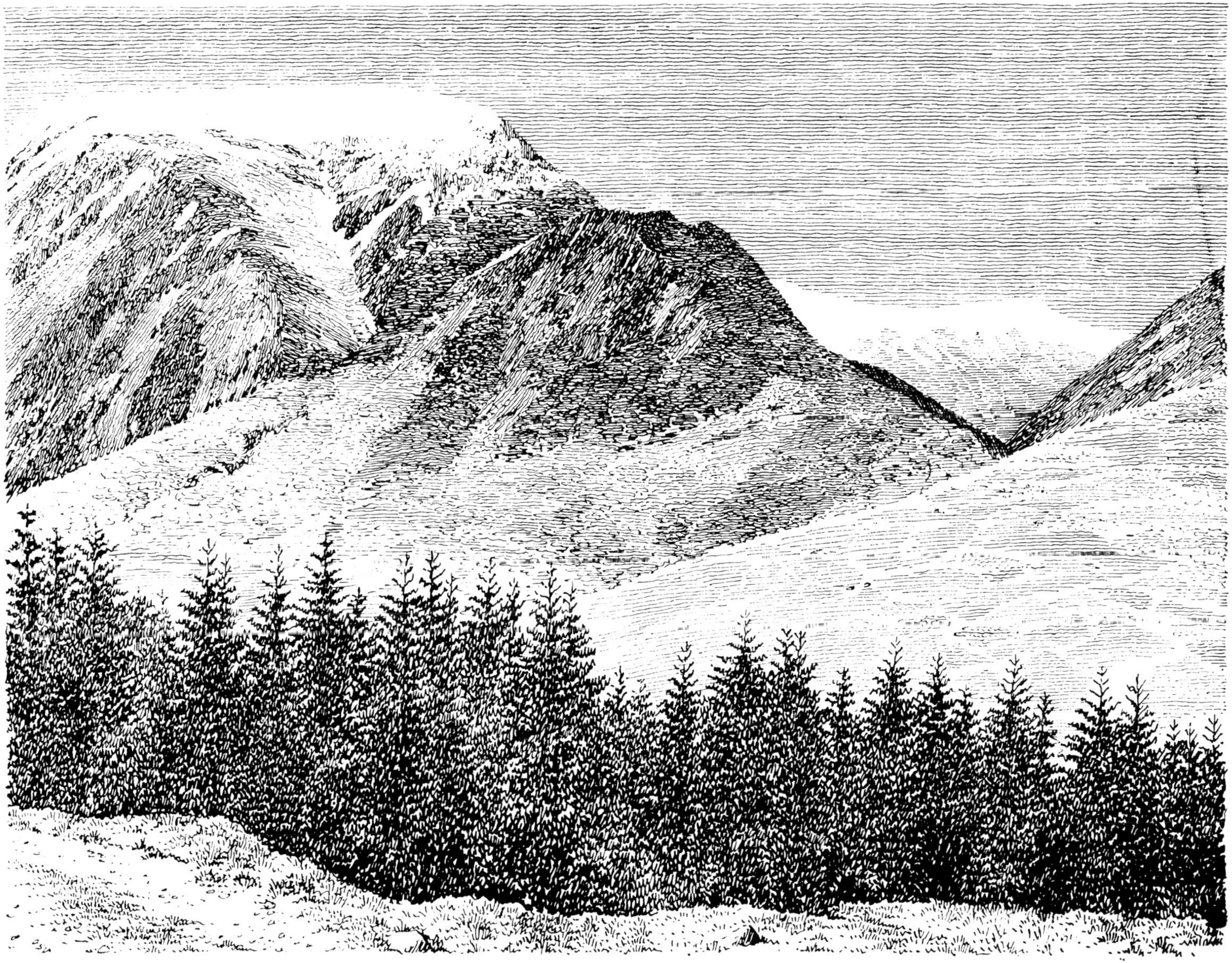

Esthwaite Water is one of the quietest of the lakes, rarely in the news, yet a lovely sheet of water in wooded surroundings. Its appearance is gentle, its disposition tranquil, and it lacks the exciting appeal of lakes set amongst mountains.

But it is a gem in its own right.

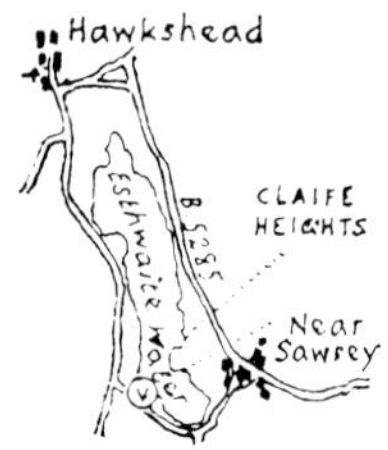

323 Esthwaite Water

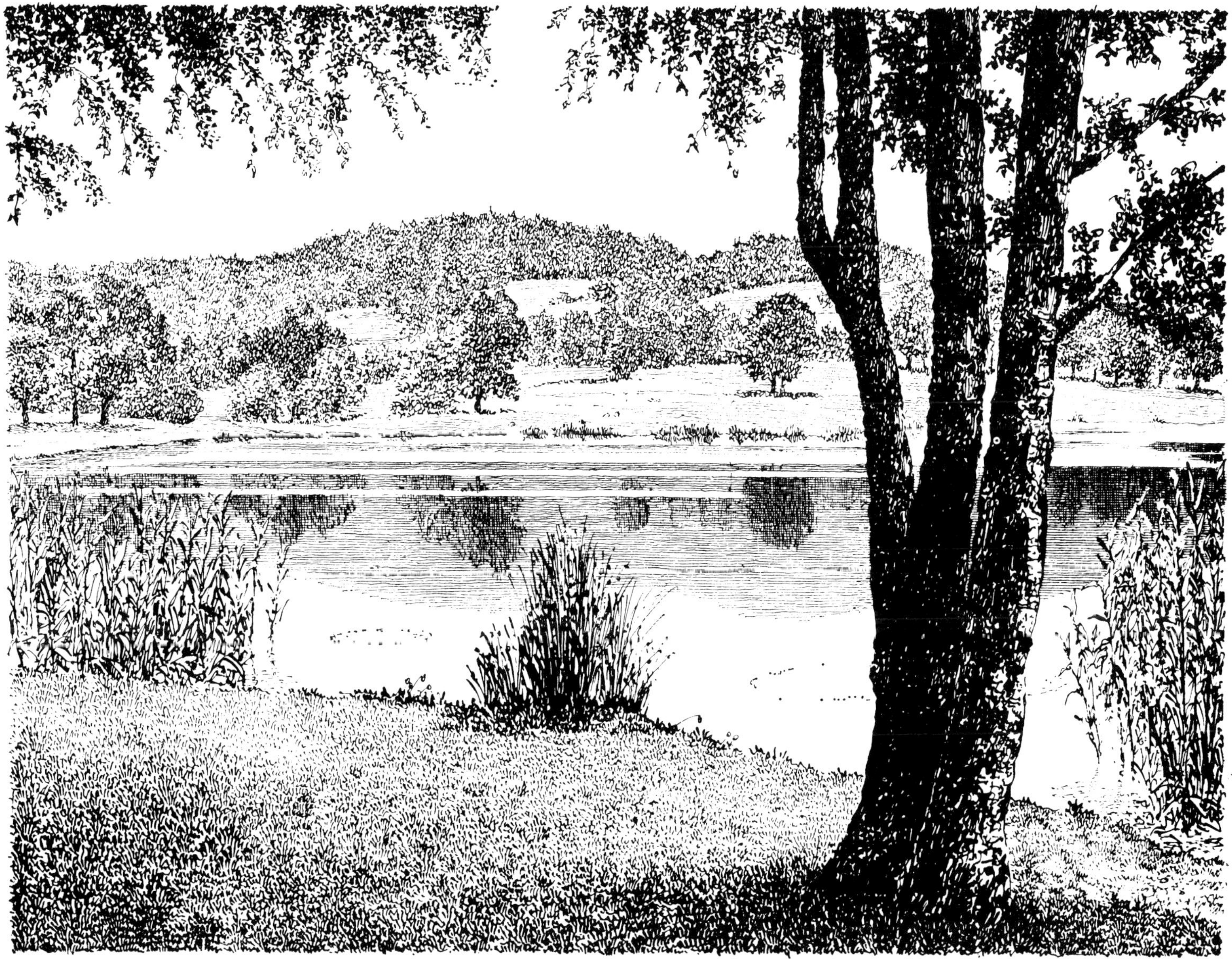

324 **Great Gable, from Haystacks**

Great Gable towers grandly over the head of Ennerdale and is well viewed across the gulf from the top of Haystacks, which has, in addition to many interesting natural features, a series of iron posts marking the boundary of the Lonsdale estate.

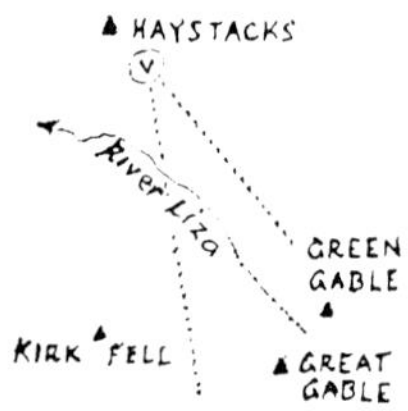

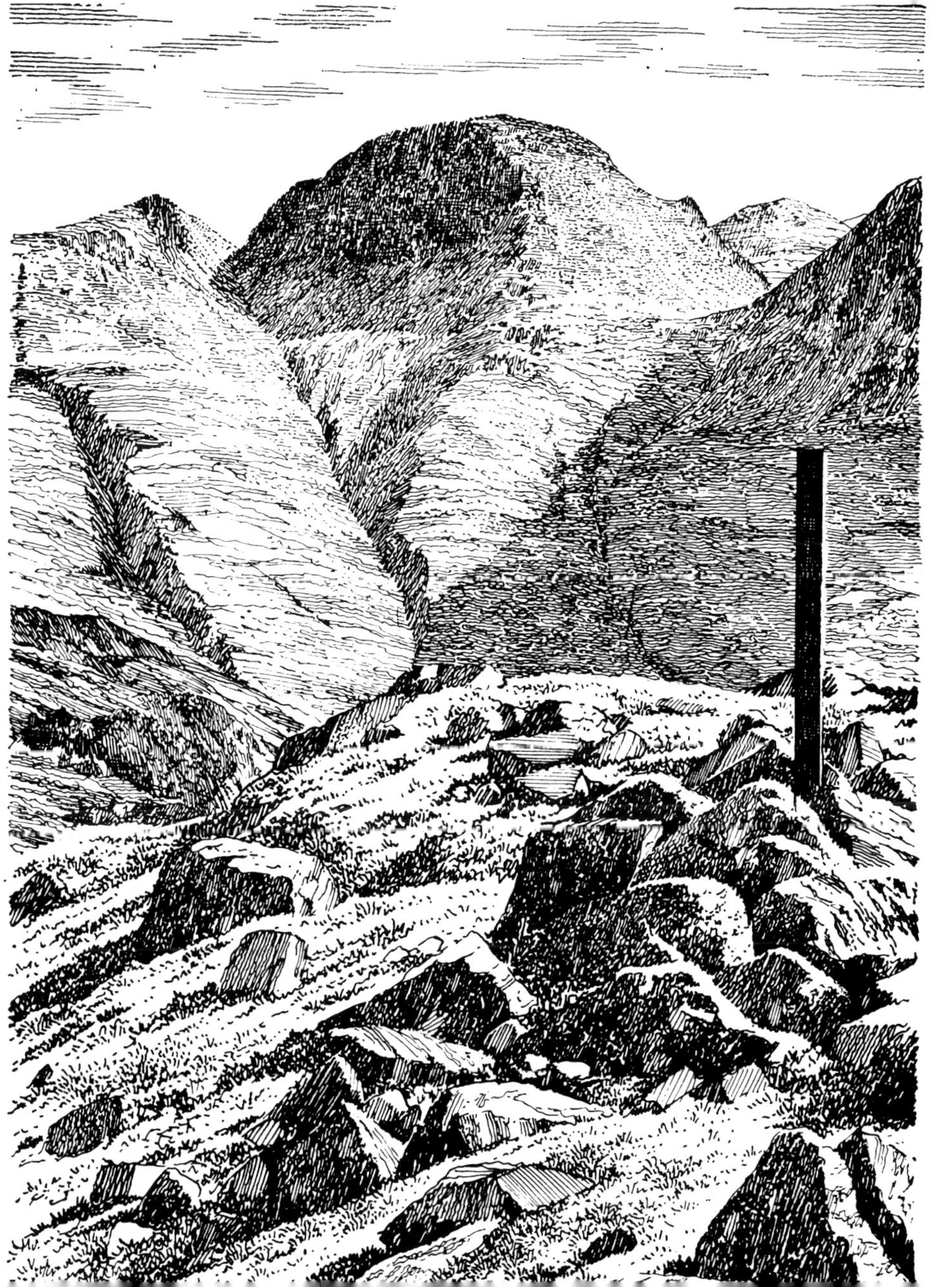

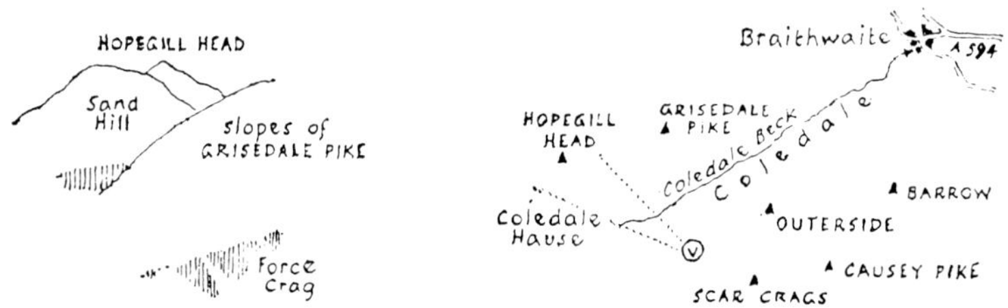

325 The head of Coledale

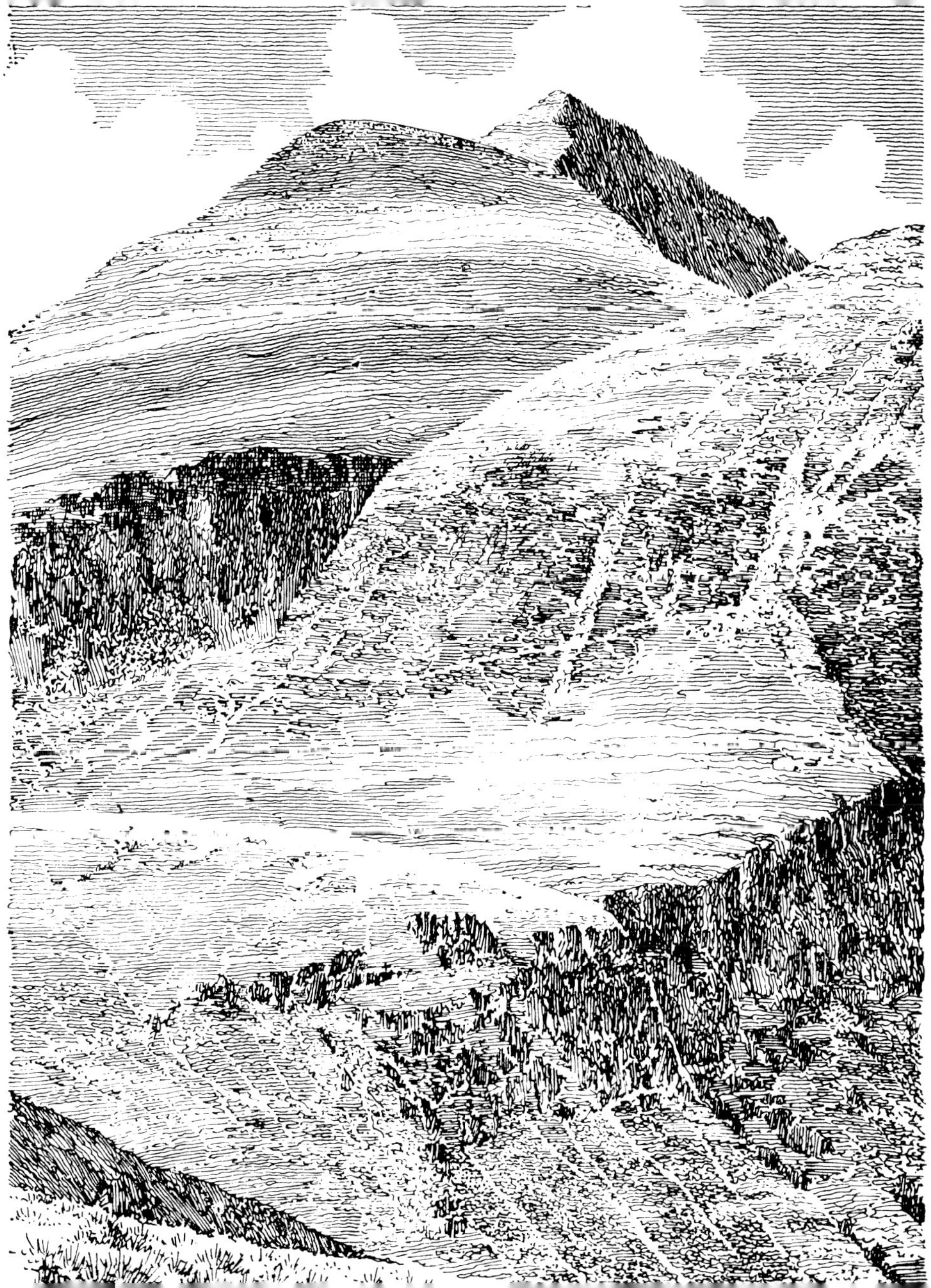

326 Levers Water

Levers Water, in a wild hollow of the Coniston Fells, provided a water supply for the old copper mines, a feature being the massive dam, still serviceable, under which the outflow passes along a tunnel. The rocks bordering the reservoir are an interesting study for the mineralogist.

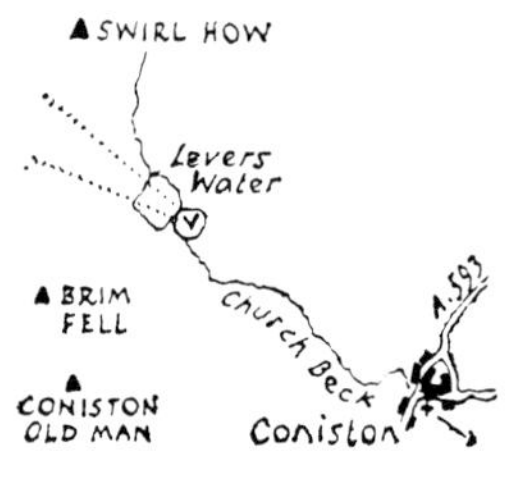

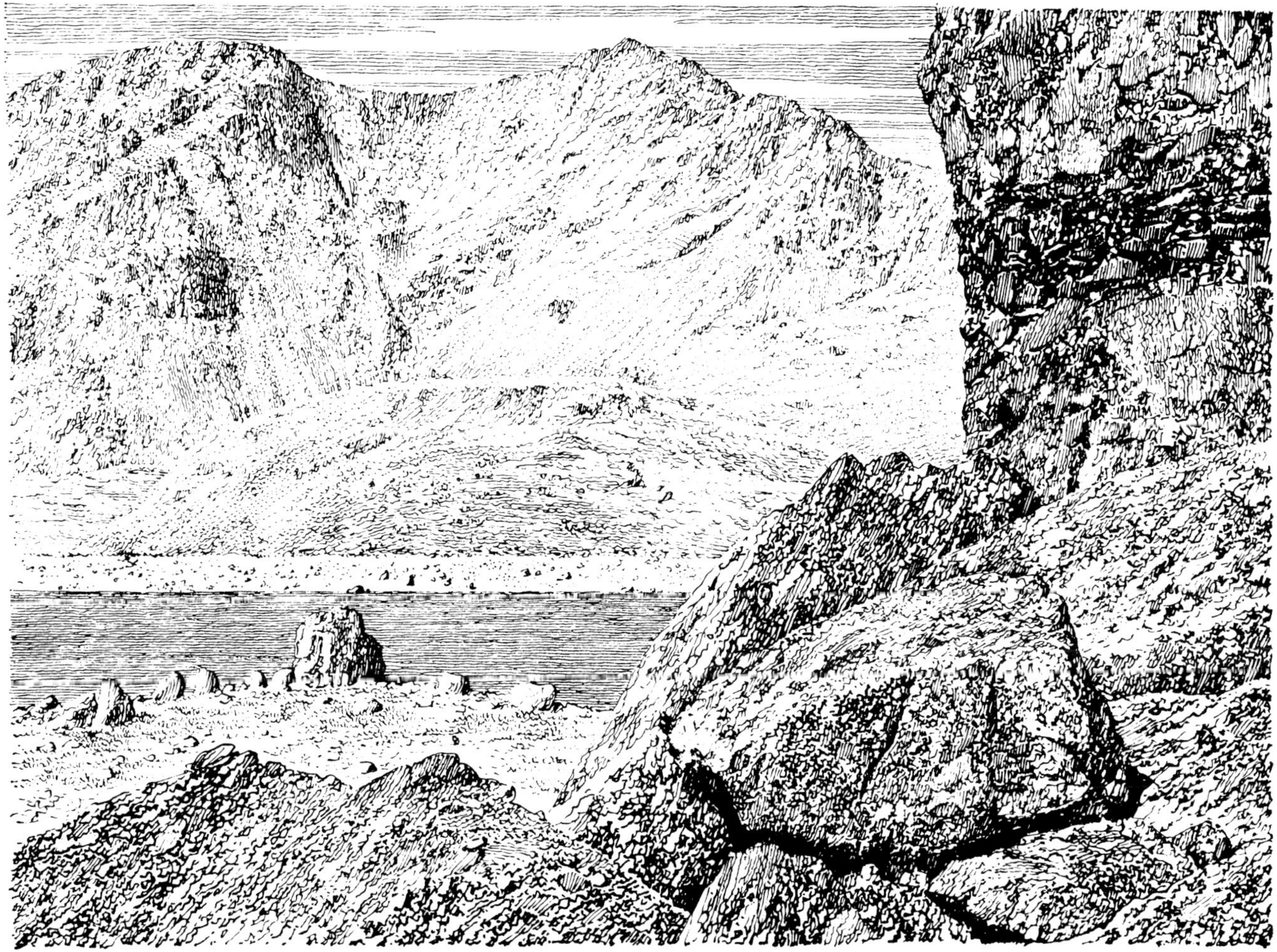

The Stone Circle at Castlerigg, often wrongly referred to as the Druids' Circle, is the best-known prehistoric monument in the district, being within easy reach of Keswick and two main roads. Owned by the National Trust and in Government care the site commands a beautiful and extensive view, Blencathra being especially prominent.

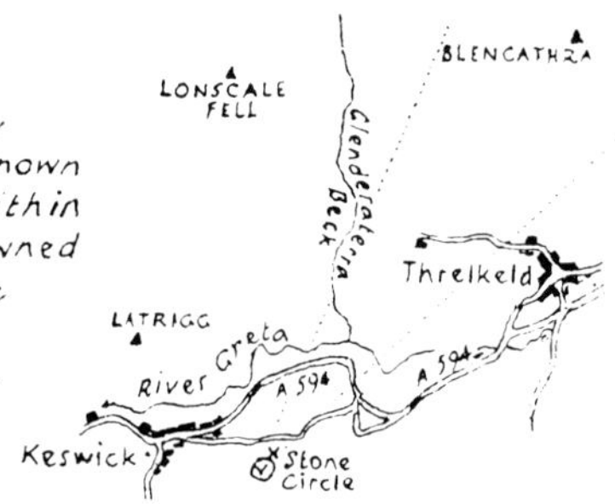

327 Blencathra,
from Castlerigg Stone Circle

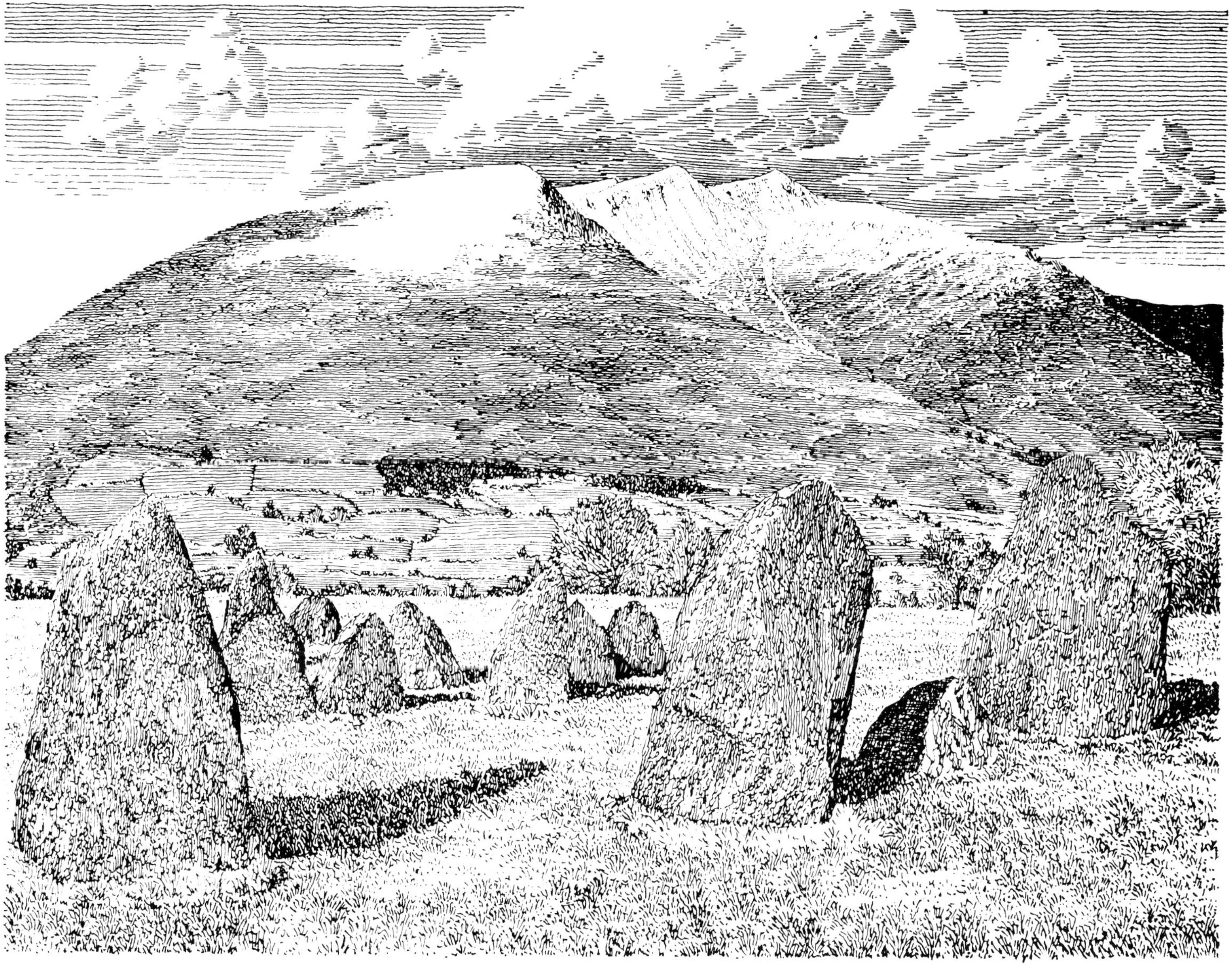

328 Swindale Head

Not many visitors to Lakeland know Swindale and few find it, there being no signpost to its three-mile strip of tarmac. Although shyly hidden, it has not escaped the notice of Manchester's engineers, who take its water through a tunnel to Haweswater — commendably, if the alternative was a reservoir. Swindale Head is the highest farmstead in the valley.

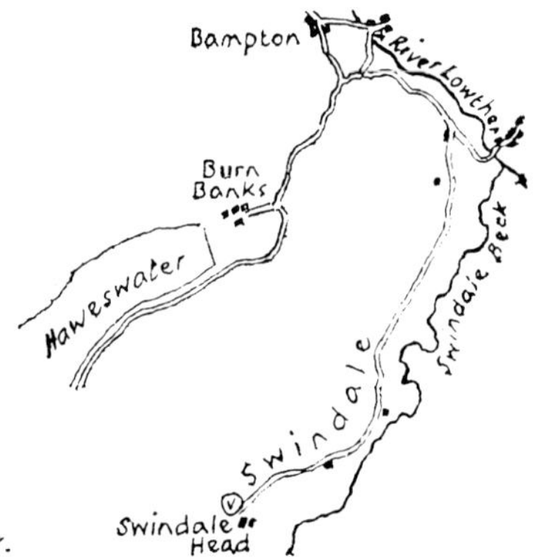

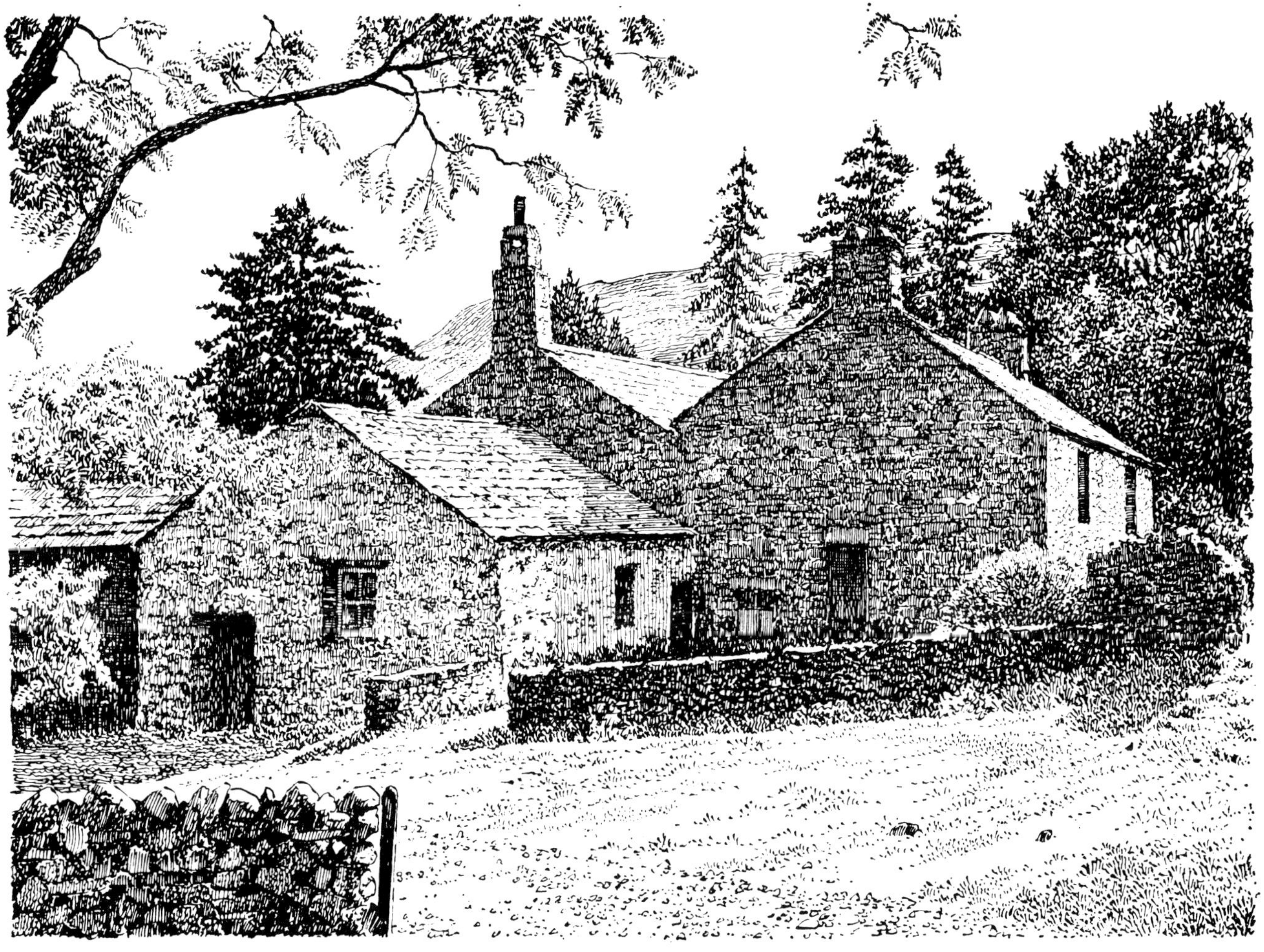

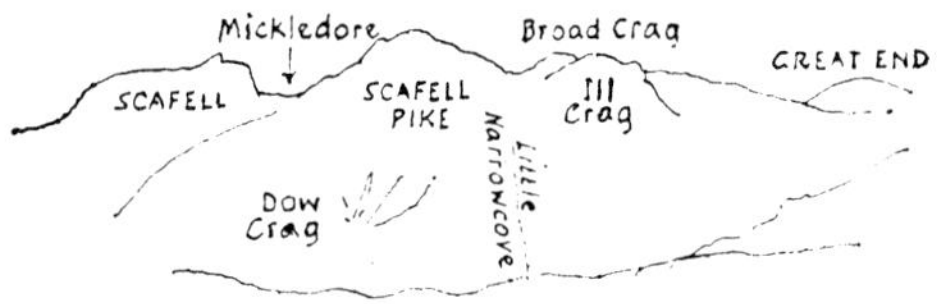

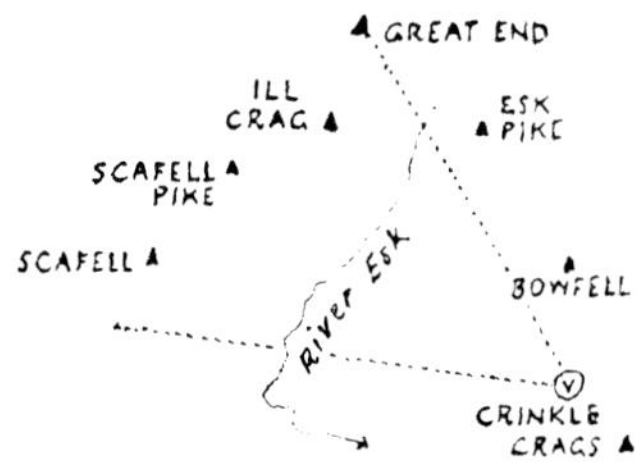

329 The Scafells, from Crinkle Crags

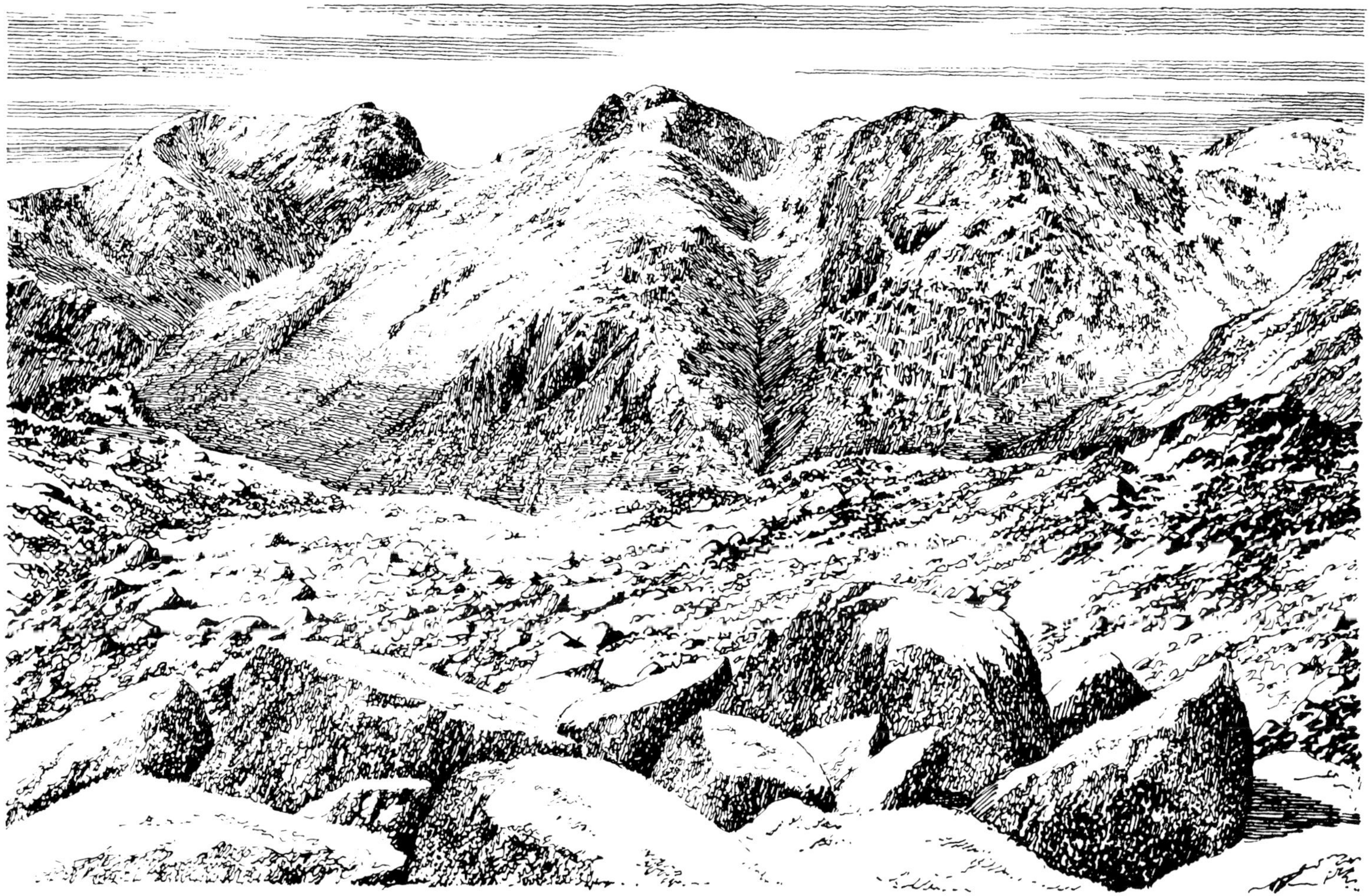

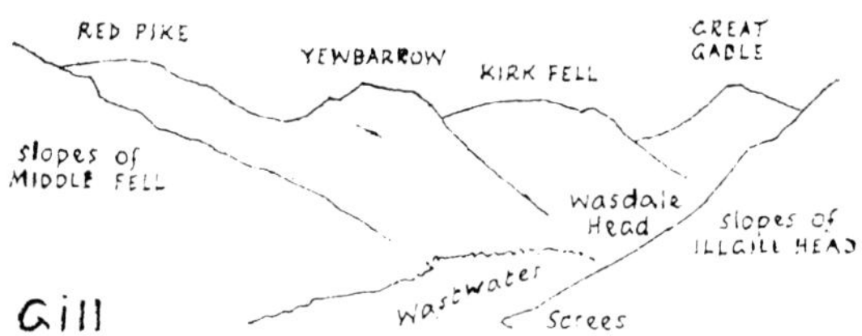

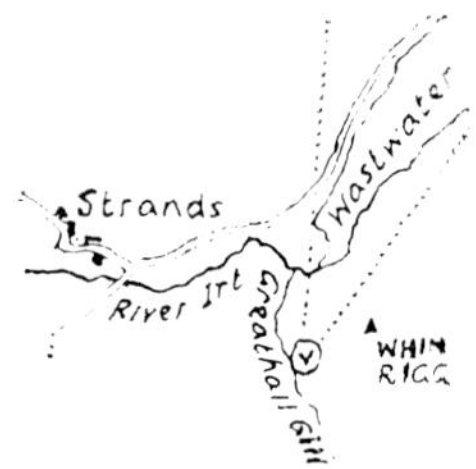

330 Wastwater, from Greathall Gill

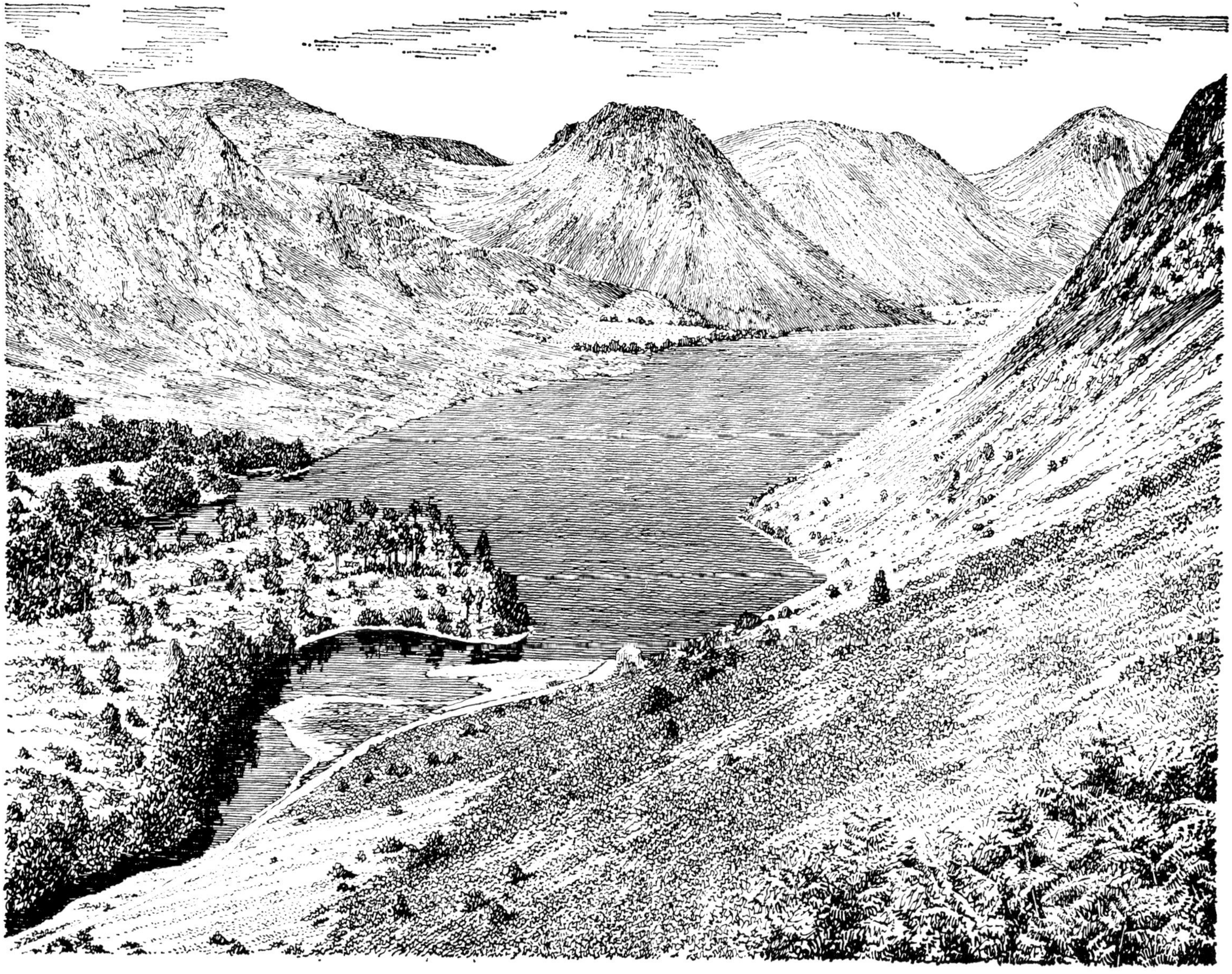

Amongst Kendal's many attractive features is the natural limestone woodland overlooking the town on the west. Here pleasant paths lead to the open heights beyond and a golf course with spectacular views.

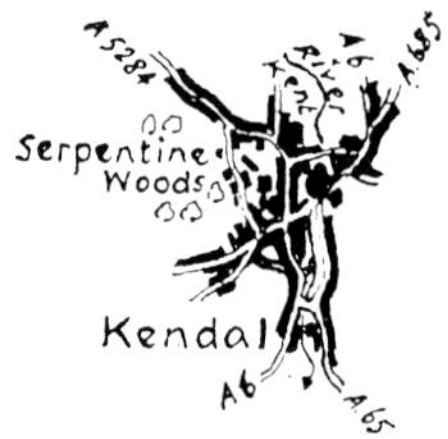

331 Serpentine Woods, Kendal

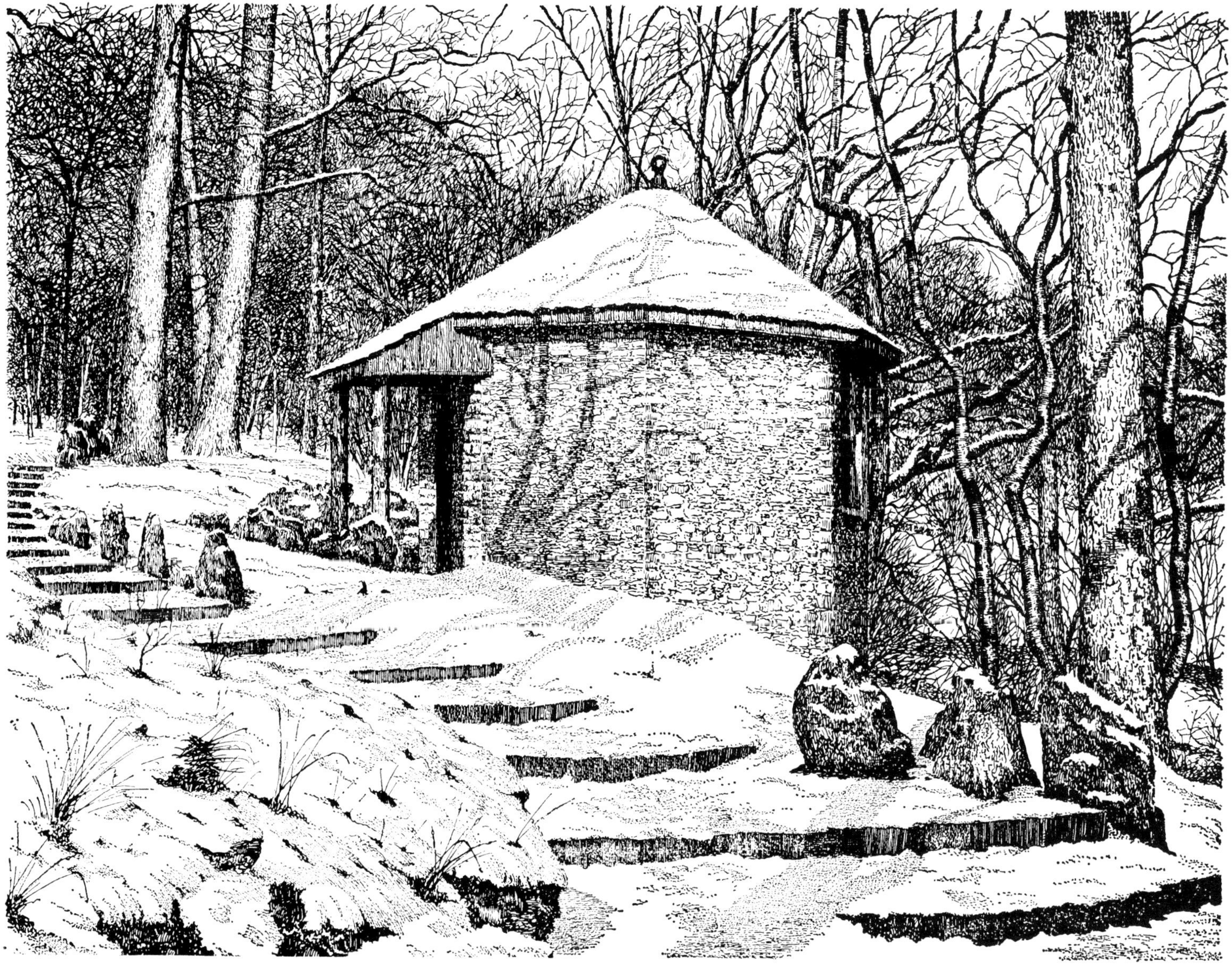

332 Clappersgate

A short mile out of Ambleside on the exciting road to Coniston and the Langdales is the trim cluster of buildings forming the small hamlet of Clappersgate, a place familiar to all visitors but (in view of what lies beyond) where only those tarry who seek the lovely seclusion of the rock gardens adjoining.

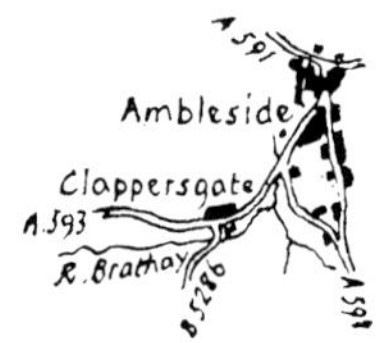

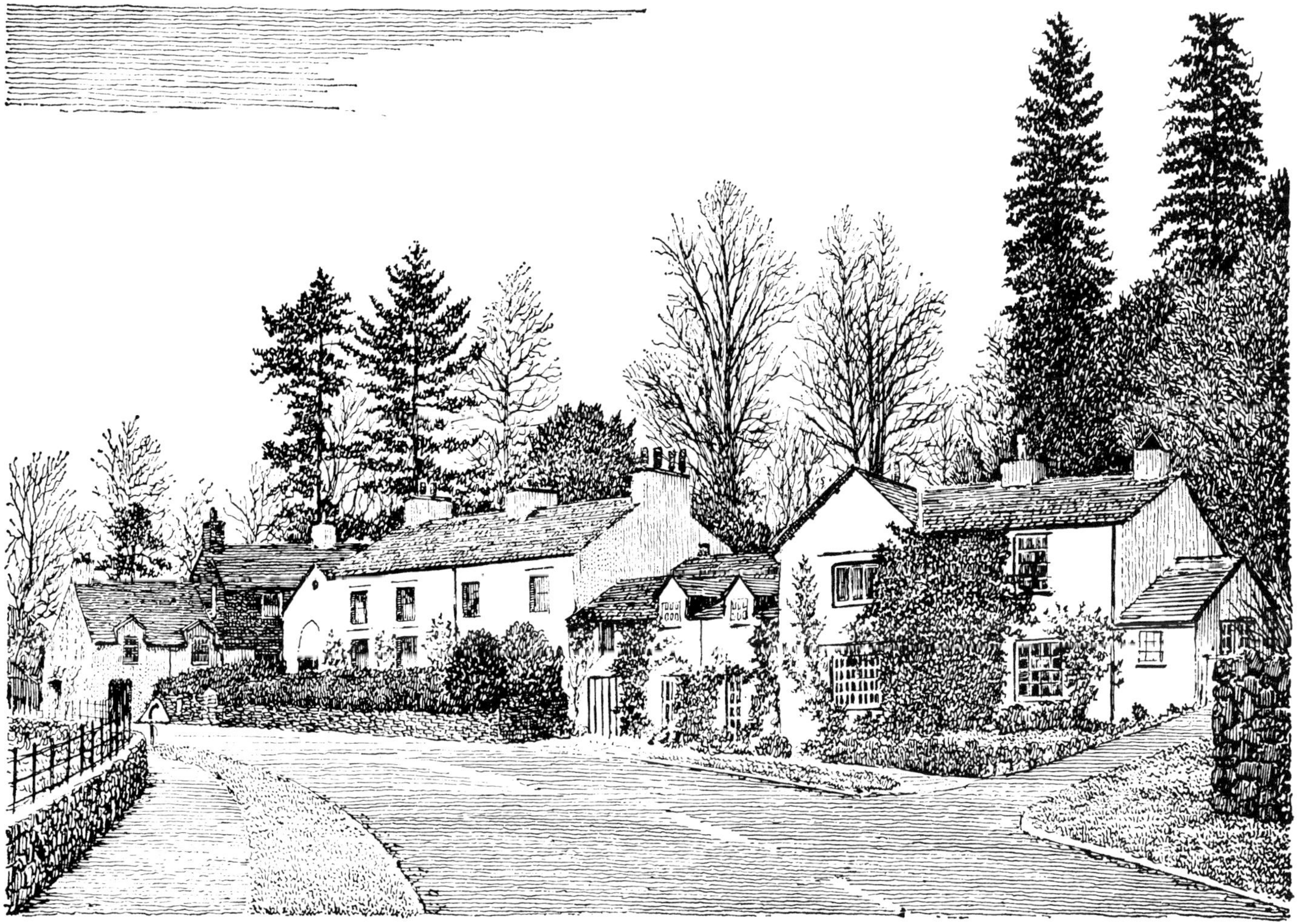

333 **Scout Scar**

Scout Scar is the popular name of the long limestone escarpment indicated on Ordnance maps as Underbarrow Scar. As a pleasant promenade the grassy walk along the edge of the cliff is second to none. The views over the Lyth Valley to the Kent Estuary and the Lakeland hills are truly superb.

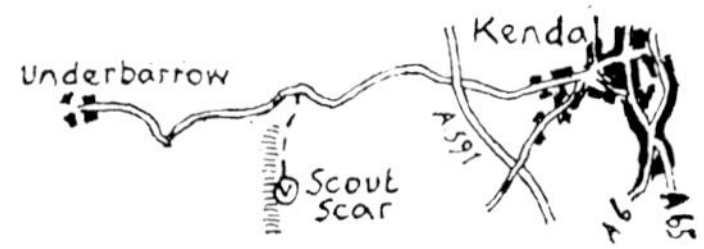

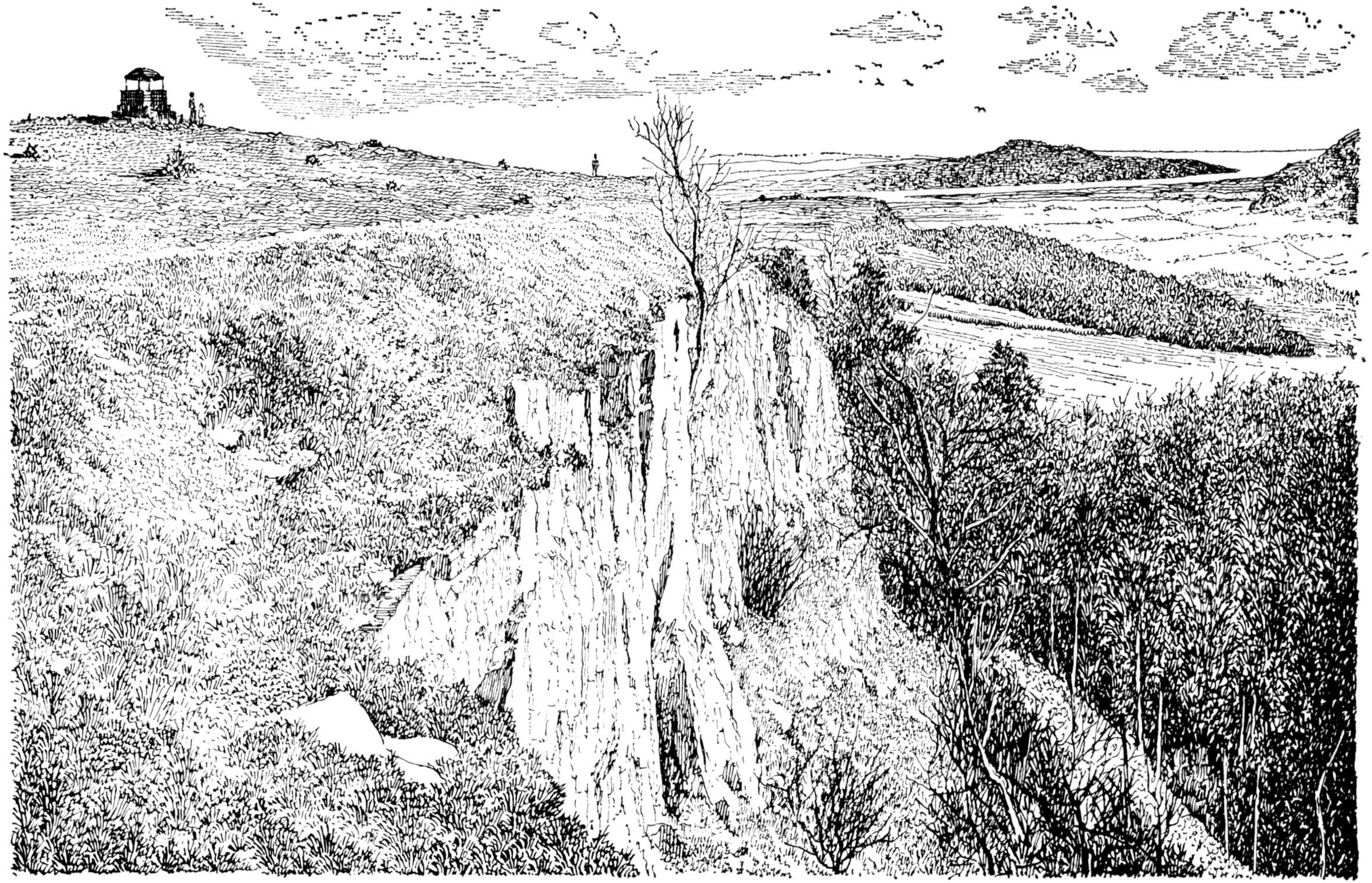

334 Cottage, Low Hartsop

Low Hartsop remains unspoiled as a characteristic centuries-old Lakeland hamlet built of the native stone and seeming thereby to have erupted from the rough ground: it blends into the landscape perfectly. The mossy stone walls, the barns, the cottages (two of which retain their spinning galleries), the packhorse bridge, survive unchanged.

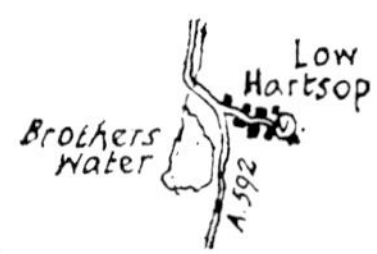

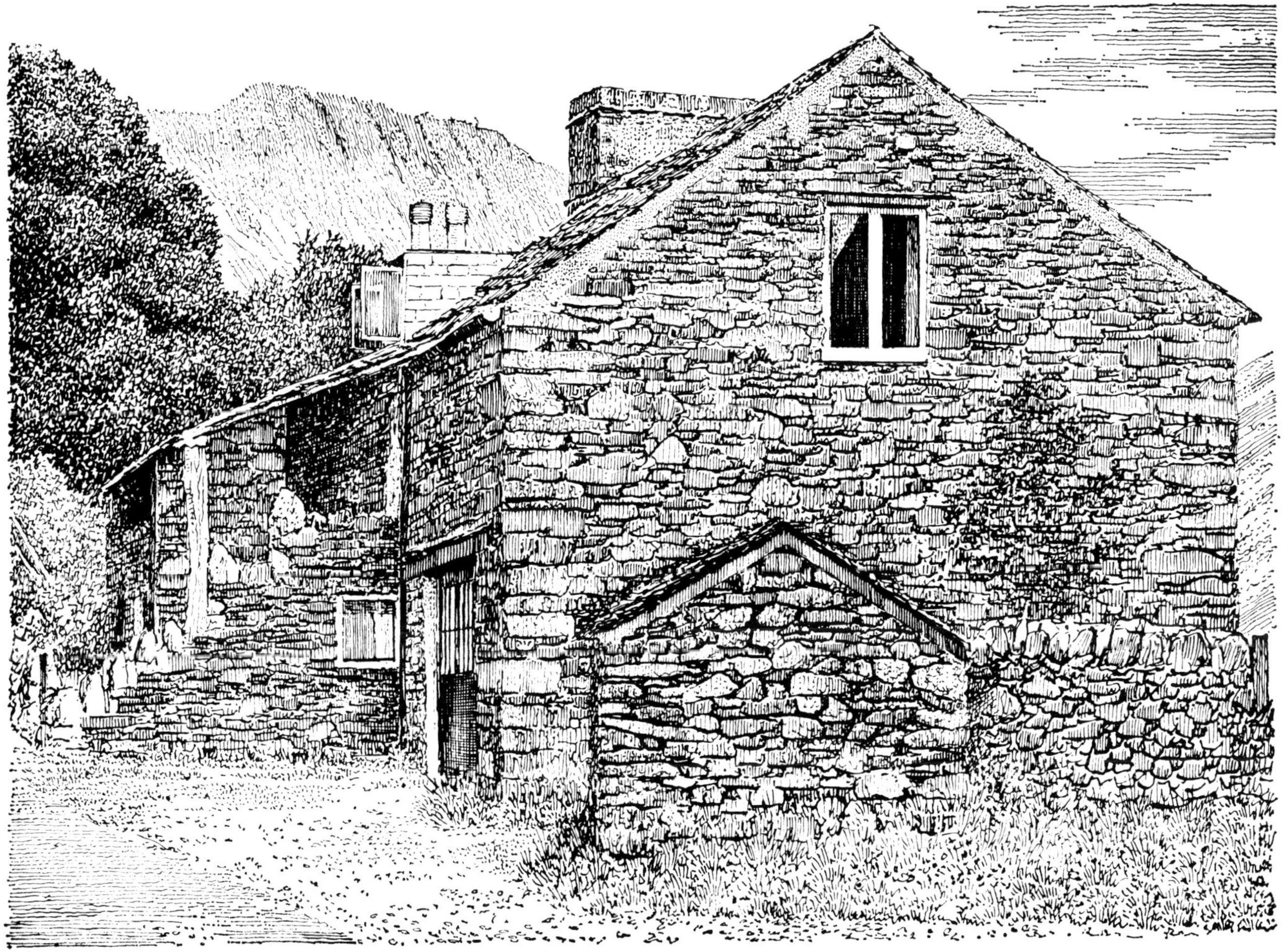

Bowness Bay presents a scene of animation alien to Lakeland, and discerning visitors (in the minority, judging by the Bowness crowds) search for natural beauty elsewhere. Before the tourists came Bowness Bay must have been very lovely. It is still actually rather better than Blackpool.

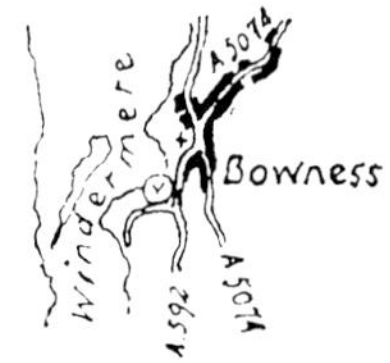

335 Bowness Bay, Windermere

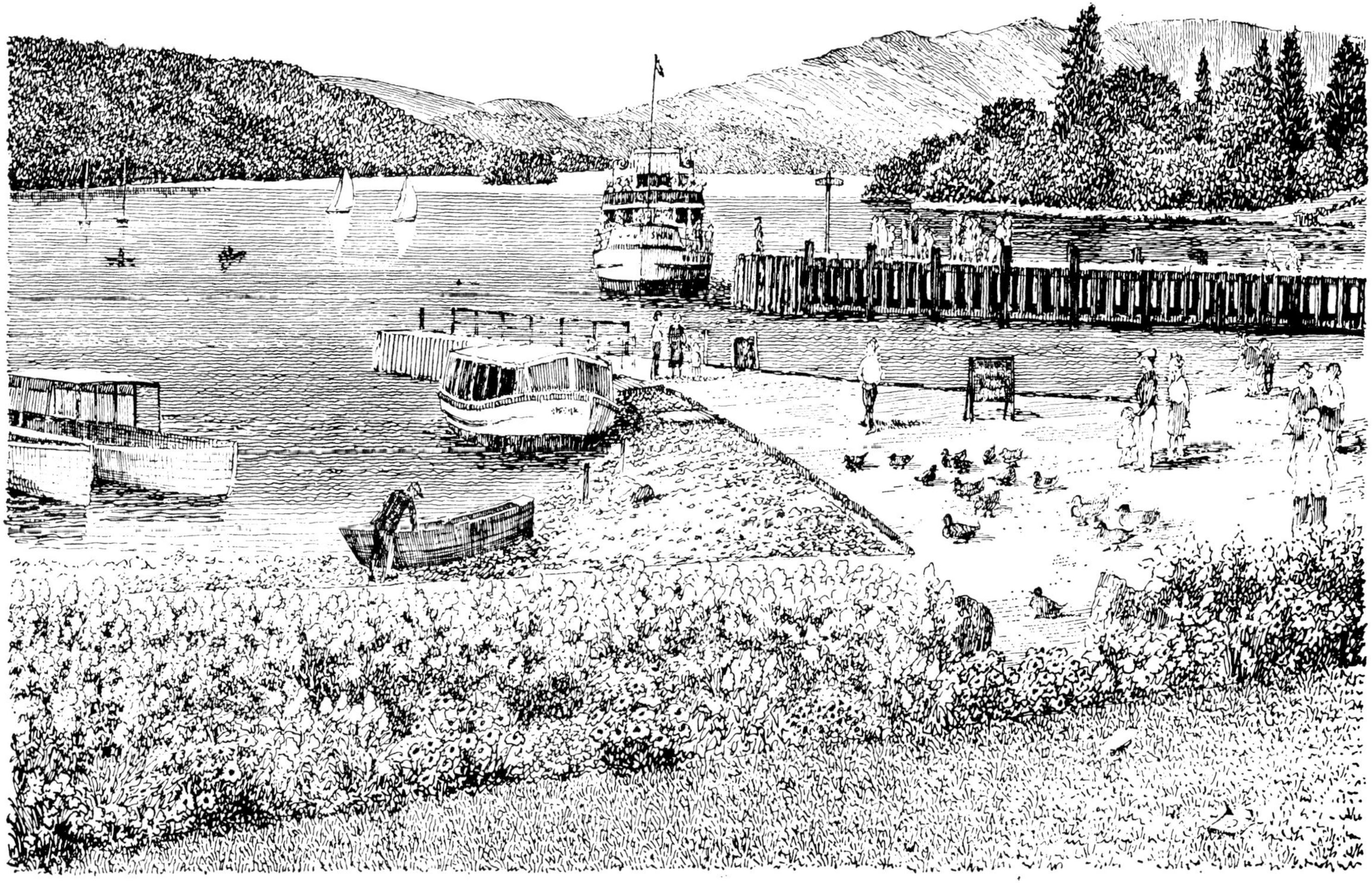

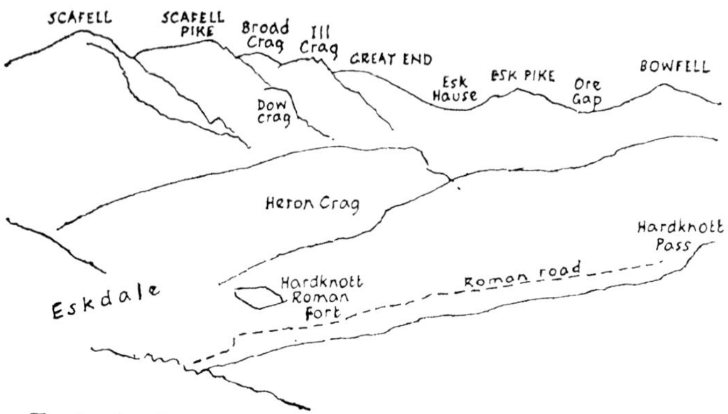

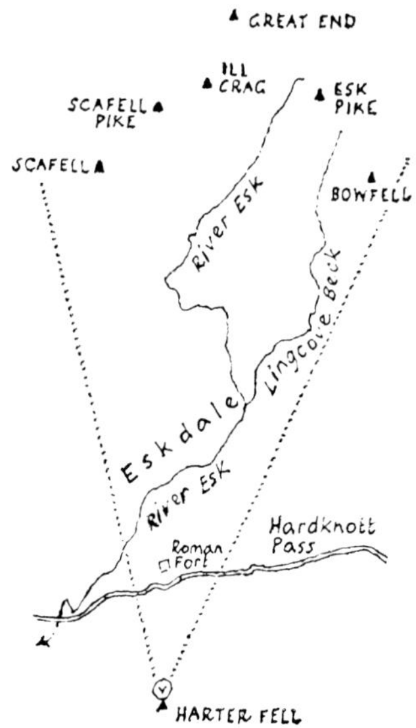

336 Upper Eskdale

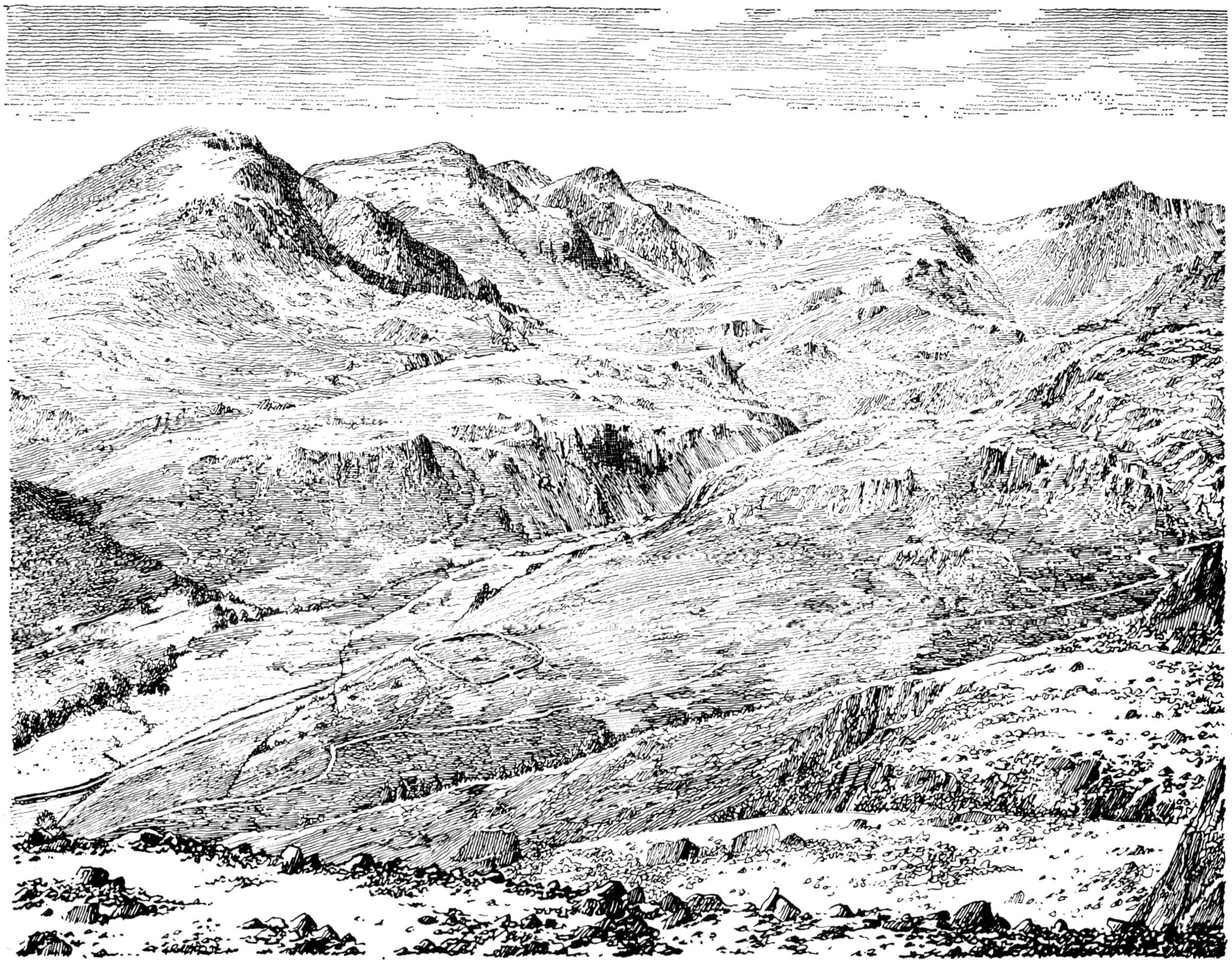

337 Wasdale Head

Of all the remote daleheads, Wasdale Head is, always has been and always will be, the most impressive. Hemmed in by the grandest mountains in the district, the atmosphere is truly Alpine. Day trippers disturb the peace and seclusion, but in the quiet of early morning and evening there is still no place like Wasdale Head for the walker and climber. This view is down-valley to Illgill Head and Wastwater.

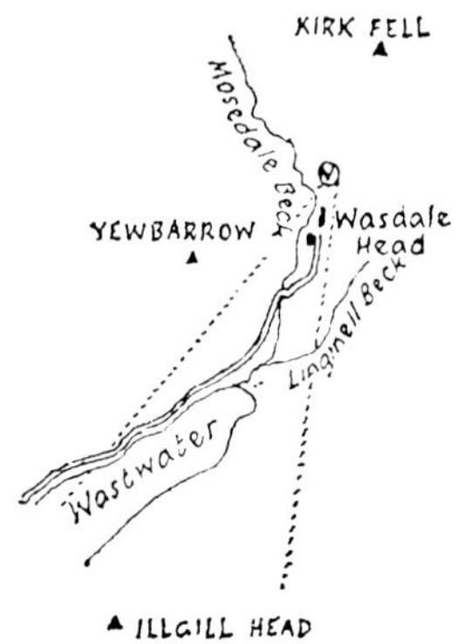

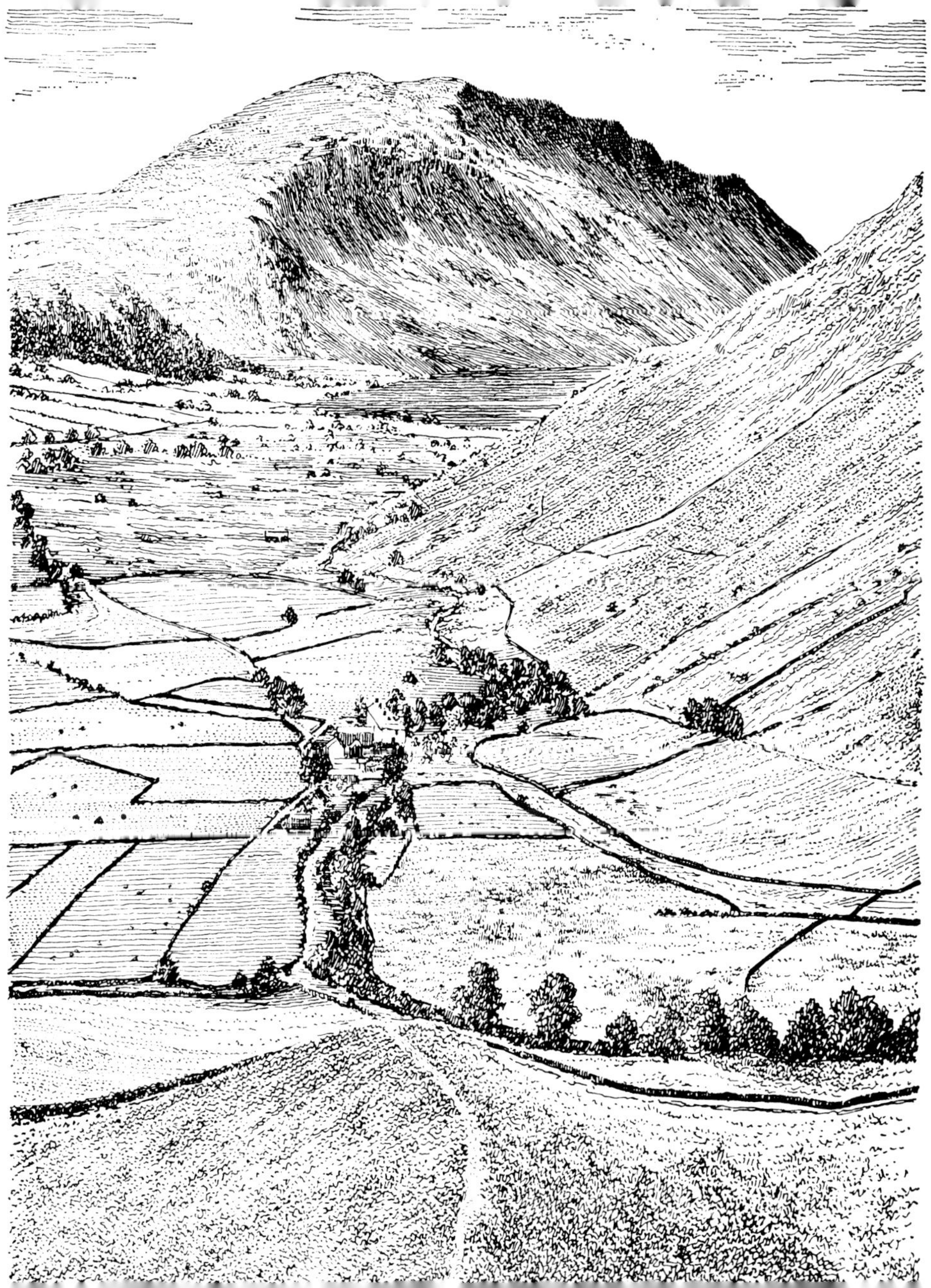

1 : DOVE CRAG
2 : RED SCREES
3 : CAUDALE MOOR
4 : THORNTHWAITE CRAG
5 : ILL BELL
6 : HARTER FELL

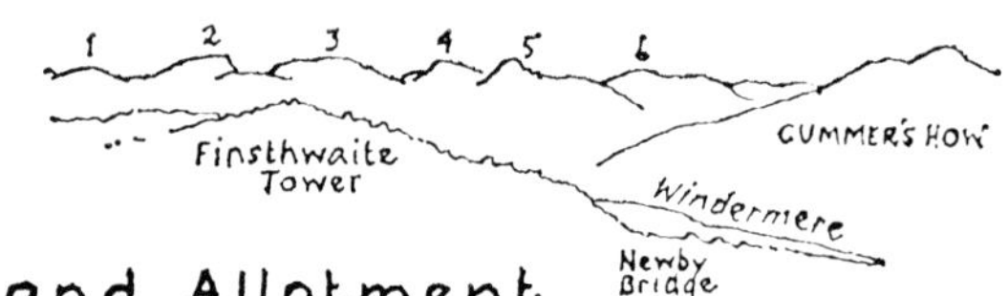

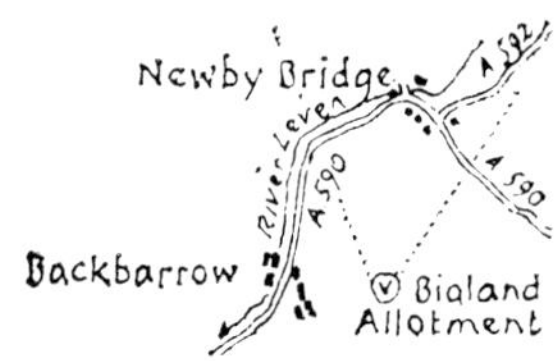

 North from Bigland Allotment

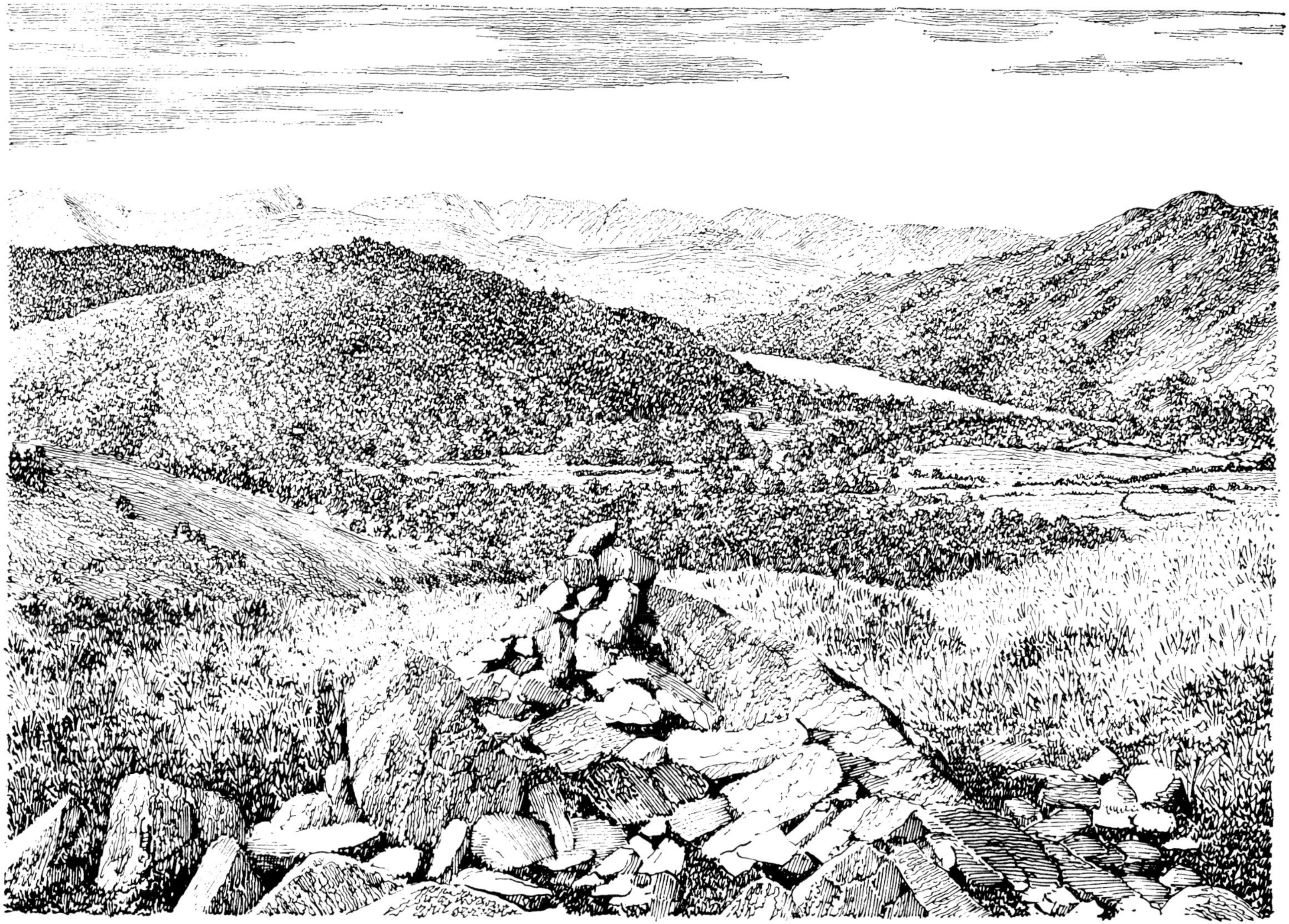

Coniston Old Man is a rough but simple climb in summer and its top is a place of popular resort. But in the conditions here pictured sheets of ice on the final steep rise may make the ascent virtually impossible and certainly dangerous.

339 The summit of Coniston Old Man

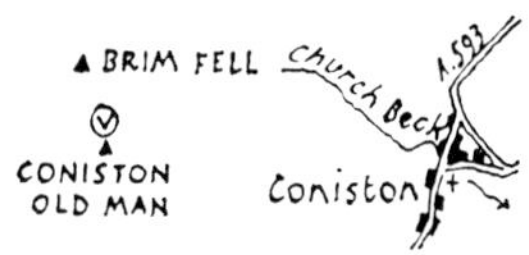

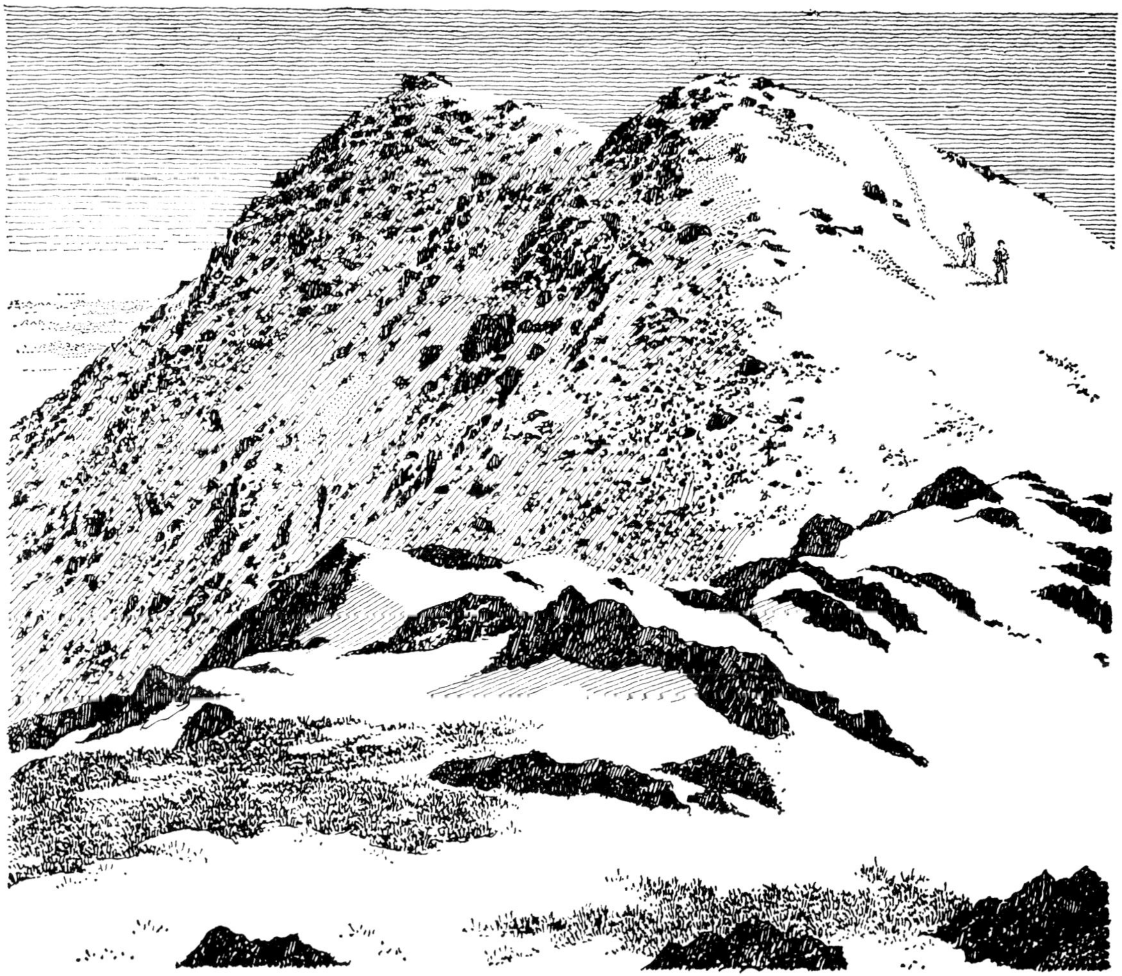

A wall of rock, seamed by steep and stony gullies and bounded by rivers of scree, is the finest feature of Great Gable's south flank overlooking Wasdale Head. Known as the Napes, its star attraction is the Needle, a remarkable obelisk of naked rock.

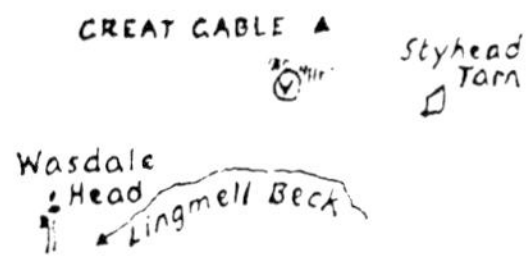

340 The Napes, Great Gable

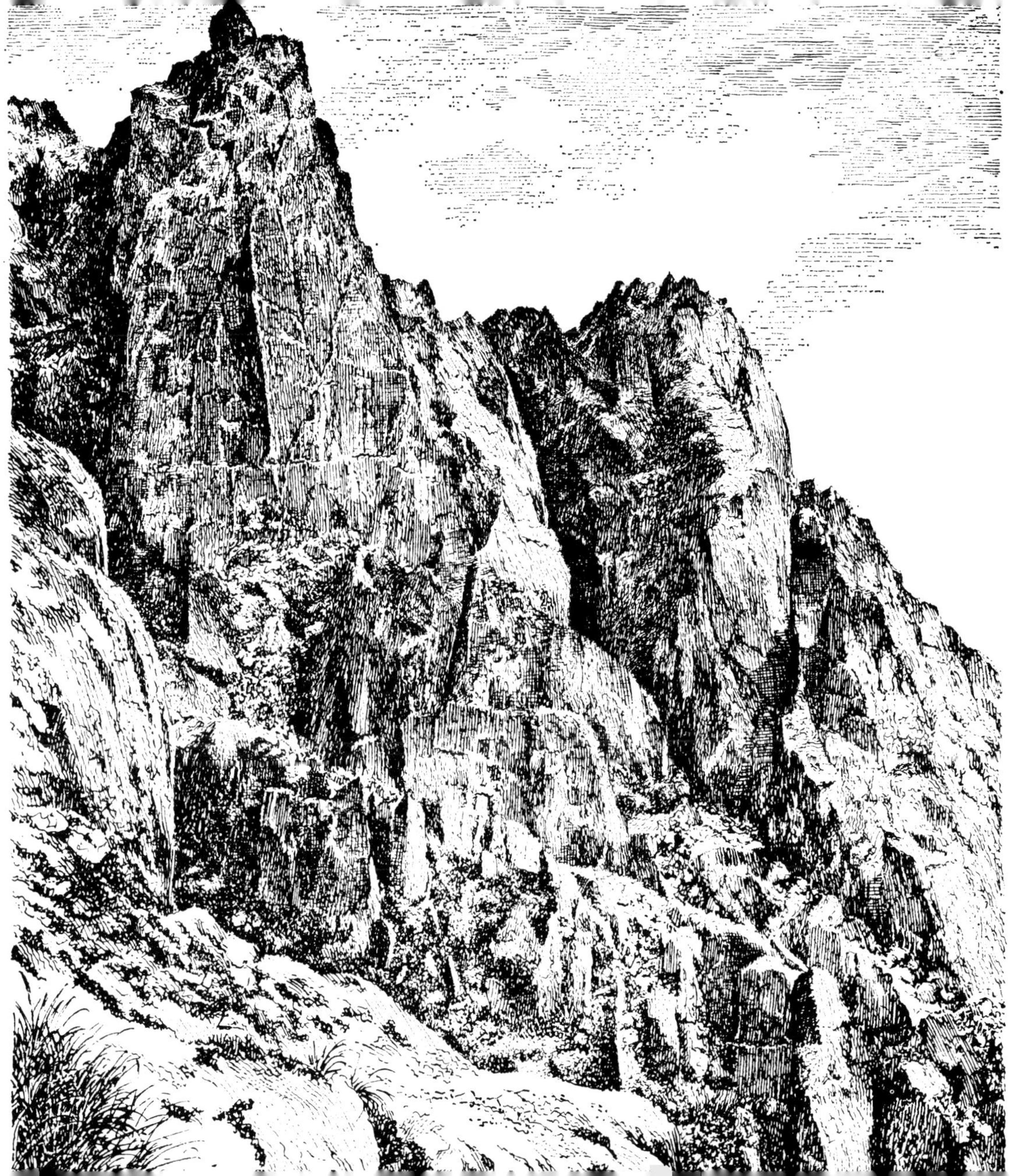

Not the largest fallen boulder in the district but the most spectacular and best known, the Bowder Stone occupies a narrow shelf of flat ground and overlooks and seemingly threatens the road through the Jaws of Borrowdale. But it is safe enough. This is its chosen resting place.

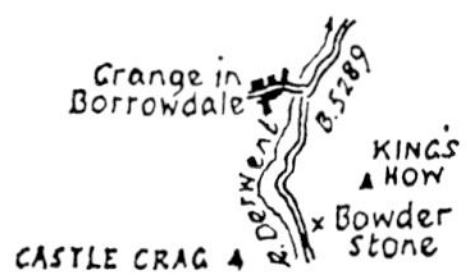

341 The Bowder Stone, Borrowdale

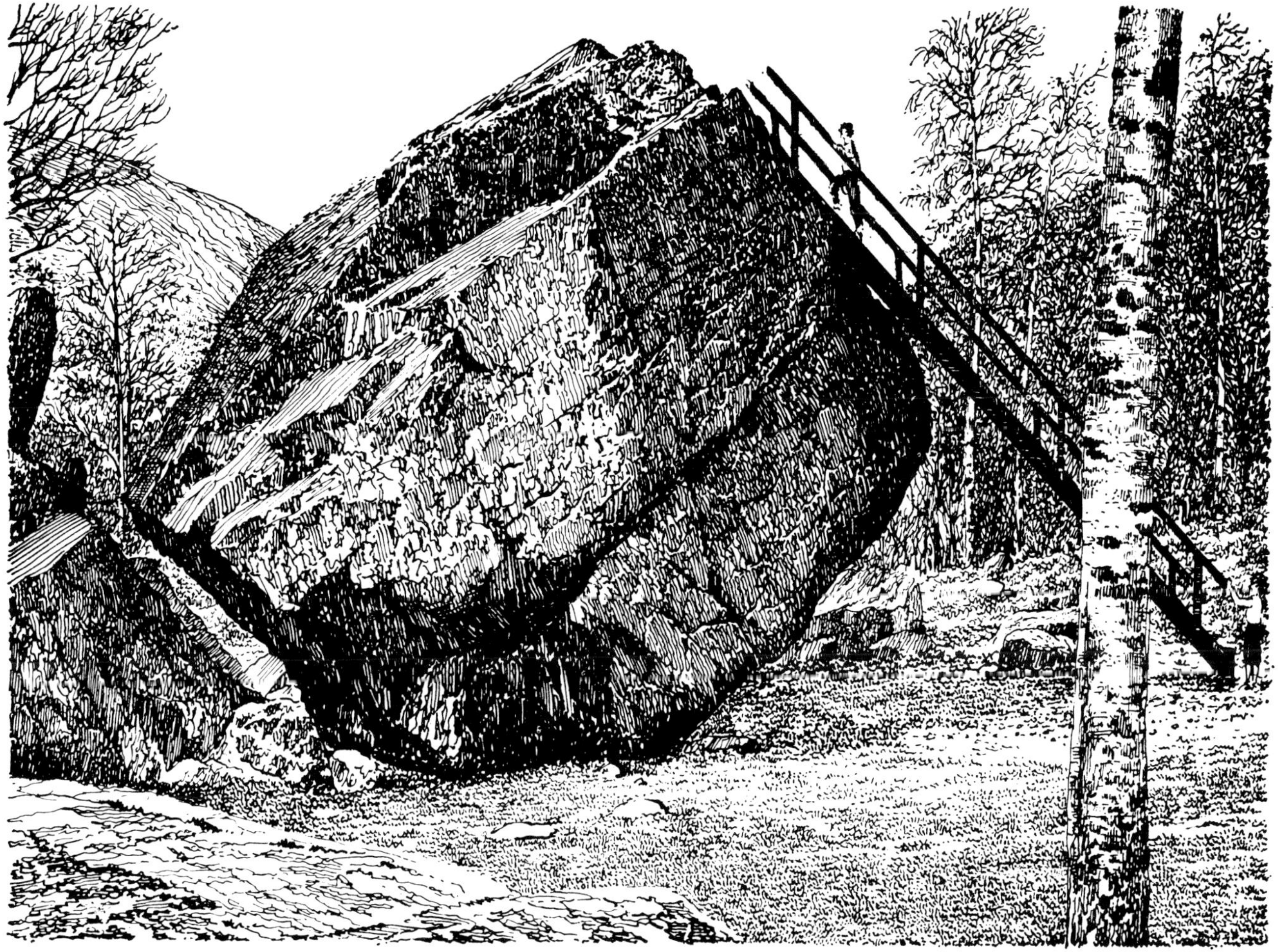

342 At Caldbeck

Caldbeck is a pleasant village on the band of limestone bordering Lakeland in the north, with a fame derived from its associations with the great John Peel, whose ornate memorial stands in the graveyard of the lovely church.

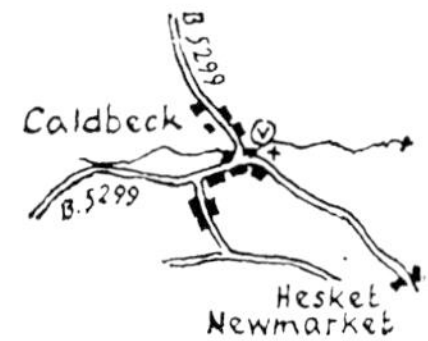

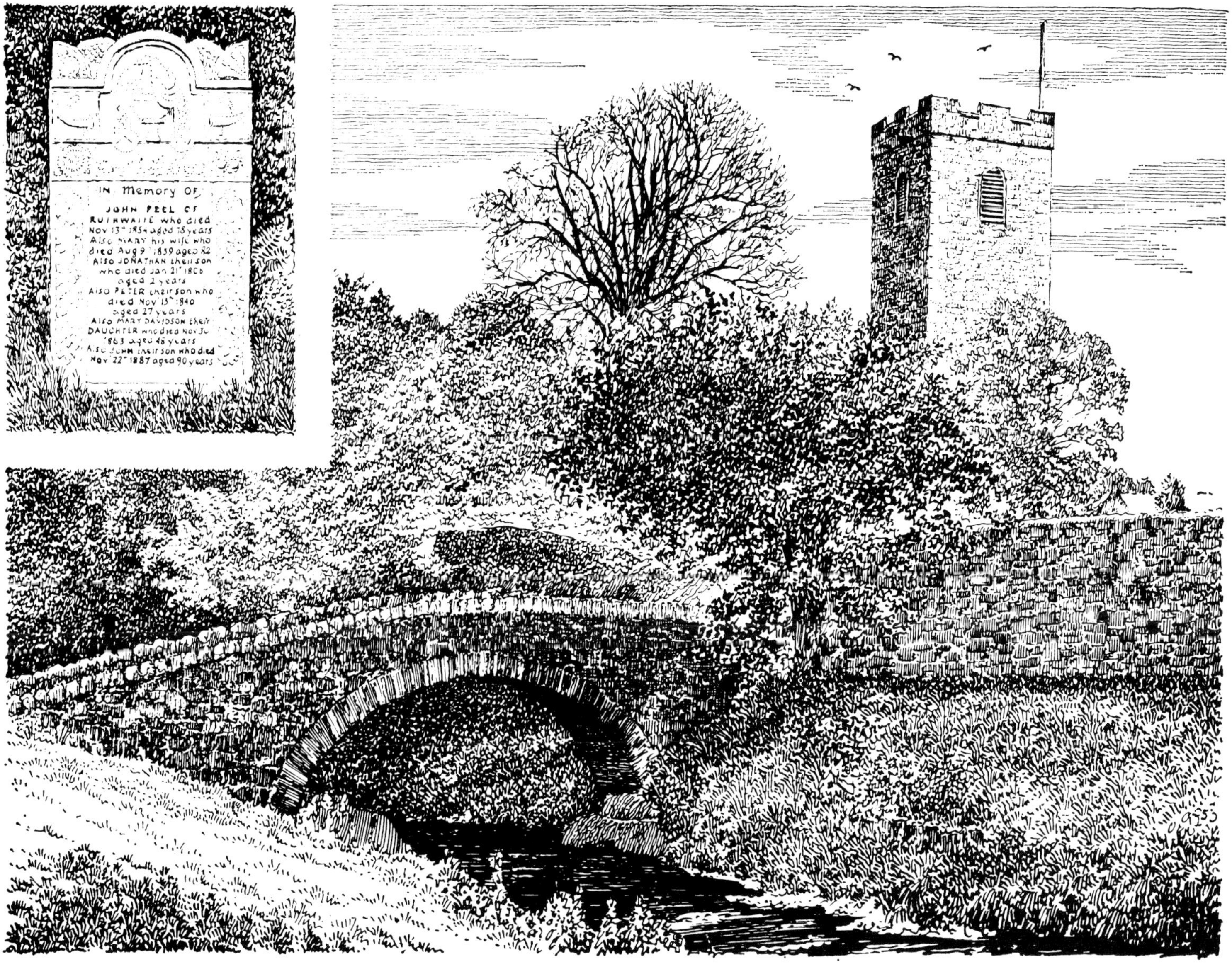
IN Memory OF
JOHN PEEL OF
RUTHWAITE who died
Nov 13 1854 aged 78 years
Also MARY his wife who
died Aug 9 1859 aged 82
Also JONATHAN their son
who died Jan 21 1806
aged 2 years
Also PETER their son who
died Nov 13 1840
aged 27 years
Also MARY DAVIDSON their
DAUGHTER who died Nov 30
1863 aged 48 years
Also JOHN their son who died
Nov 22 1887 aged 90 years

343 Sty Head, from Great End

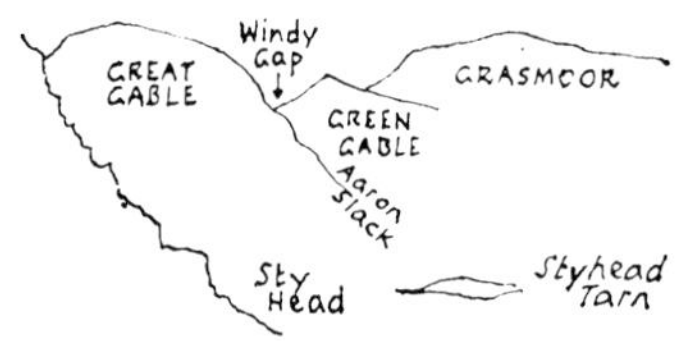

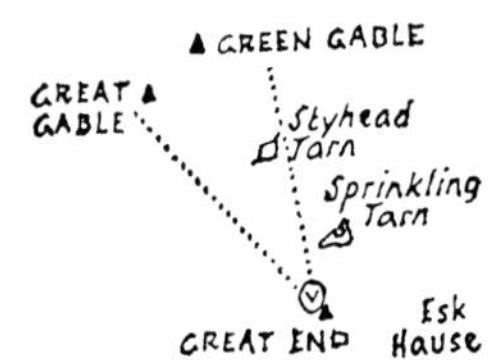

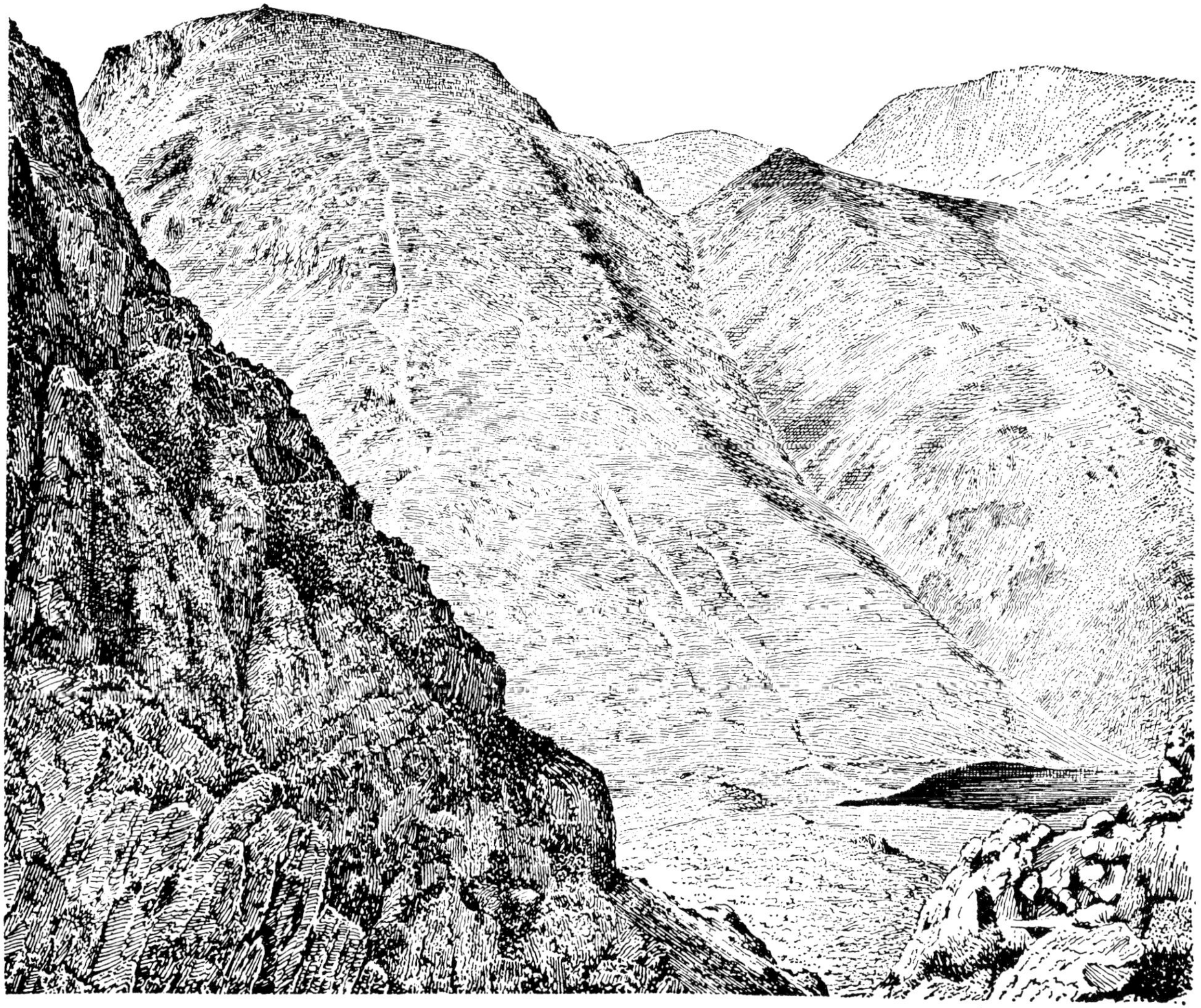

1 : WHITELESS PIKE
2 : DALE HEAD
3 : FLEETWITH PIKE
4 : GREEN GABLE
5 : GREAT GABLE
6 : HIGH CRAG
7 : HIGH STILE
8 : RED PIKE
9 : HAYSTACKS
10 : RANNERDALE KNOTTS

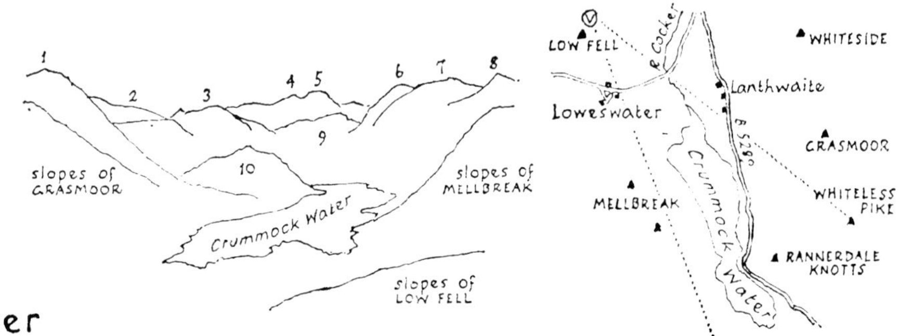

344 Crummock Water

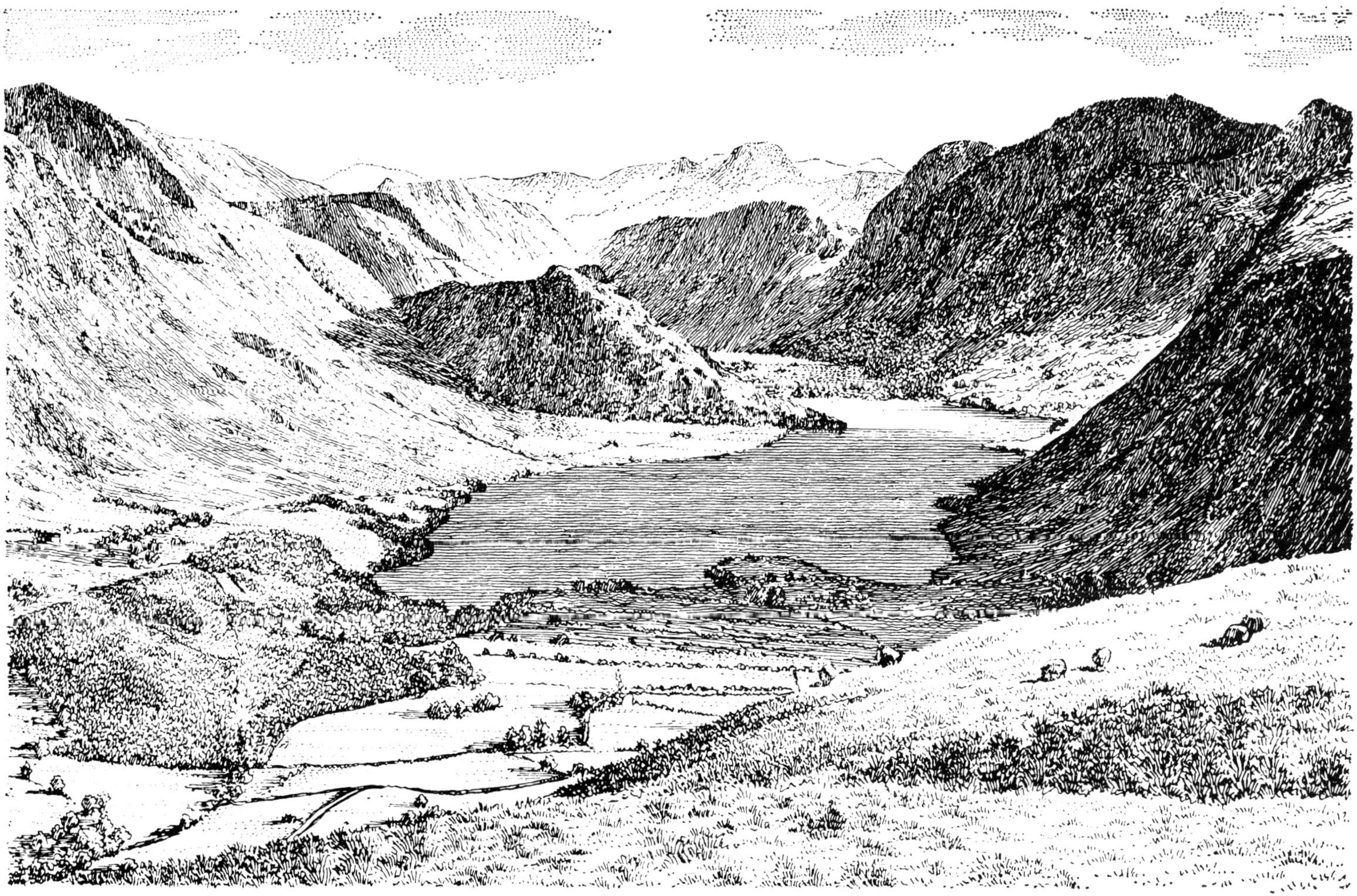

The Swinside Stone Circle ranks second to the Castlerigg Stone Circle, but whereas the latter is almost a suburb of busy Keswick the Swinside one is in the midst of wild moorland and the more impressive because of its bleak surroundings.

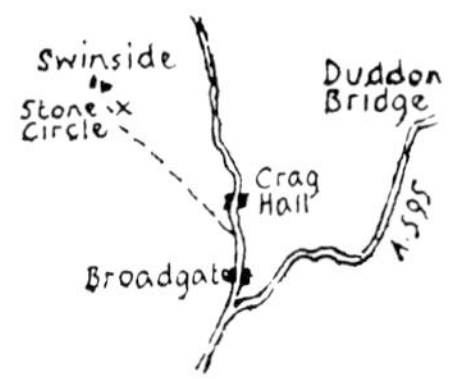

345 Swinside Stone Circle

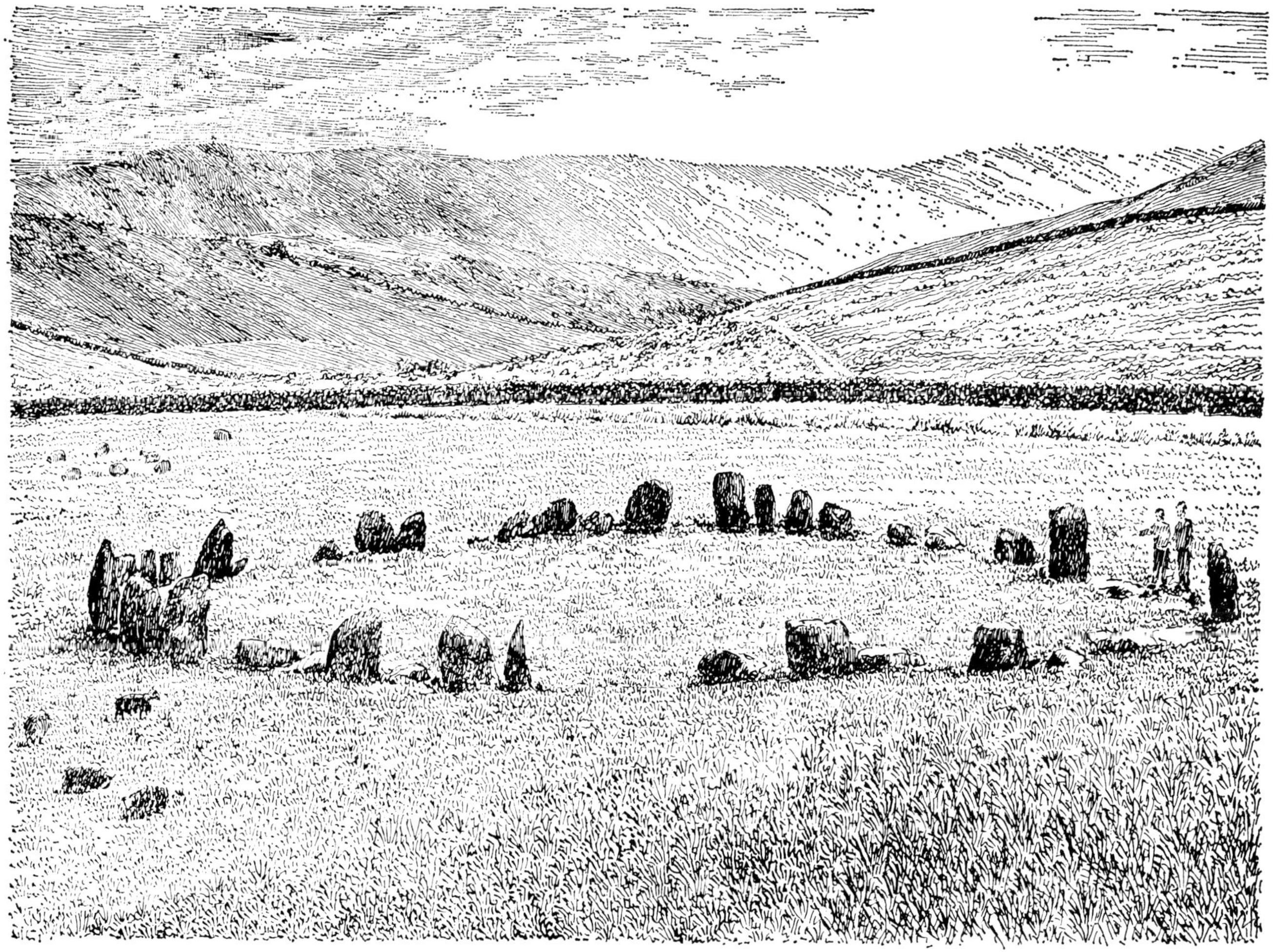

Helvellyn's east face, descending roughly to Red Tarn and flanked by Striding Edge, is the most dramatic aspect of the mountain. The view southeast looks to St. Sunday Crag over the gulf of Grisedale with the High Street range in the distance.

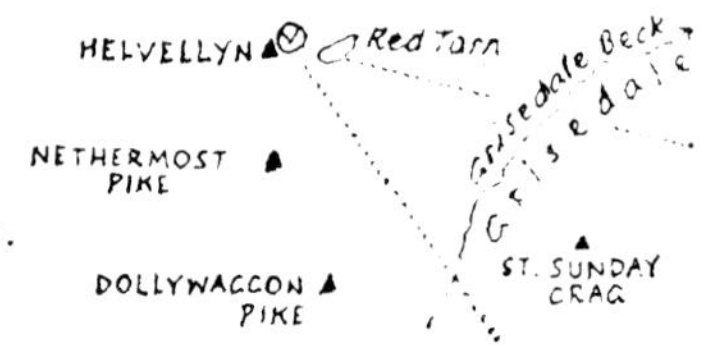

346 Southeast from Helvellyn

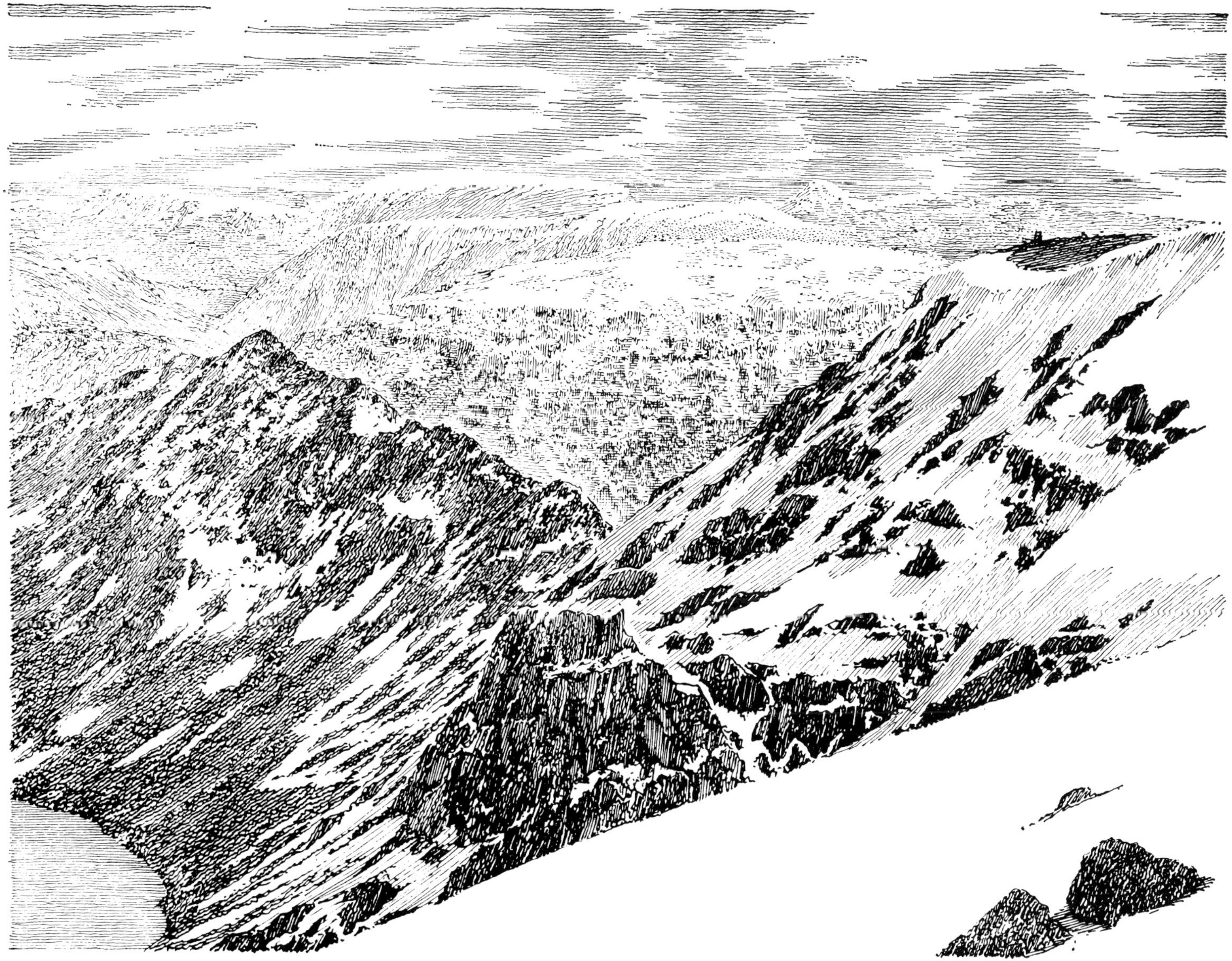

The topmost rocks of Great Gable, National Trust property and a fellwalkers' Mecca, feature the War Memorial of the Fell and Rock Climbing Club and form the sombre background to an annual November Remembrance Service.

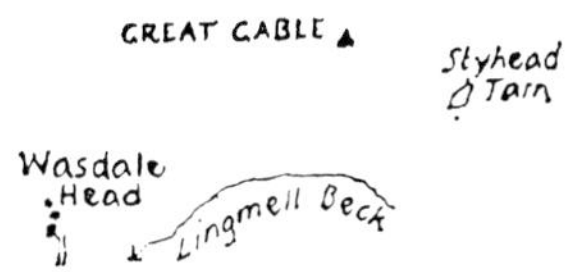

347 The summit of Great Gable

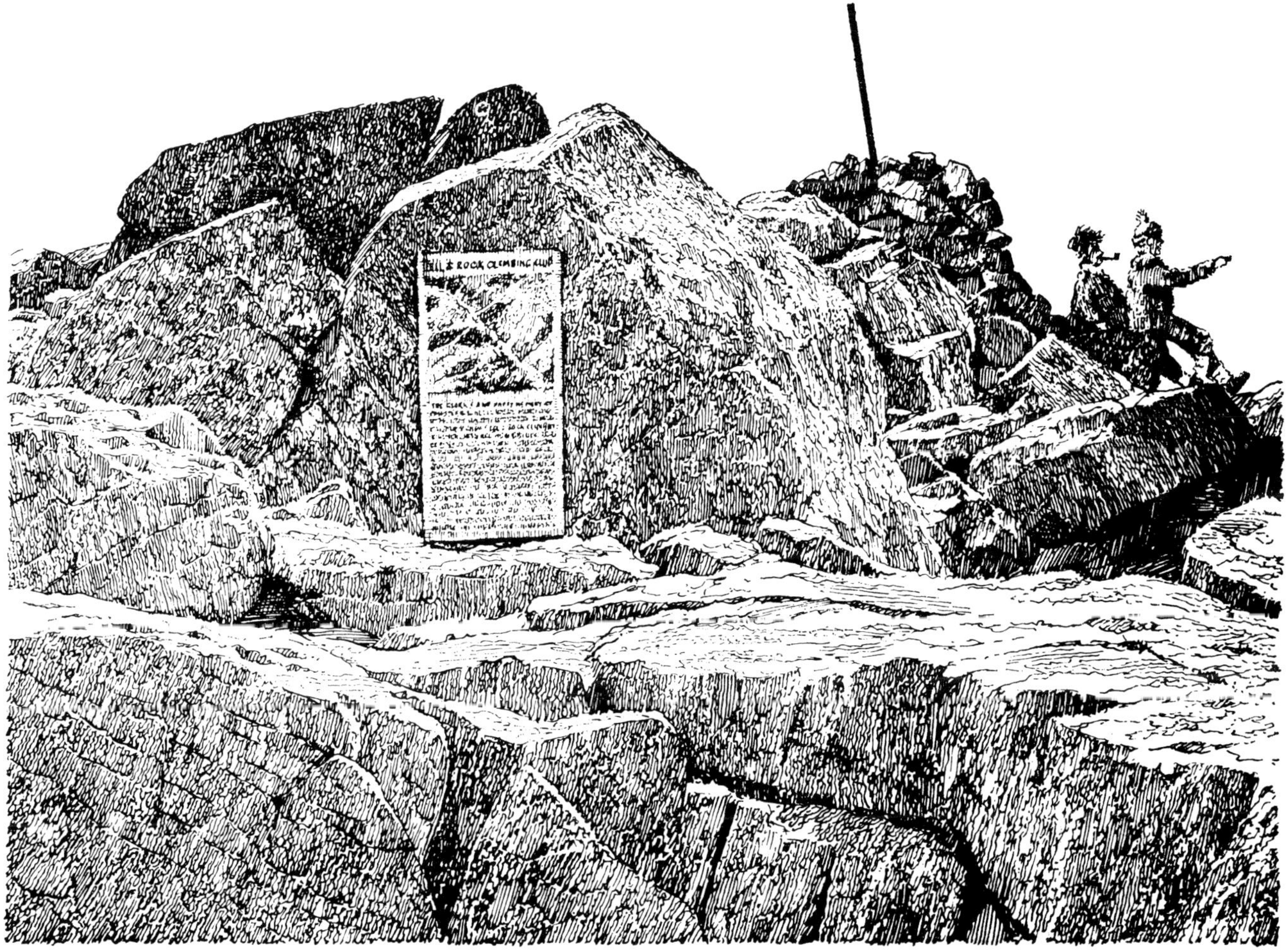
& ROCK CLIMBING CLUB

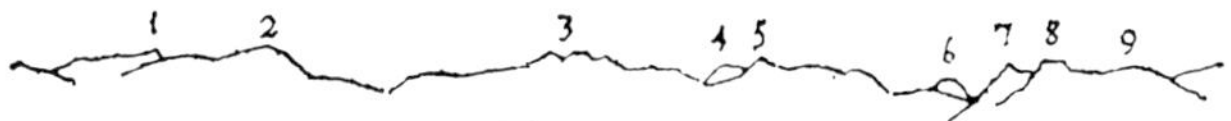

1: SWIRL HOW
2: WETHERLAM
3: CRINKLE CRAGS
4: SCAFELL PIKE
5: BOWFELL
6: GREAT GABLE
7: PIKE O'STICKLE
8: HARRISON STICKLE
9: PAVEY ARK

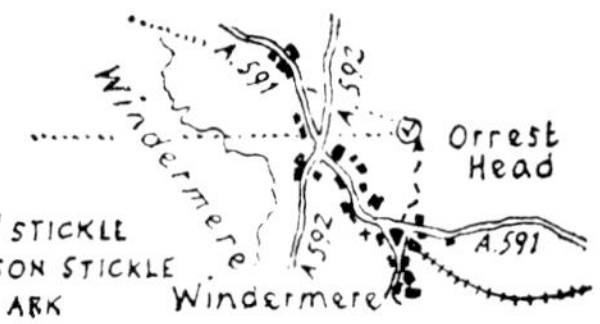

348 View from Orrest Head

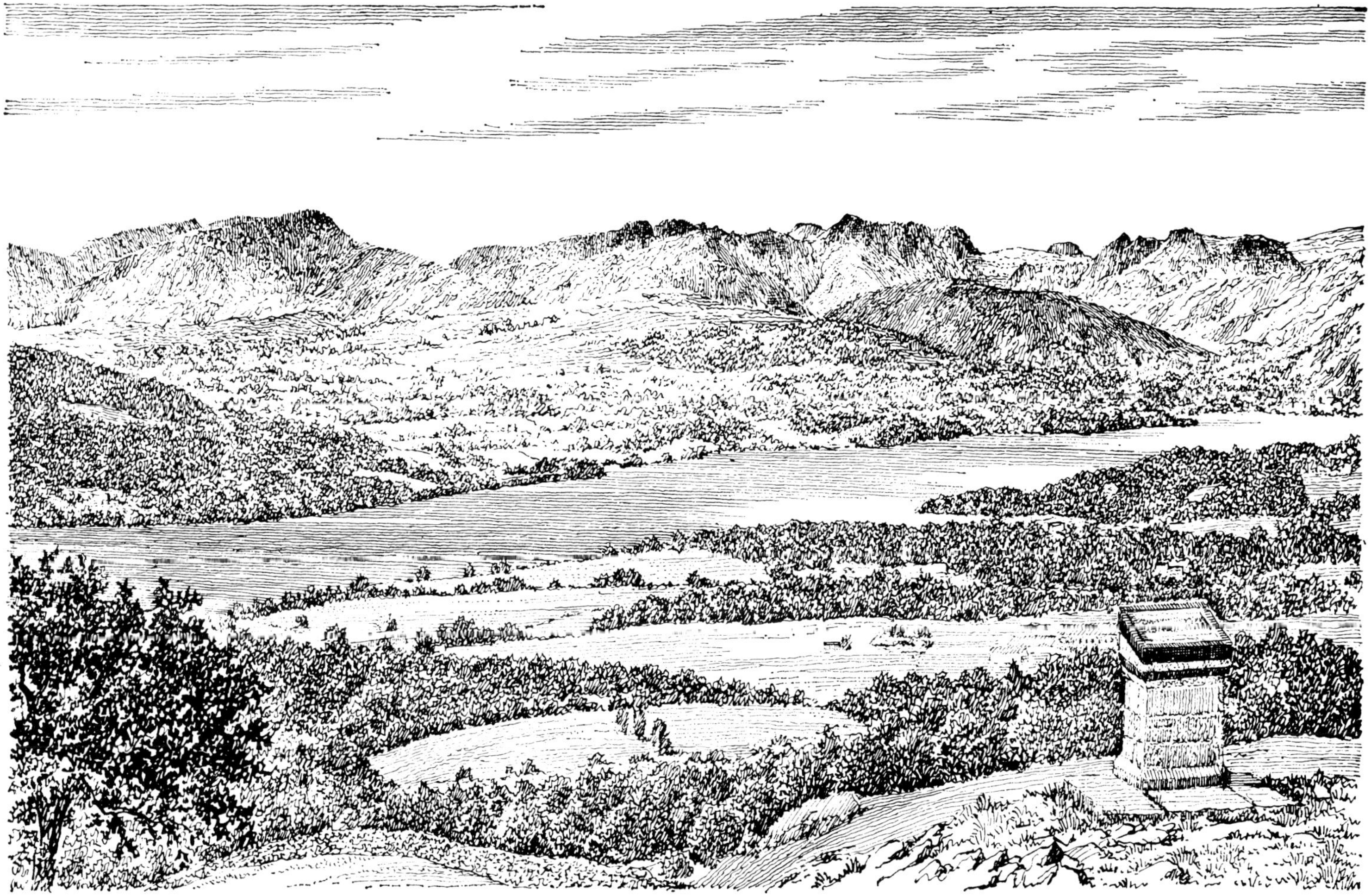

349 Langdale Pikes, from Side Pike

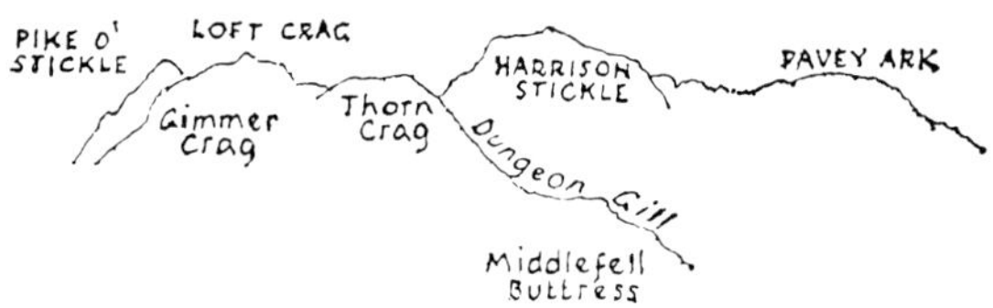

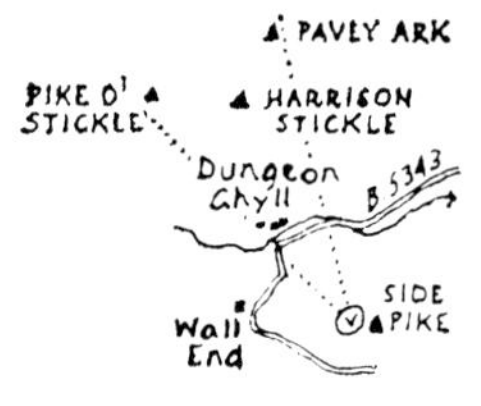

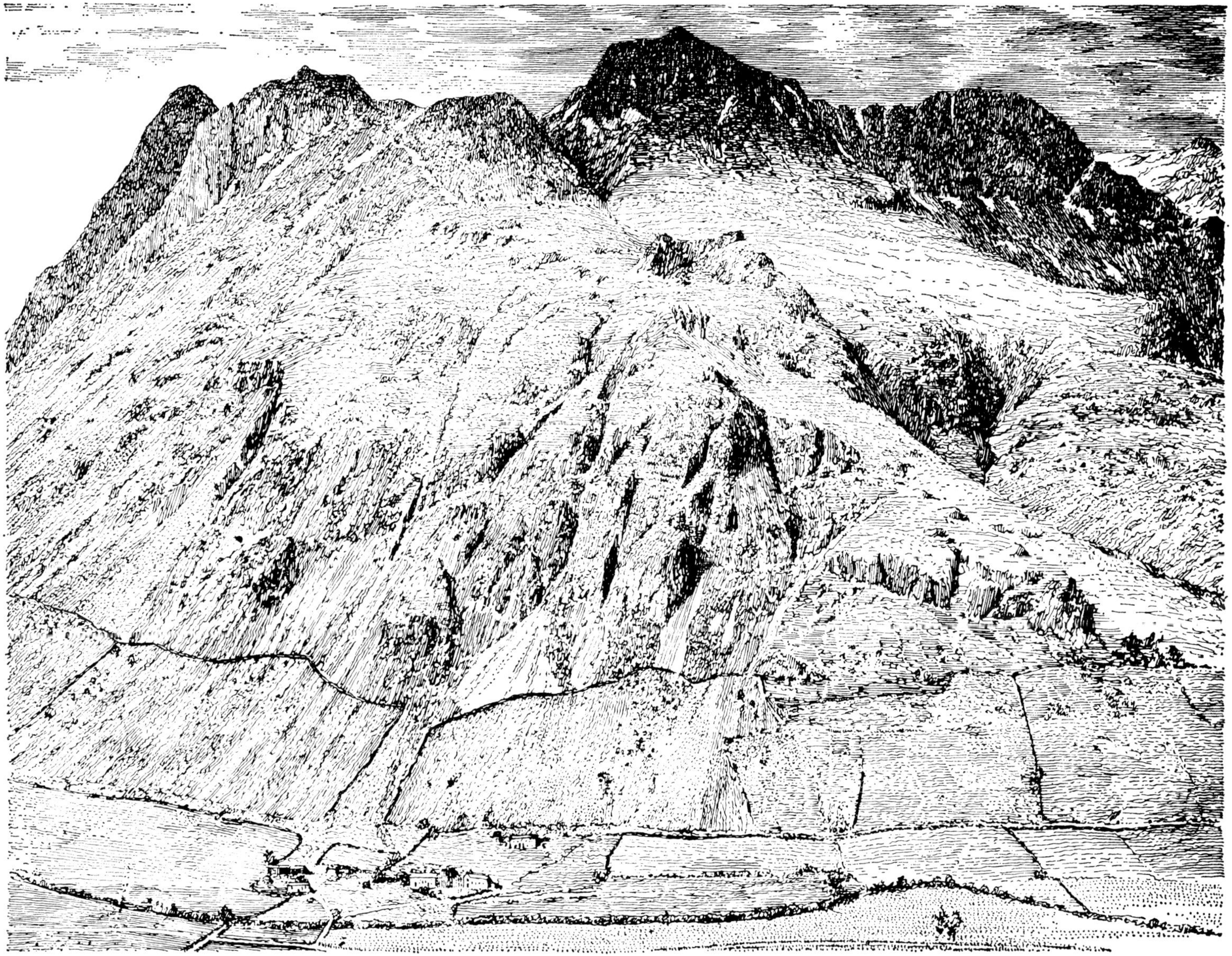

350 Grasmere Church

Grasmere Church, 'for duration built rather than raised in nice proportion', is the hallowed shrine of countless devotees of William Wordsworth who call to pay homage to the poet's memory. The graveyard is visited even more often than the church interior for in it lie his remains and those of his family and friends.

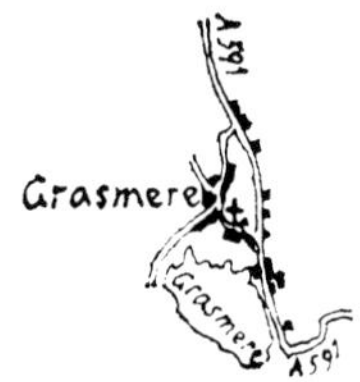

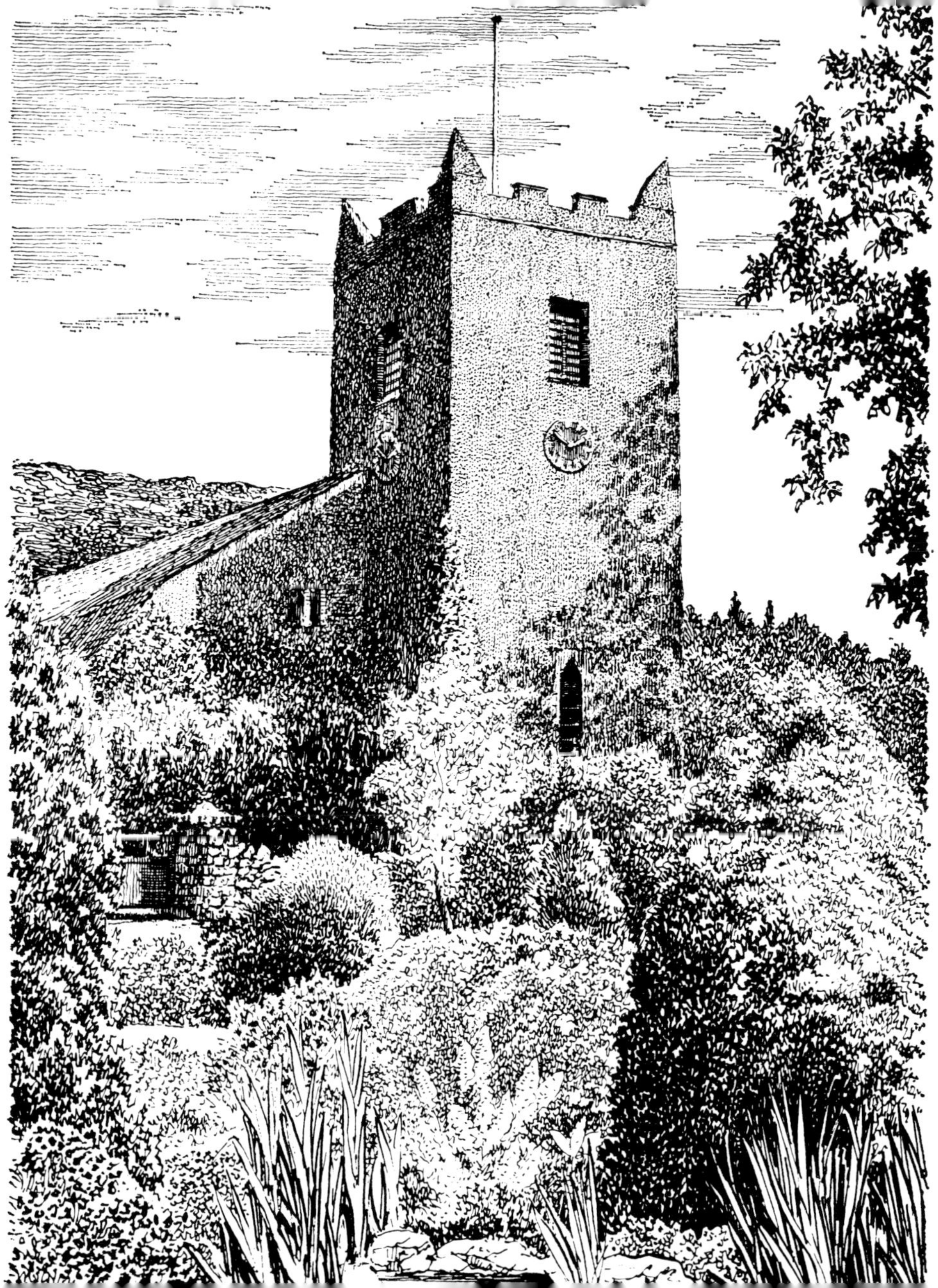

Sheffield Pike dominates the quiet side-valley of Glencoyne, where new plantings have concealed even more effectively the hidden row of miners' cottages (now 'holiday homes') known as Seldom Seen. The farmhouse of Glencoyne has notable features, particularly the round chimney stacks.

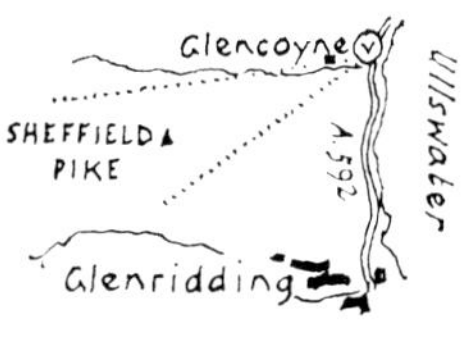

351 Sheffield Pike

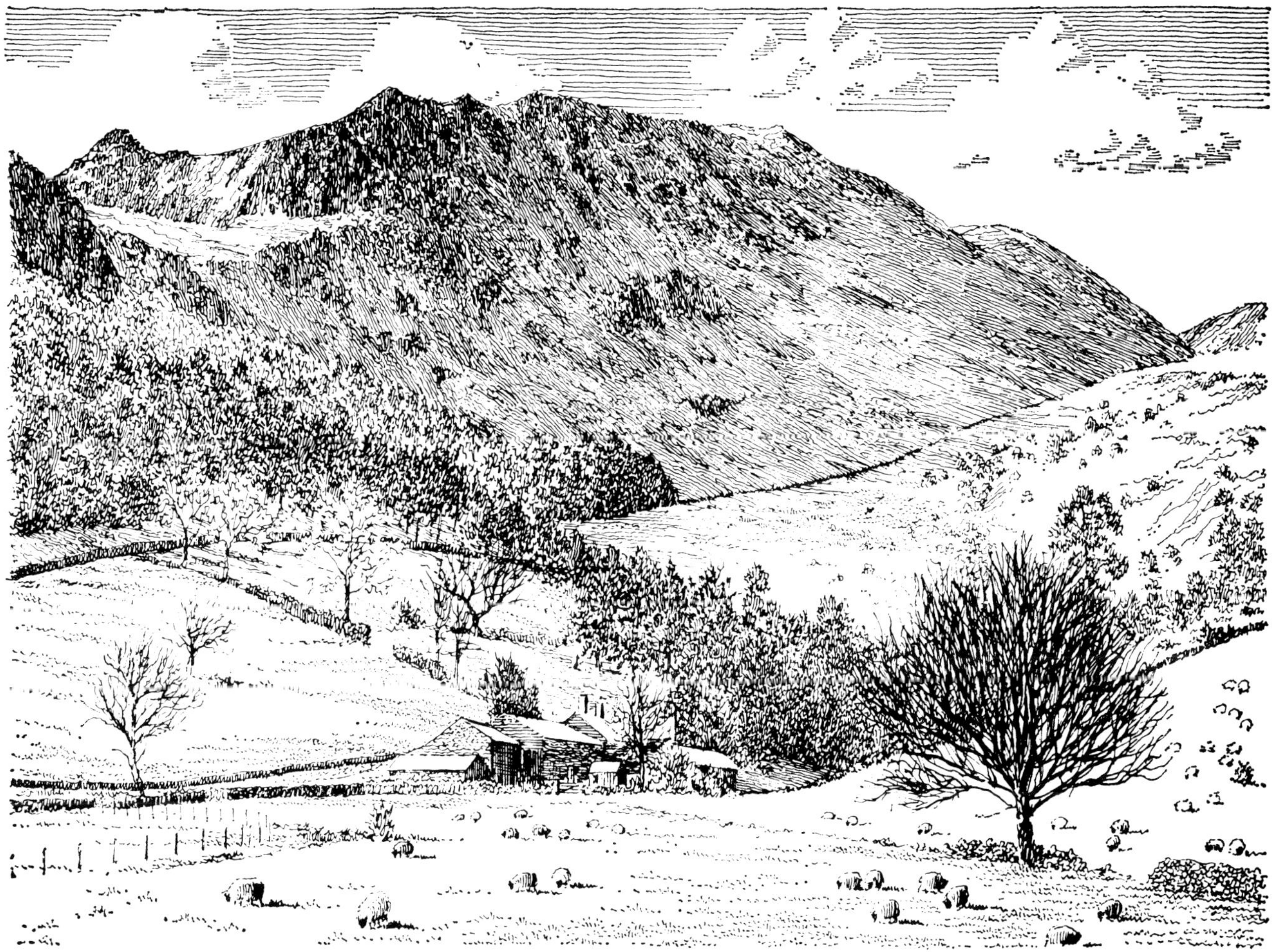

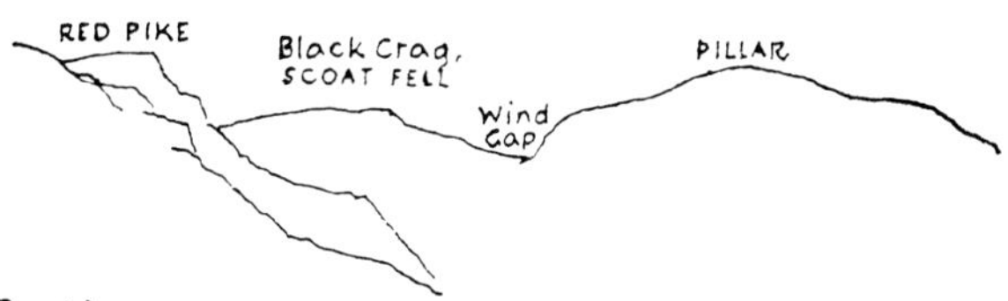
RED PIKE
Black Crag,
SCOAT FELL
Wind
Gap
PILLAR

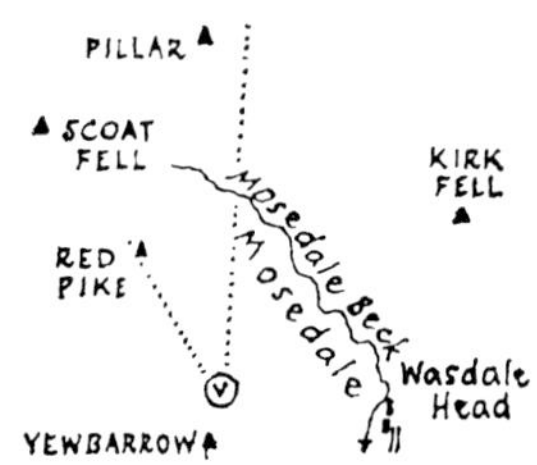
PILLAR
SCOAT
FELL
KIRK
FELL
RED
PIKE
Mosedale Beck
Mosedale
Wasdale
Head
YEWBARROW

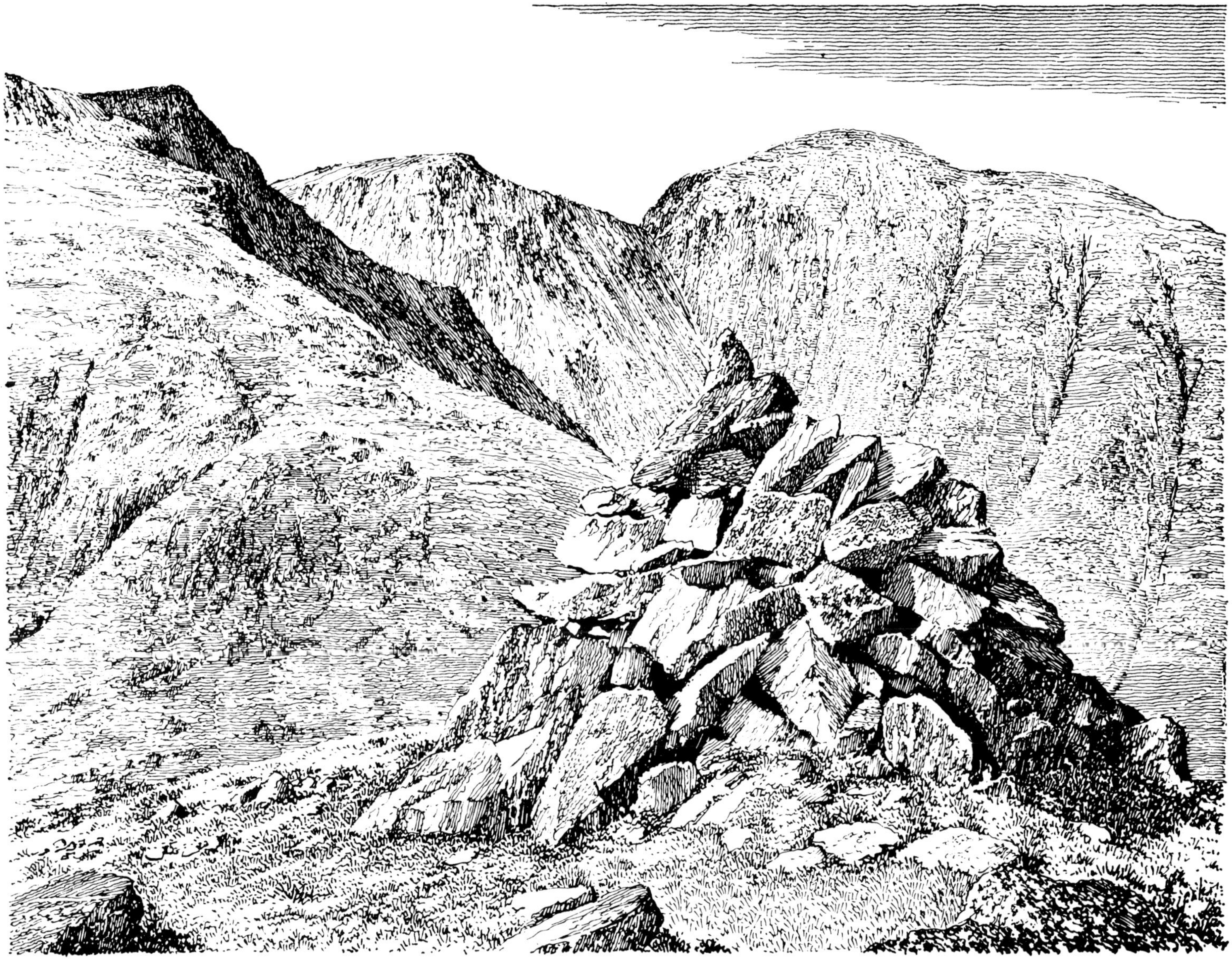

1 : PILLAR
2 : SCAFELL
3 : SCAFELL PIKE
4 : BROAD CRAG
5 : ILL CRAG
6 : GREAT END
7 : ESK PIKE
8 : BOWFELL
9 : CRINKLE CRAGS

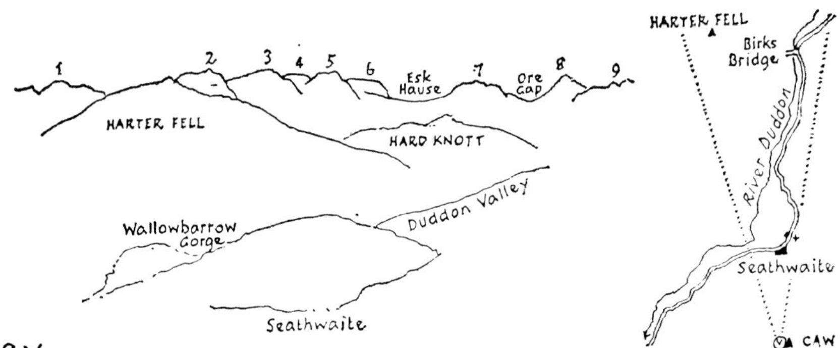

353 The Duddon Valley

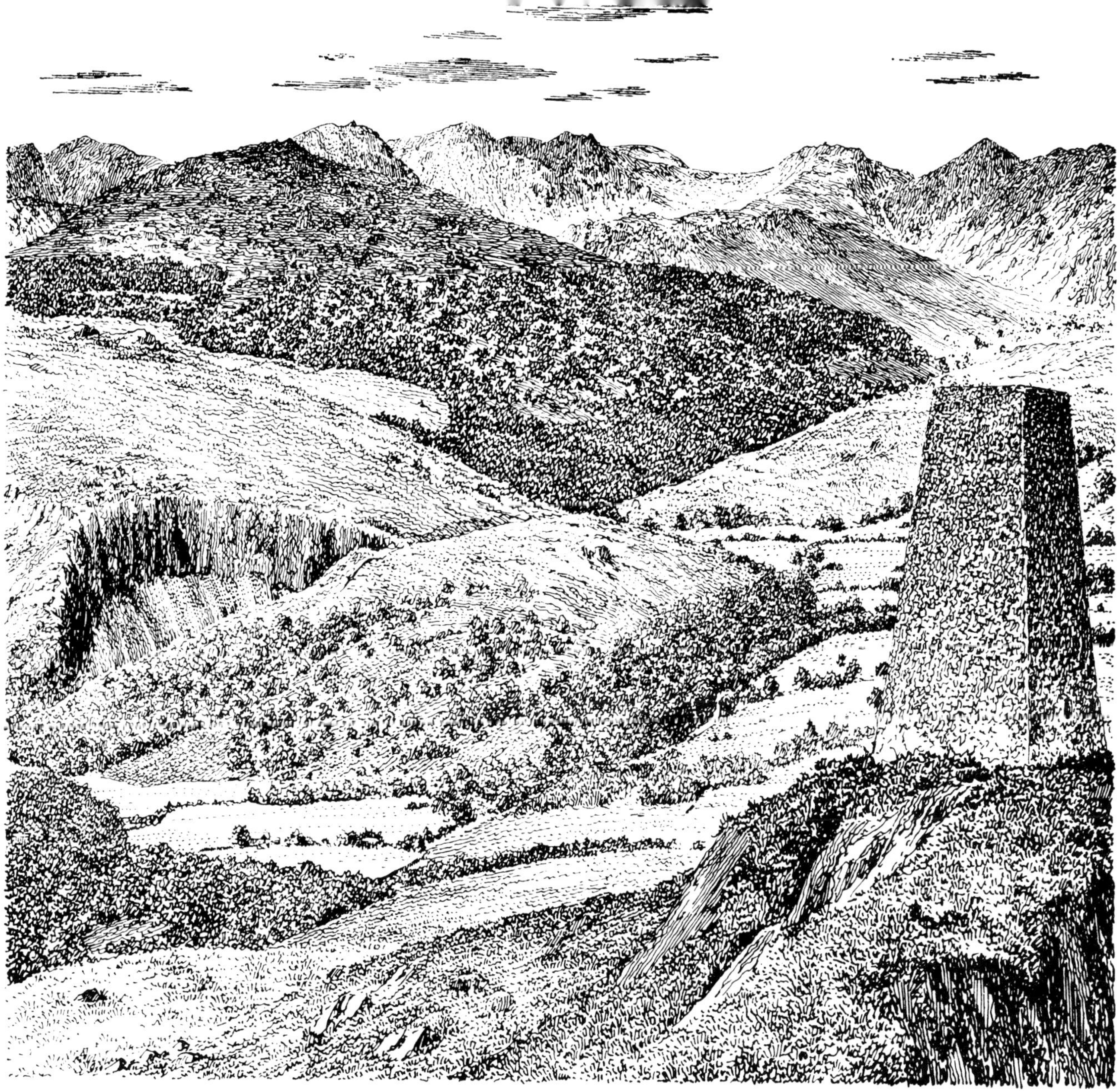

354 Easedale Tarn

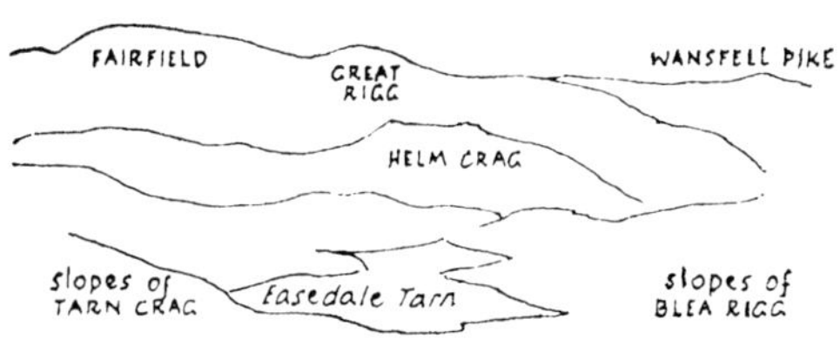

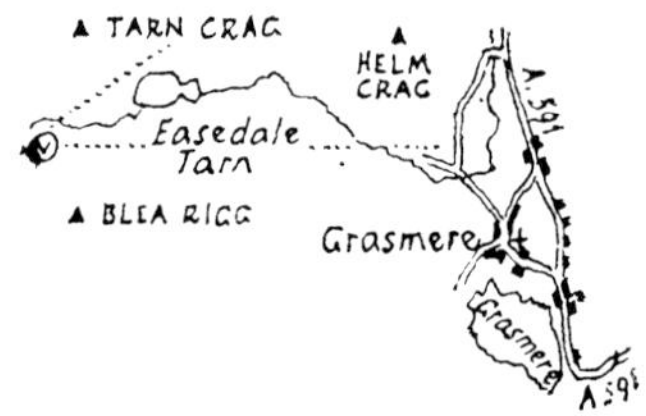

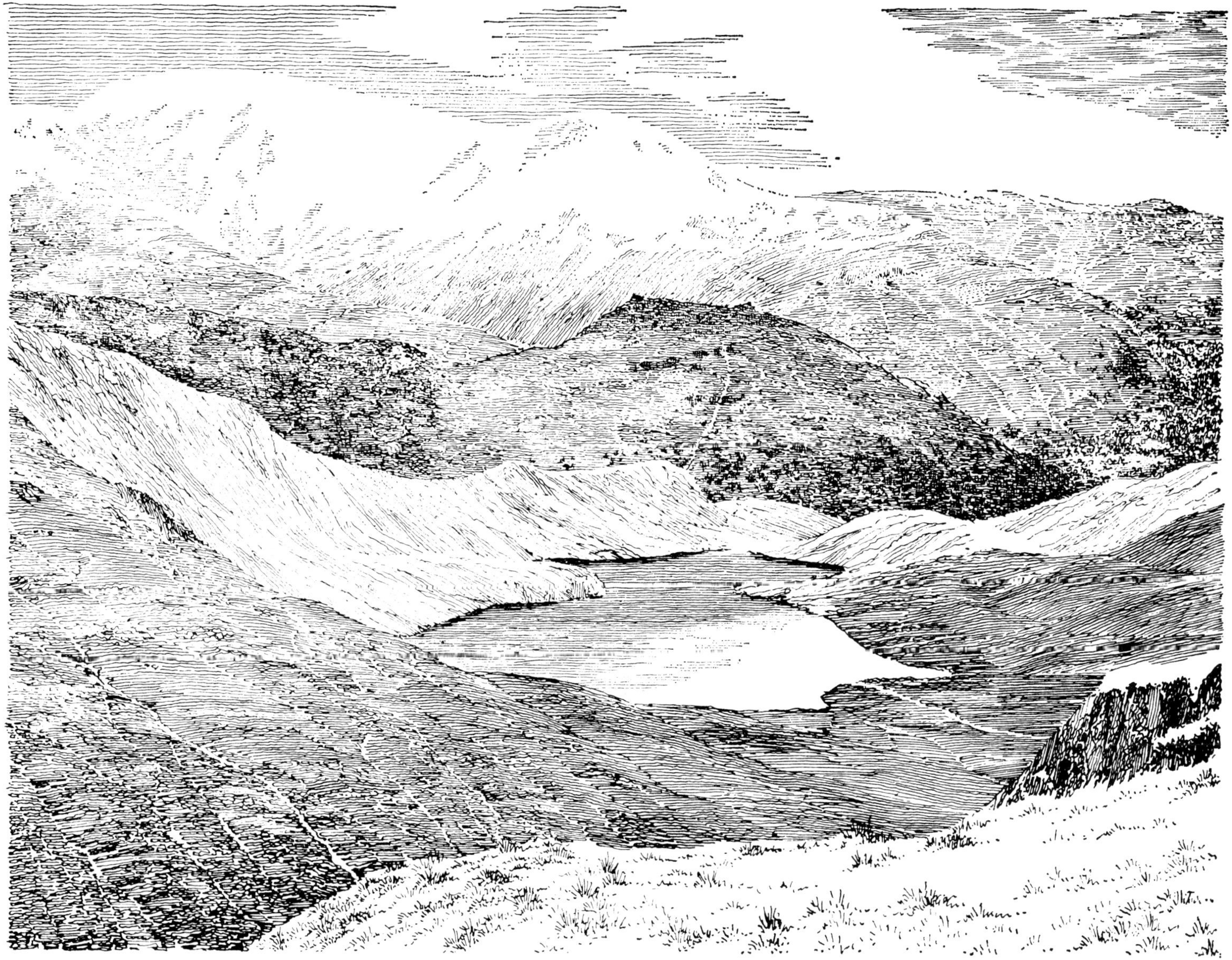

Of the two Red Pikes, the one commonly distinguished by the addition of 'Wasdale' to the name (the other being at Buttermere) overlooks not Wasdale but Mosedale, the summit towering above a rugged declivity, a tremendous downfall of cliffs: one of the least-explored fellsides in the district.

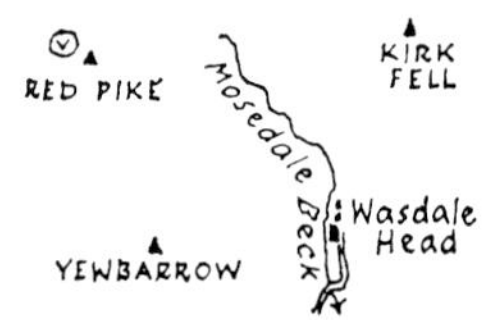

355 Red Pike, Wasdale

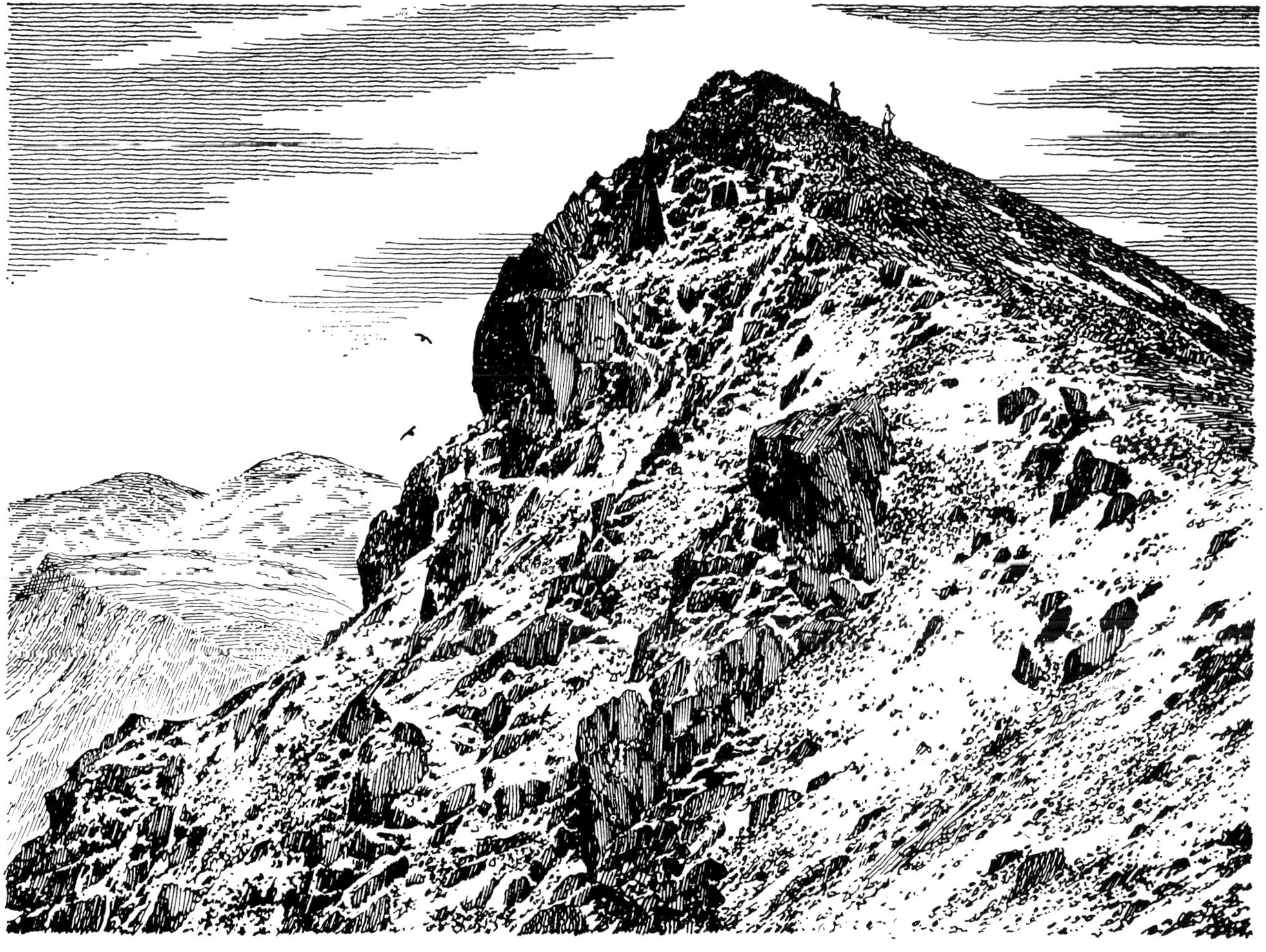

Carrock Fell comes suddenly into view along the road from Mungrisdale at the hamlet of Bowscale, a typical huddle of stone buildings that have defied improvements to the narrow road between them. Carrock Fell is remarkable for its diversity of interests.

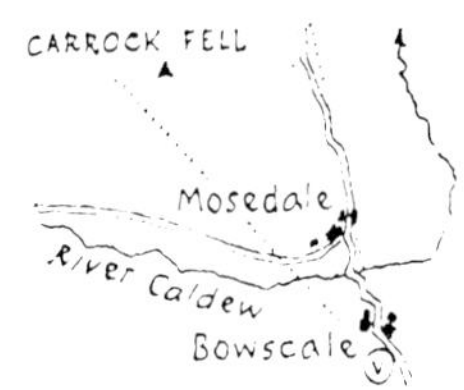

356 Bowscale and Carrock Fell

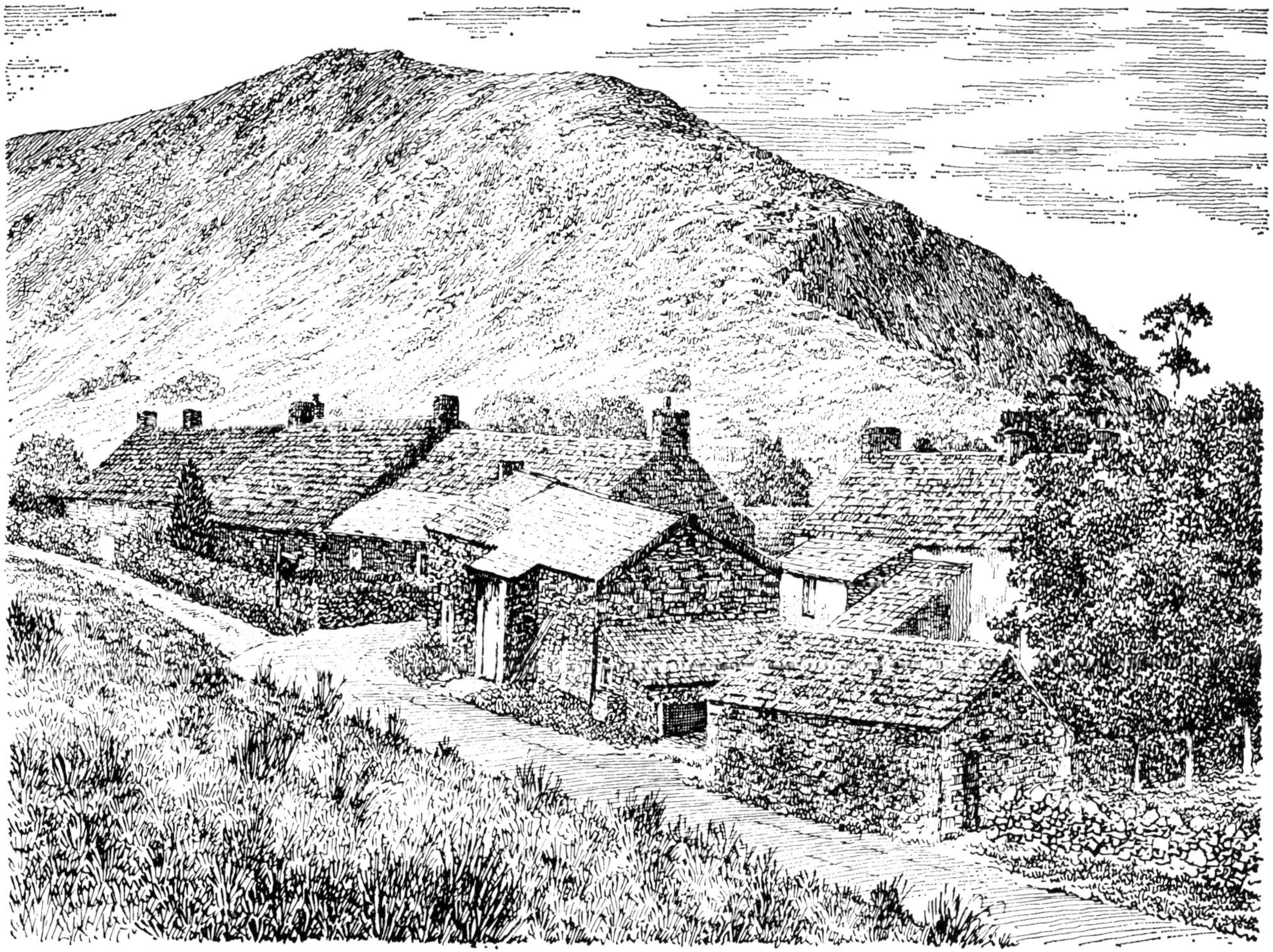

357 Demavend
— a modern residence

Up to the last war buildings in Lakeland followed traditional lines in the use of local stone and slate, quarried in the district and of a colour and texture exclusive to it, but more recently there have been wide departures in the choice of materials, not all of them so pleasing in appearance and some completely out of character. Little exception can be taken, however, (apart perhaps from the name) to the house here illustrated, built in Scandinavian style and beautifully sited on a knoll of Scots pines overlooking Windermere. This is the home of Miss Mary Burkett, Director of Abbot Hall Art Gallery, Kendal, and an authority on matters Persian — hence the name, neither Lakeland nor Scandinavian!

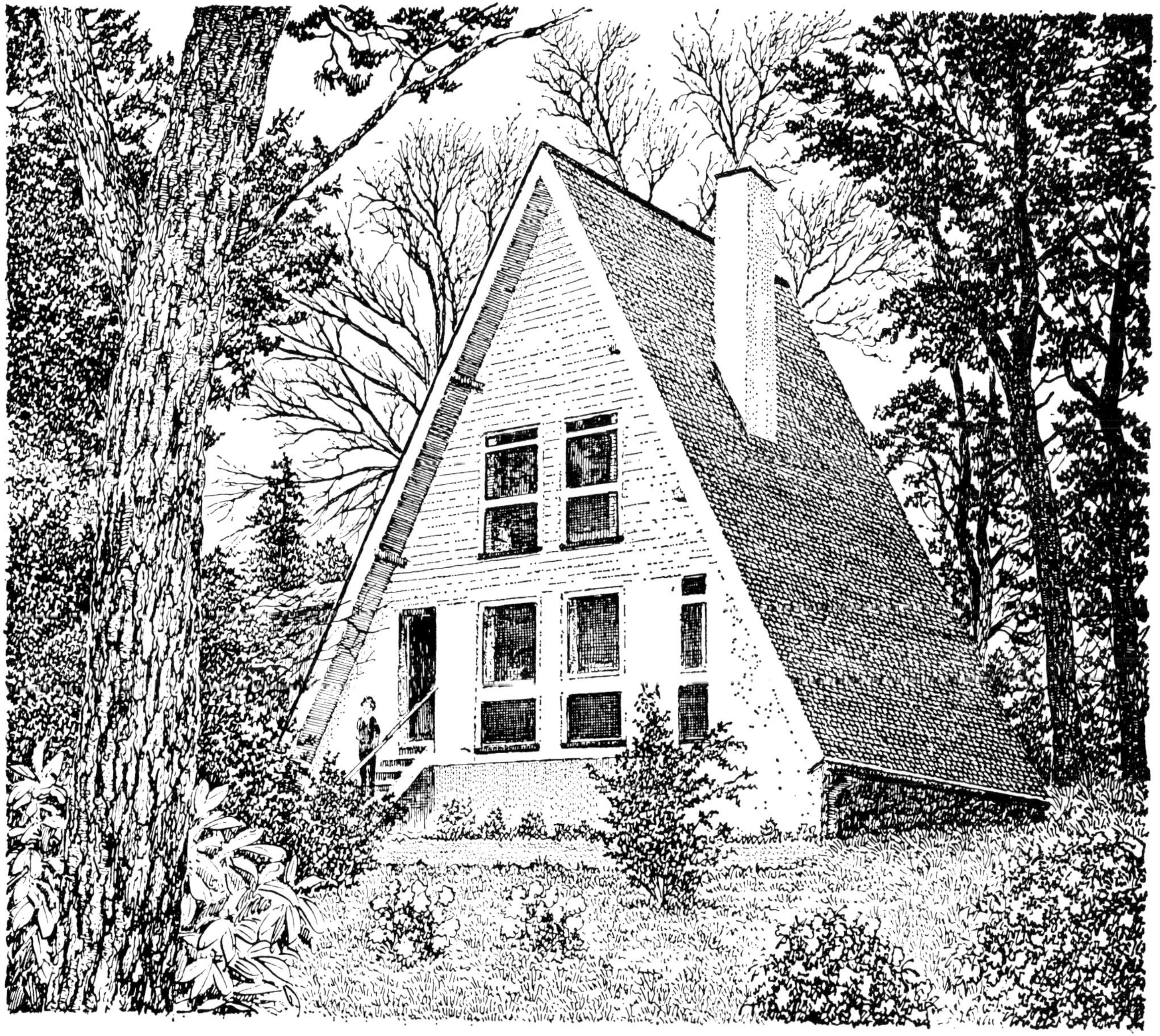

The very popular Tarn Hows has a counterpart in High Dam, which is no less lovely, and, in its favour, is too primitive to be furnished with a network of well-blazed footpaths, car parks, litter bins, toilets and other marks of sophistication. Tarn Hows draws the crowds, High Dam a discerning few.

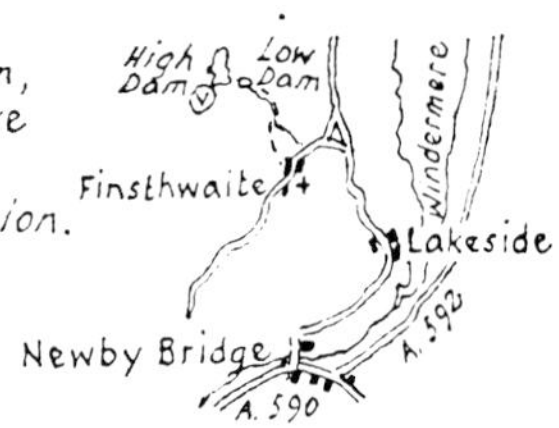

358 High Dam, Finsthwaite

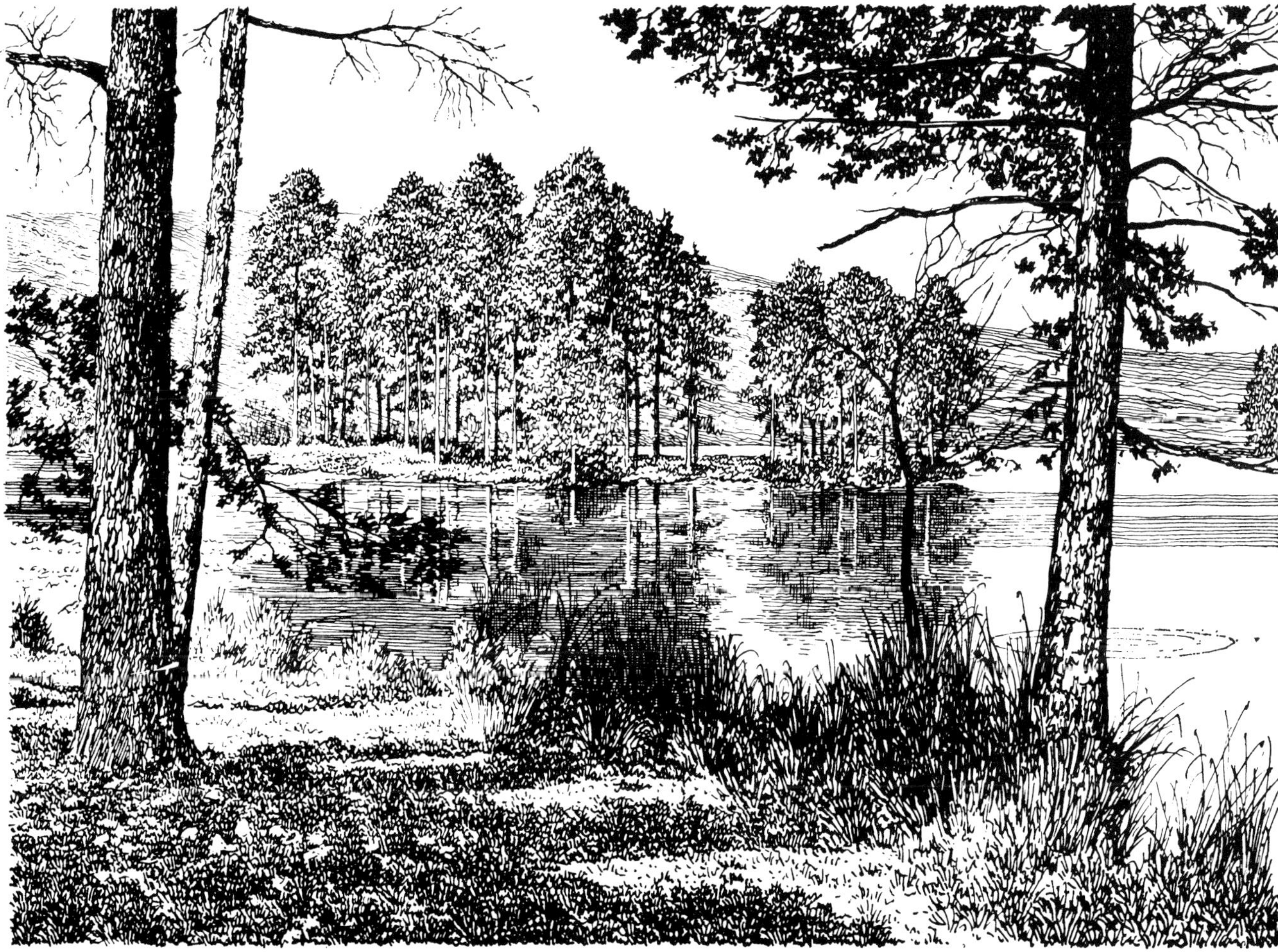

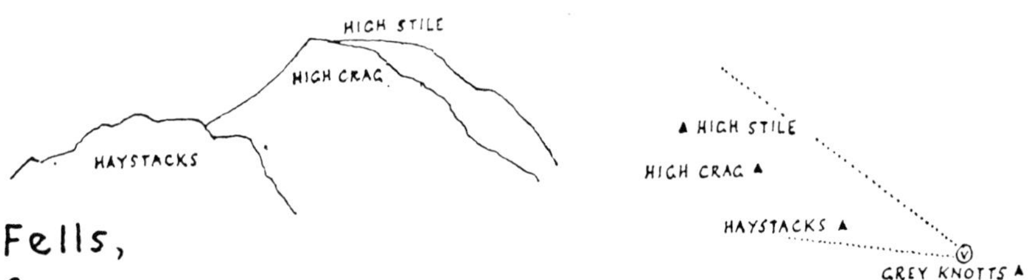

359 The Buttermere Fells,
from Grey Knotts

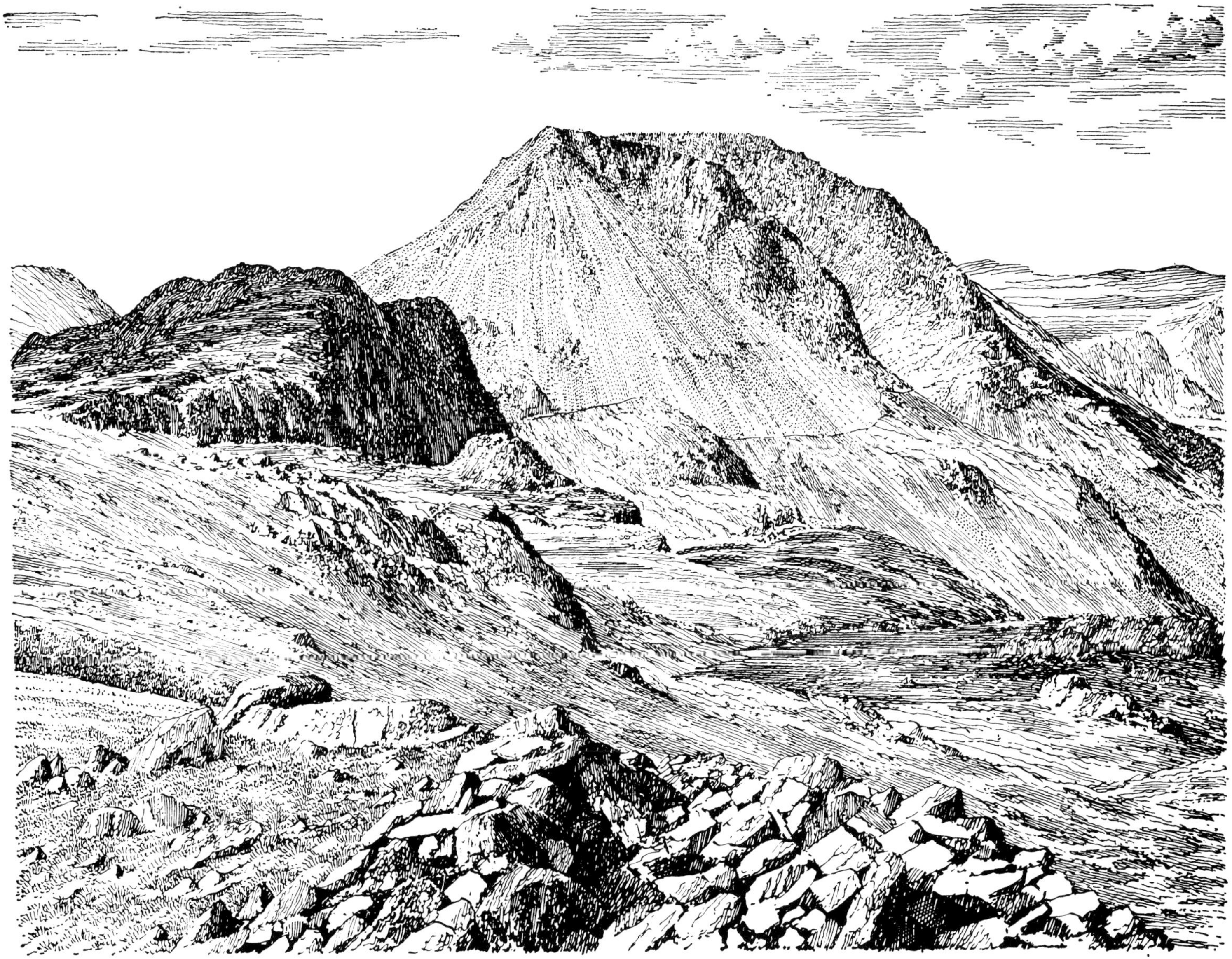

An upland desert of stones, a sterile wilderness, a wasteland: this is Nature's design for the highest ground in England. Man's contributions to the scene are a massive cairn, a War Memorial tablet, a survey column, and litter. There is nothing of beauty on the top of Scafell Pike.

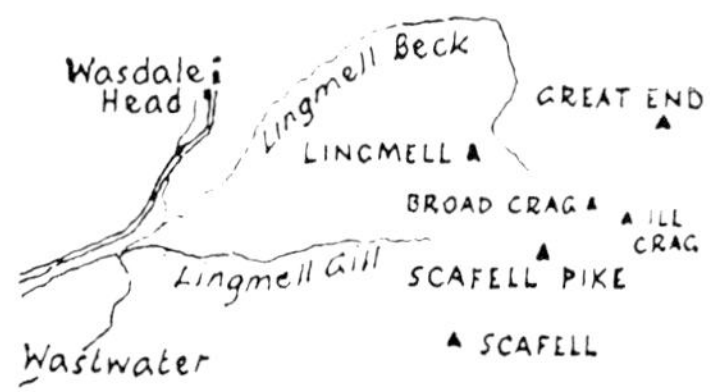

360 The summit of Scafell Pike

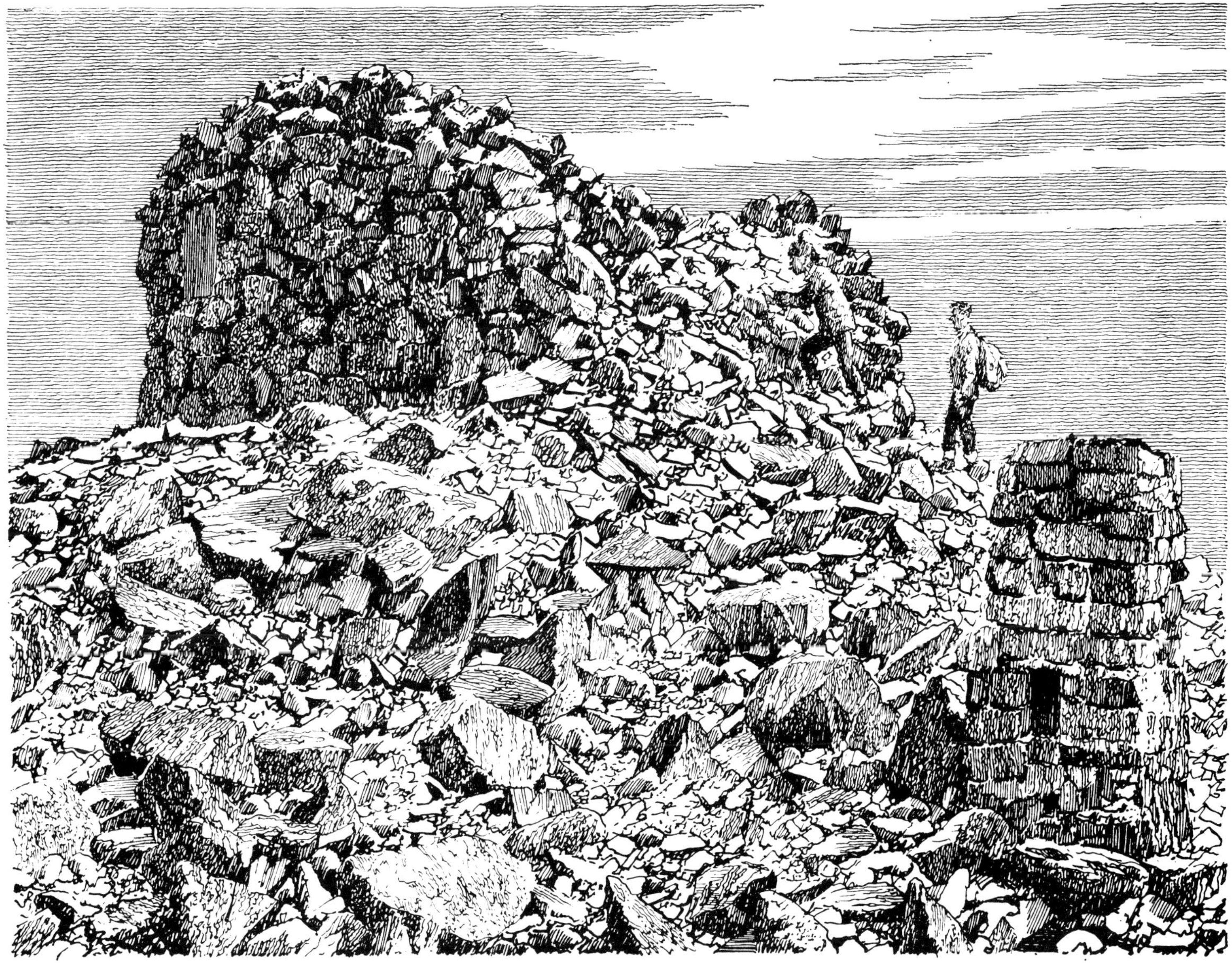

A : Walkers' path B : Rake's Progress C : Mickledore Ridge
1 : Broad Stand
2 : Mickledore Chimney
3 : Central Buttress
4 : Moss Gill 5 : Steep Gill
6 : Scafell Pinnacle
7 : Deep Gill Buttress
8 : West Wall Traverse
9 : Deep Gill
10 : Lord's Rake
11 : Tower Buttress

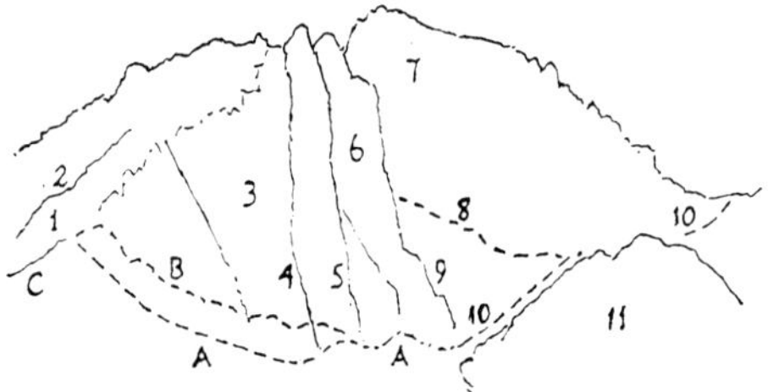

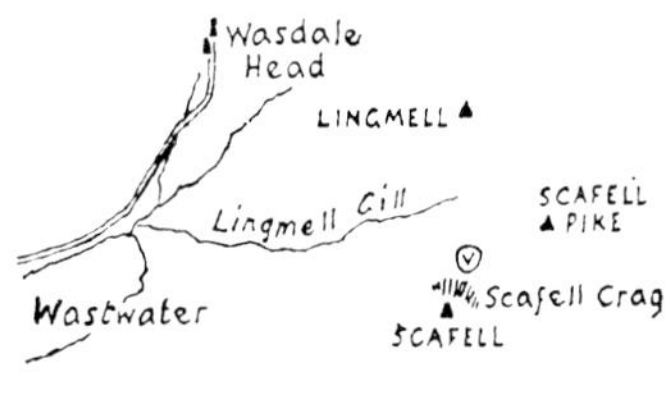

361 Scafell Crag

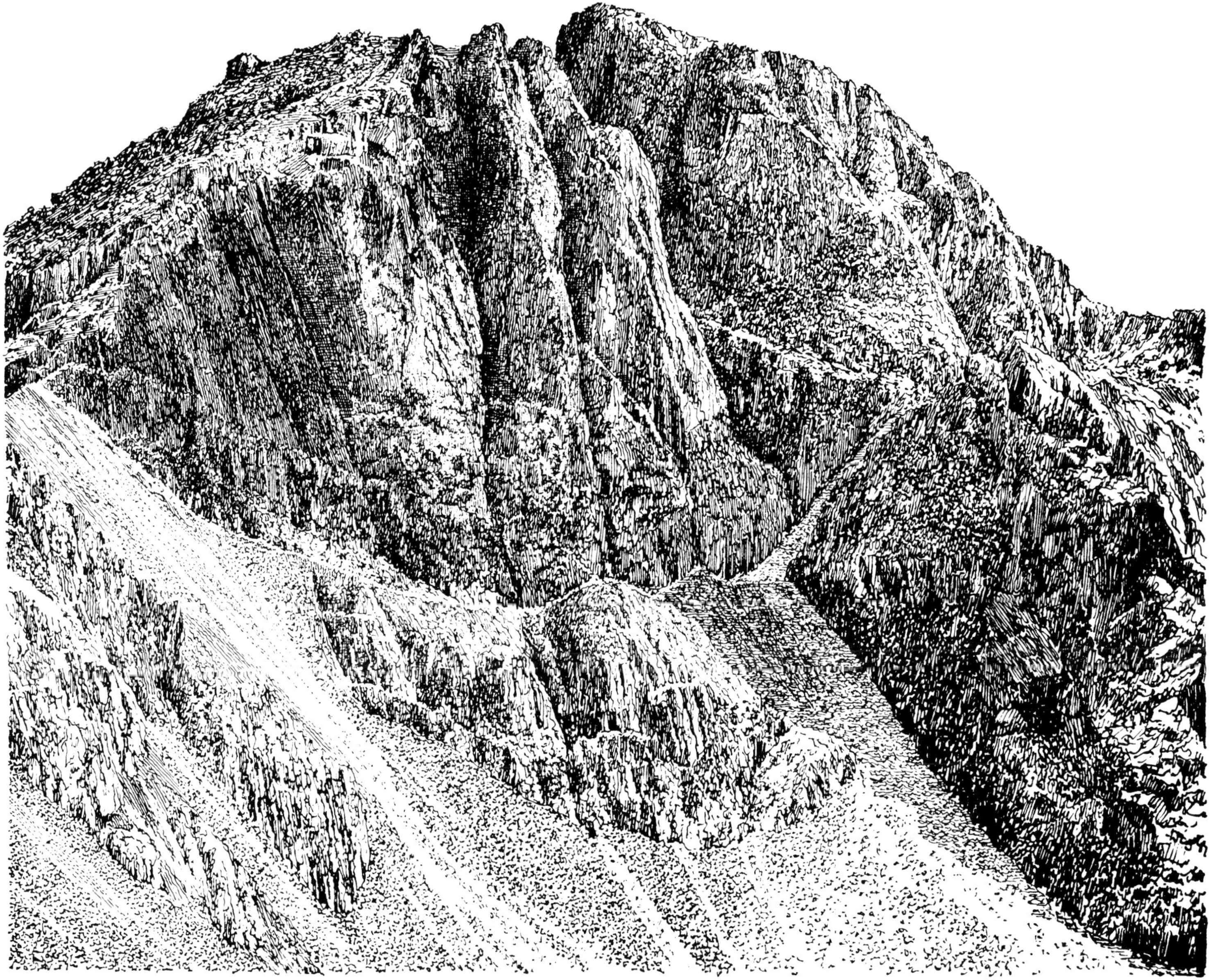

1: HIGH STILE
2: BLAKE FELL
3: CARLING KNOTT
4: MELLBREAK
5: LOW FELL
6: RANNERDALE KNOTTS
7: GRASMOOR
8: *Buttermere*
9: *Crummock Water*

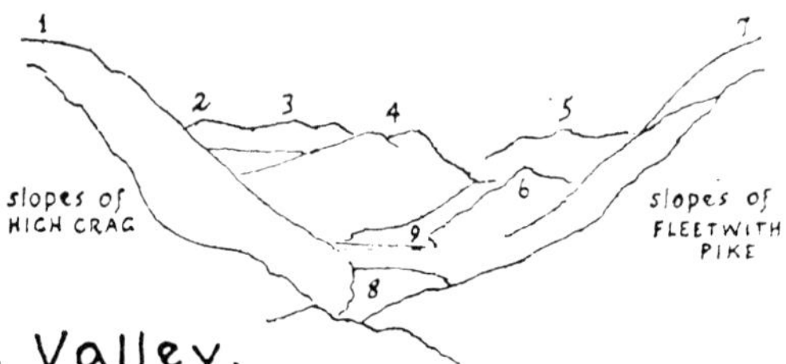

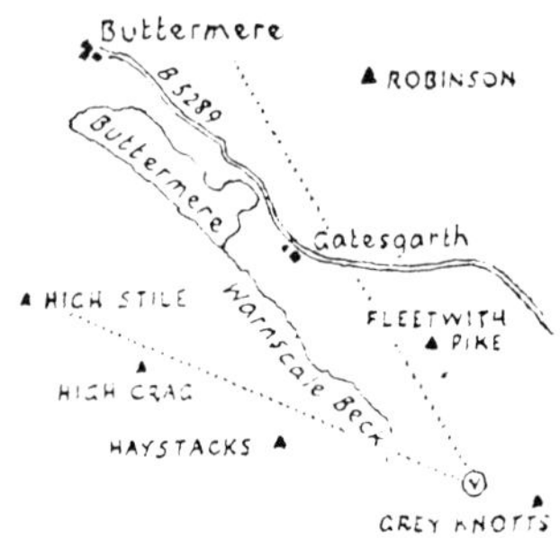

The Buttermere Valley,
from Grey Knotts

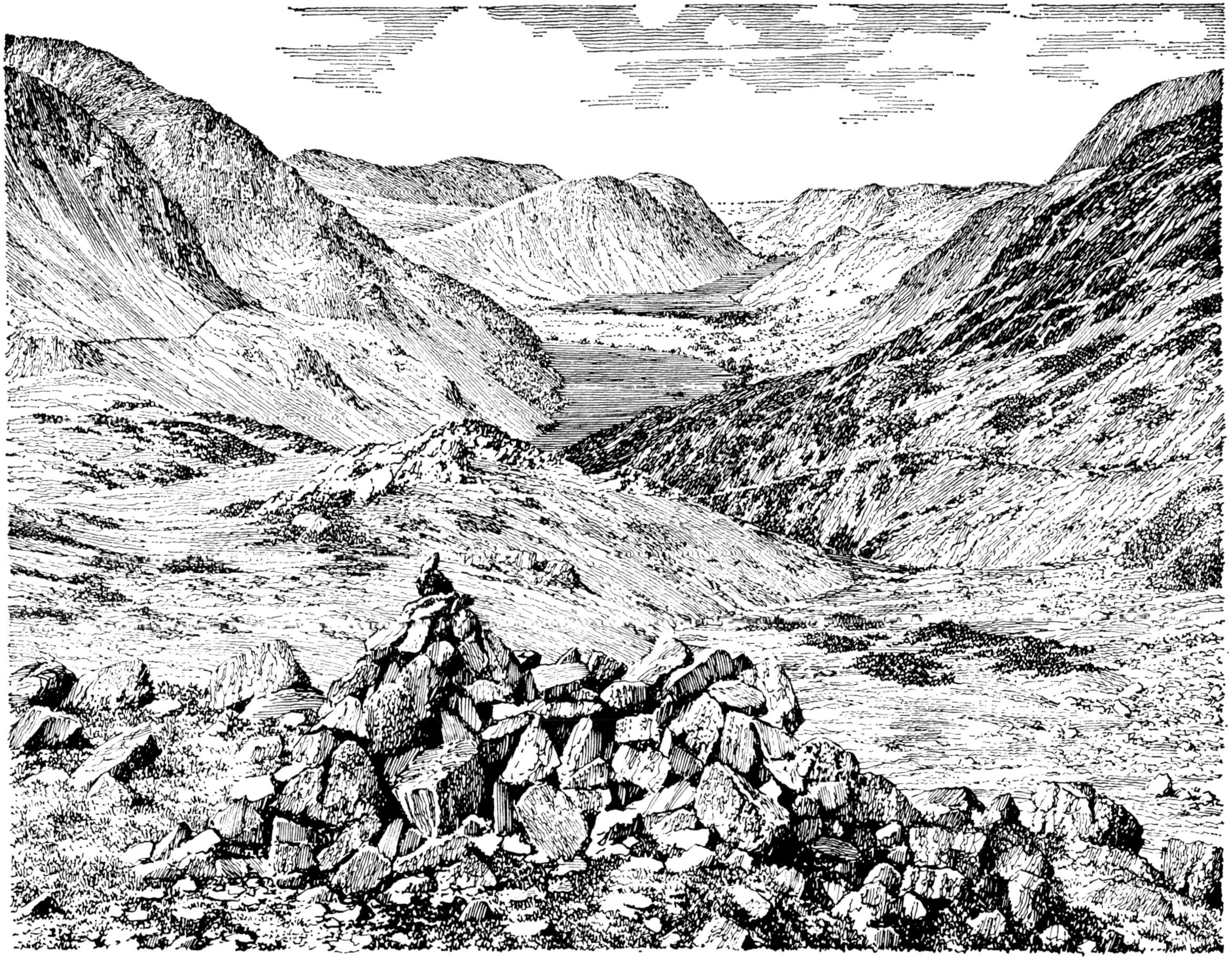

Low Dam and the neighbouring larger High Dam are still functional as reservoirs but no longer used as such with the closing of works in the valley. Low Dam is reached through woodlands on a right of way from Finsthwaite : it is small, encircled by fine trees and altogether charming.

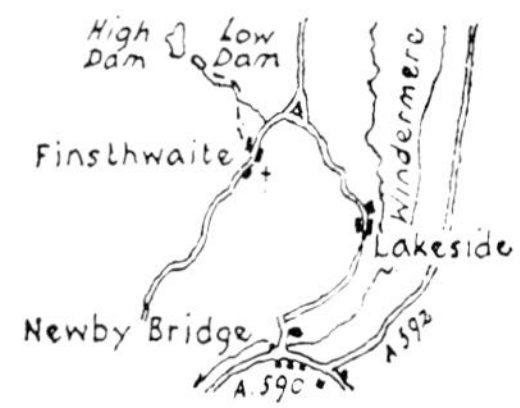

363 Low Dam, Finsthwaite

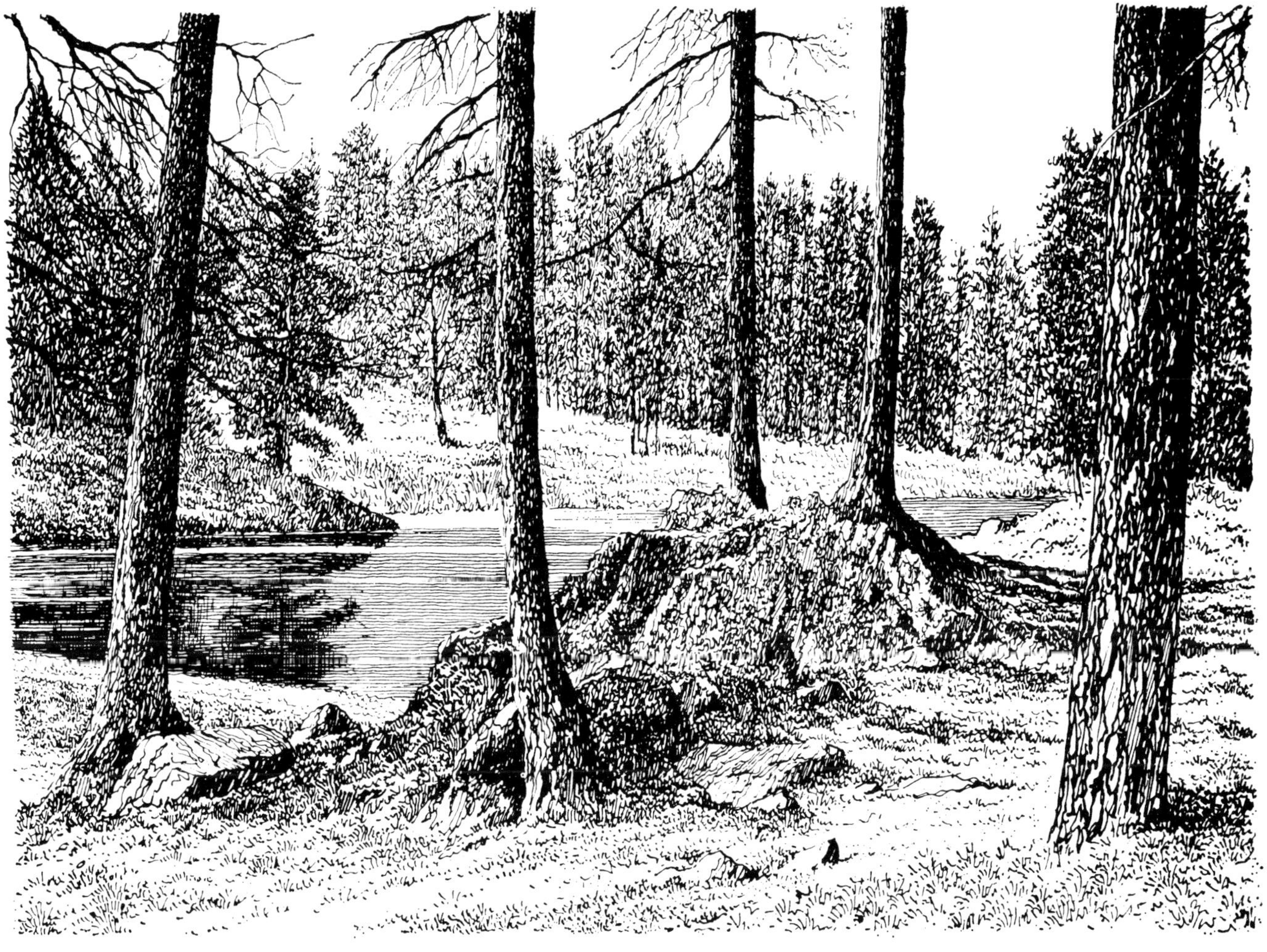

A path that is a joy on a bright summer morning is the rough track leading up the Stonethwaite valley towards the hills. It is untidy and stony, winding its way amongst boulders and tumbledown walls and bracken with the tree-fringed beck nearby, but as a prelude to a day on the tops it is perfect.

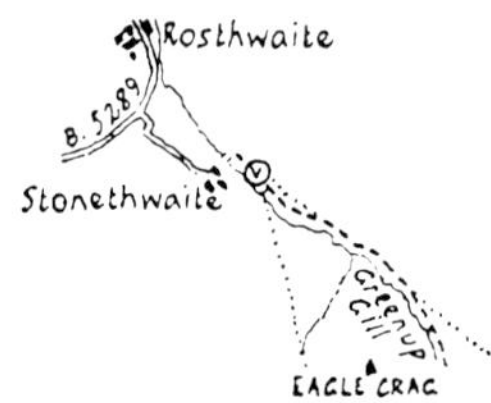

364 The path to Greenup

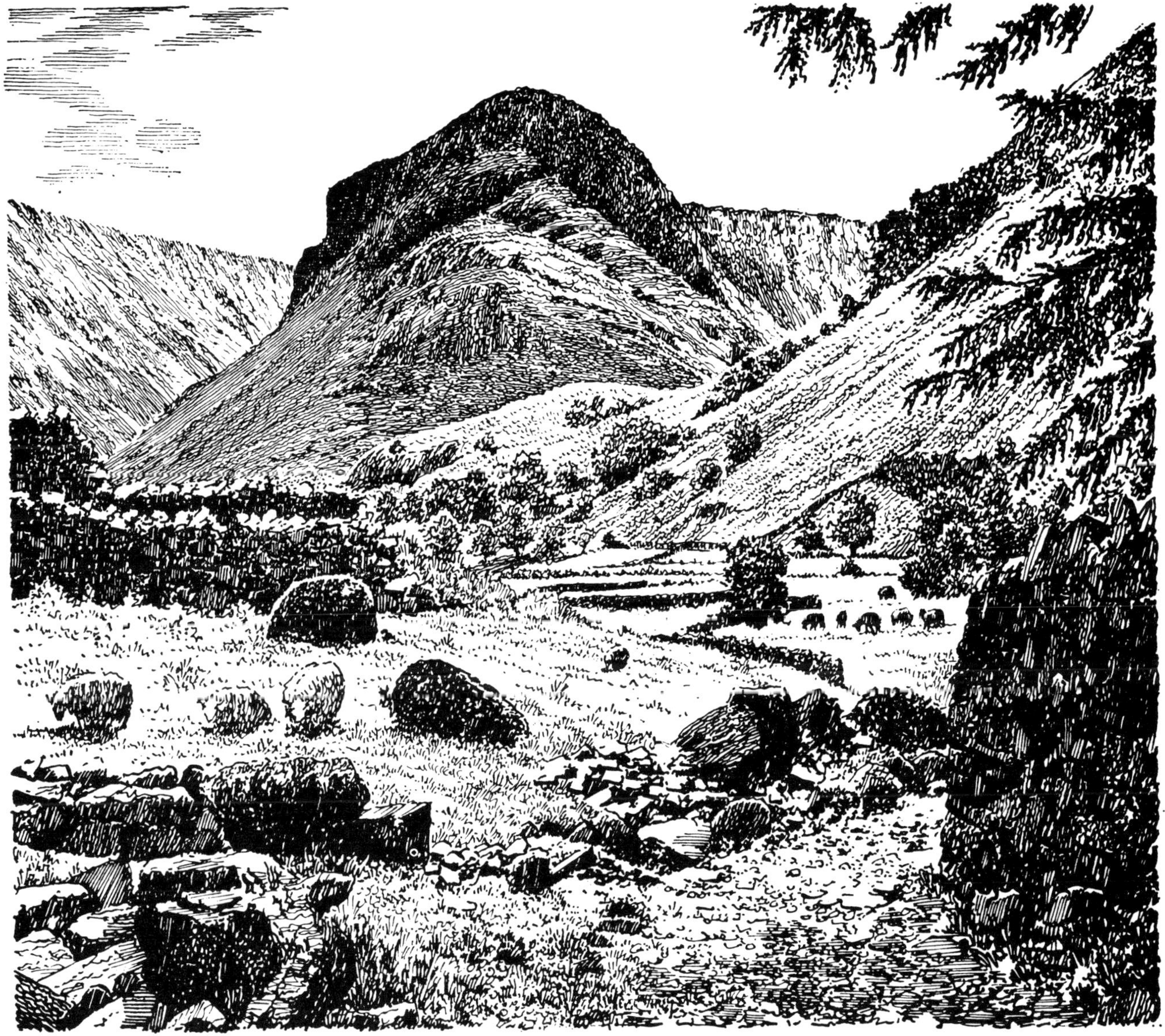

Sandwick is a motorist's dead end, a walker's springboard to a delectable path along the shore of Ullswater, the four miles to Patterdale being the most beautiful lakeside ramble of all.

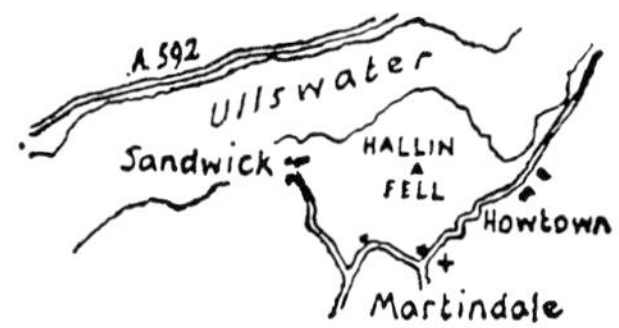

365 Sandwick

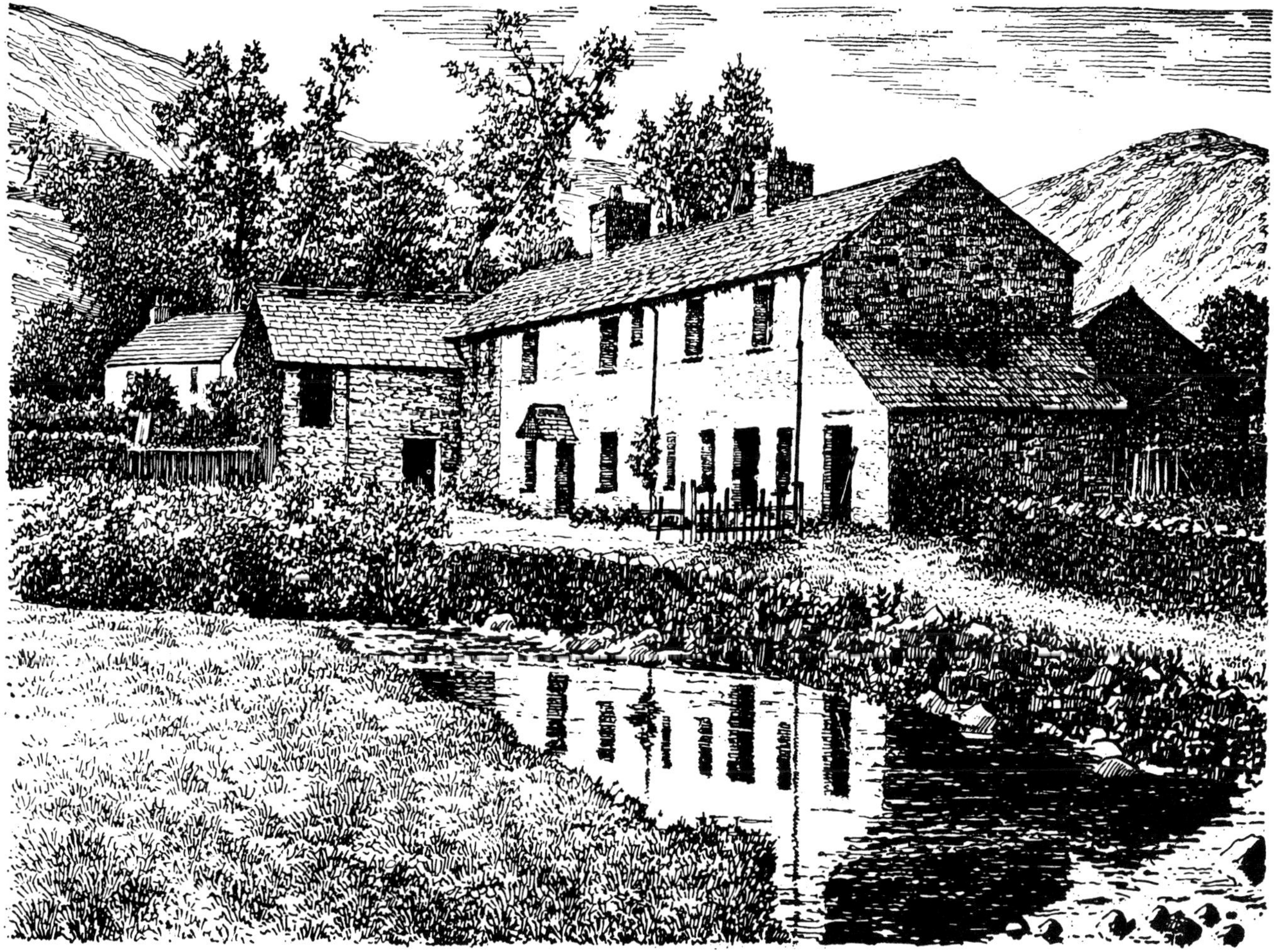

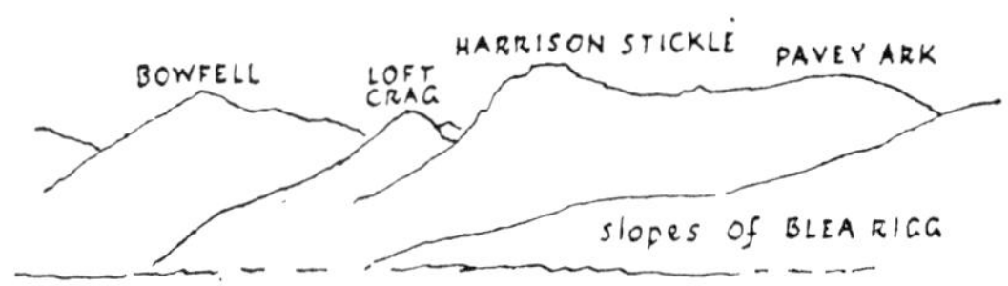

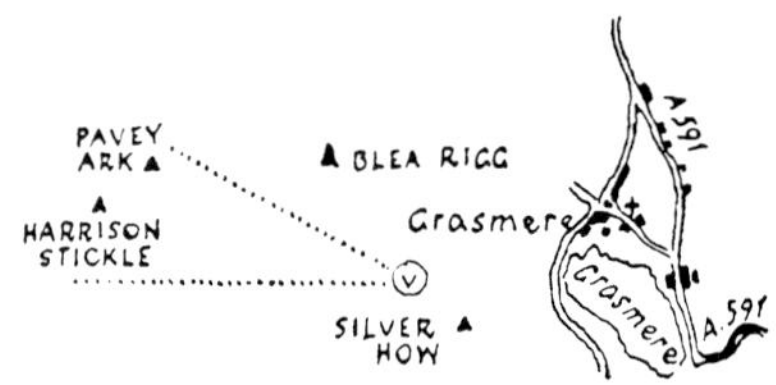

366 Tarn on Silver How

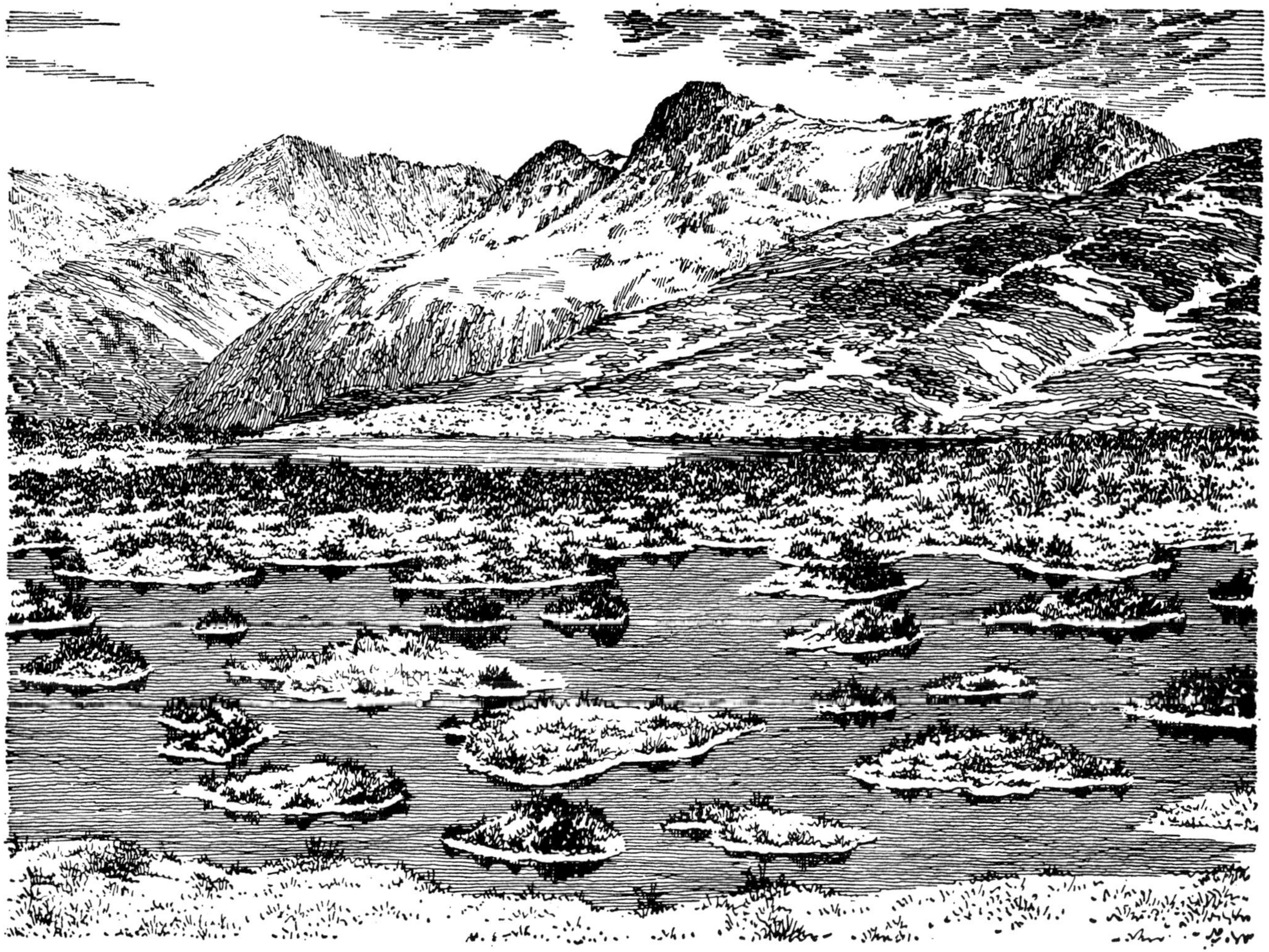

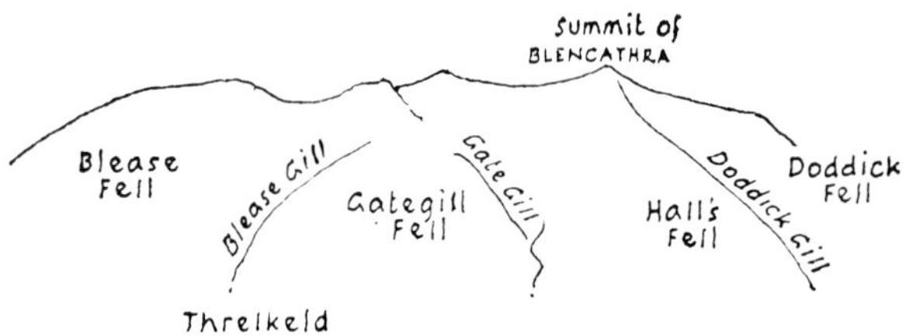

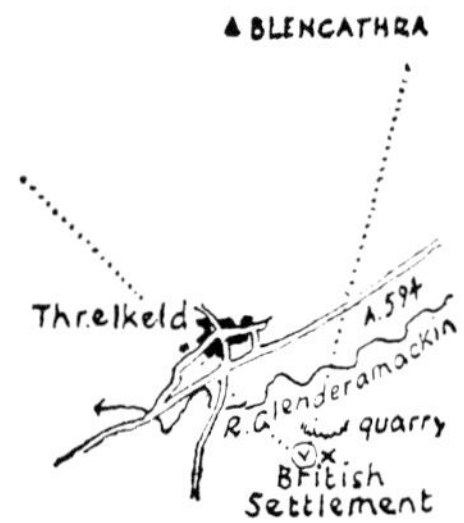

367 Blencathra, from the British Settlement

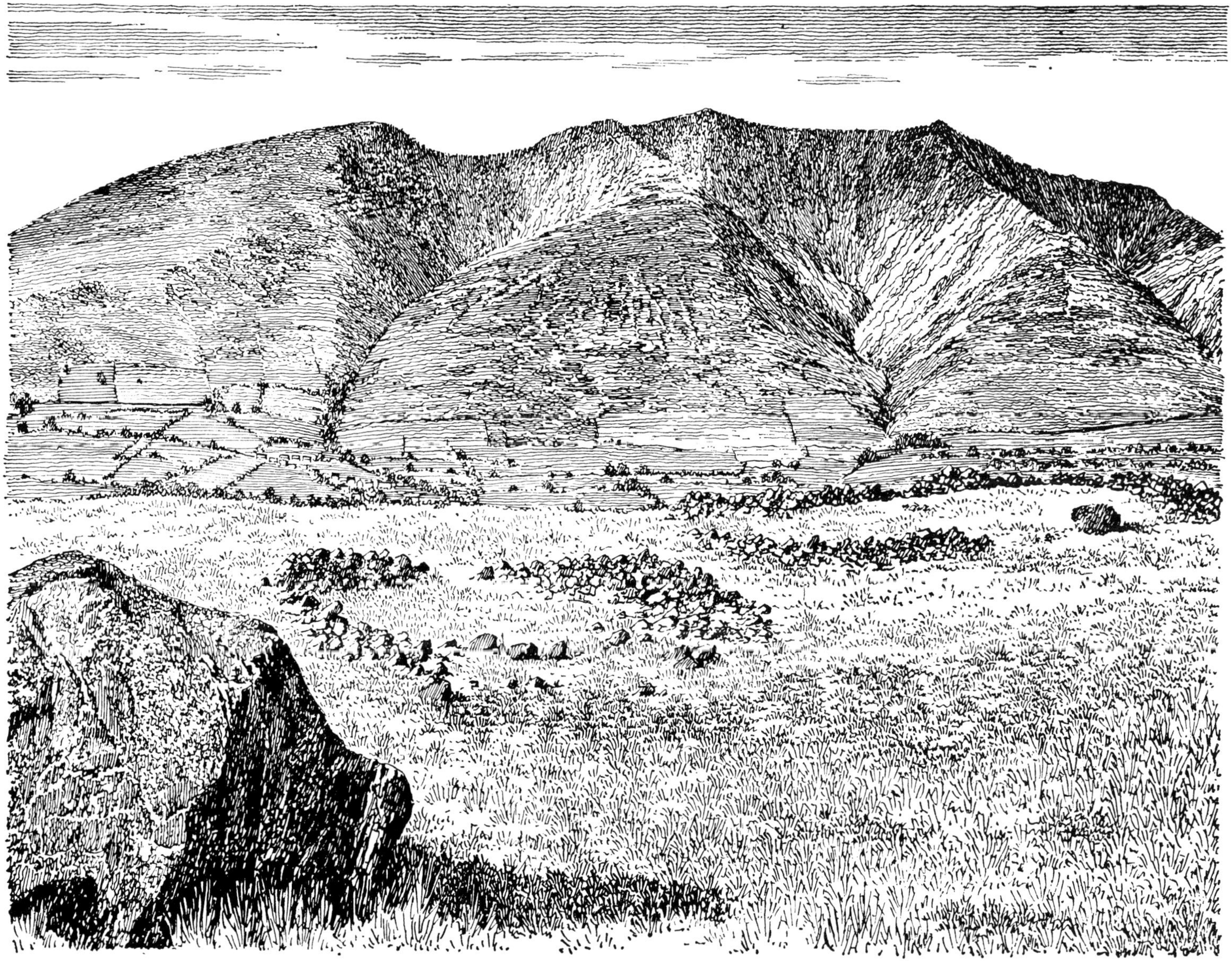

The vast slopes of scree falling into Wastwater give place, near the foot of the lake, to steep buttresses cleft by tremendous rifts — a no-man's-land for the walker and a strict preserve only for experienced climbers.

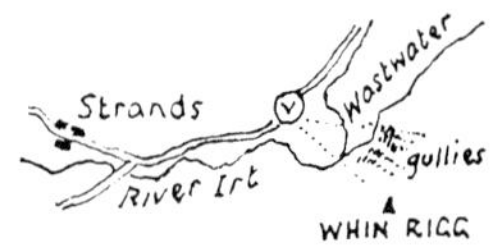

368 The Screes Gullies, Wastwater

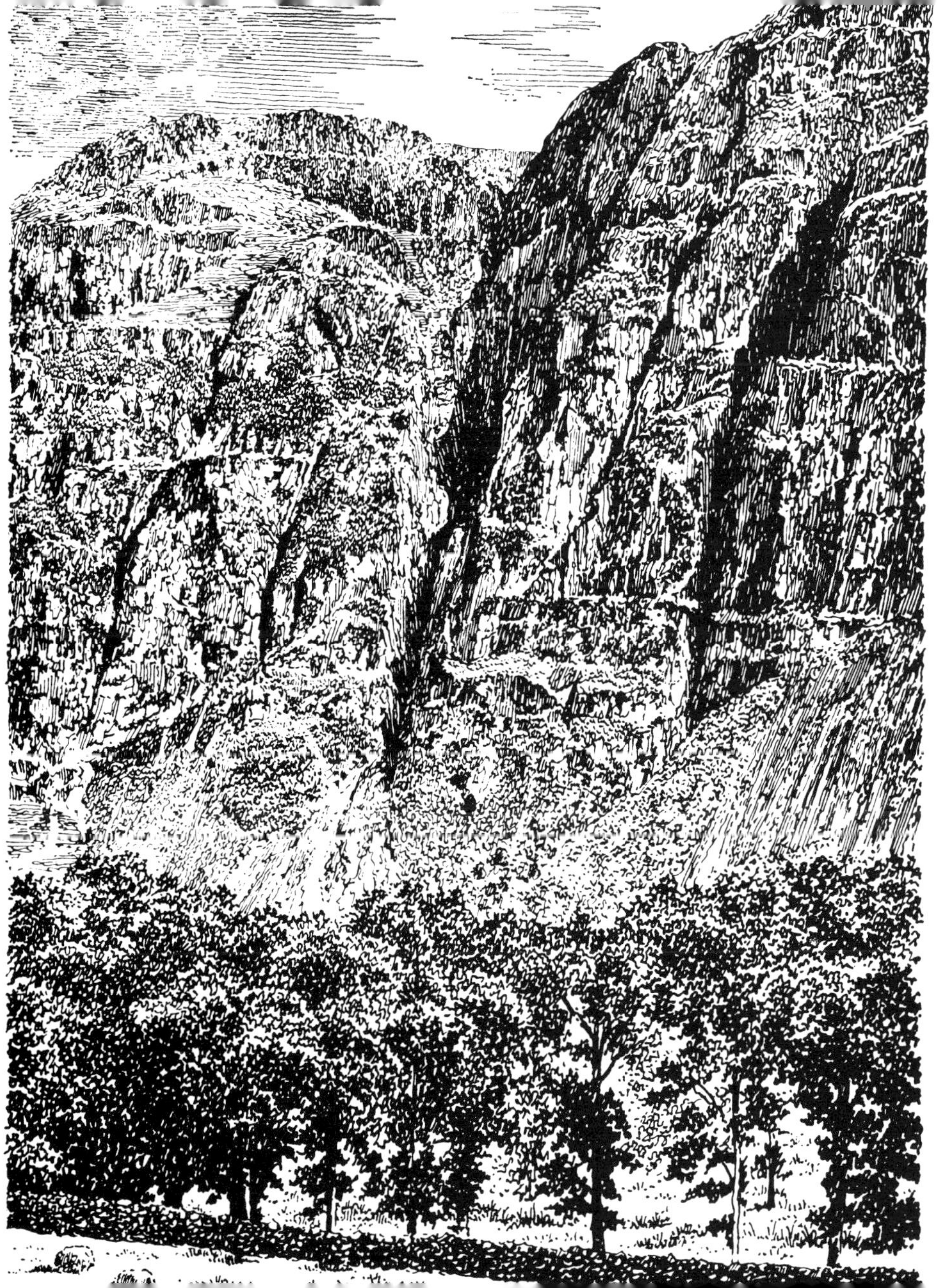

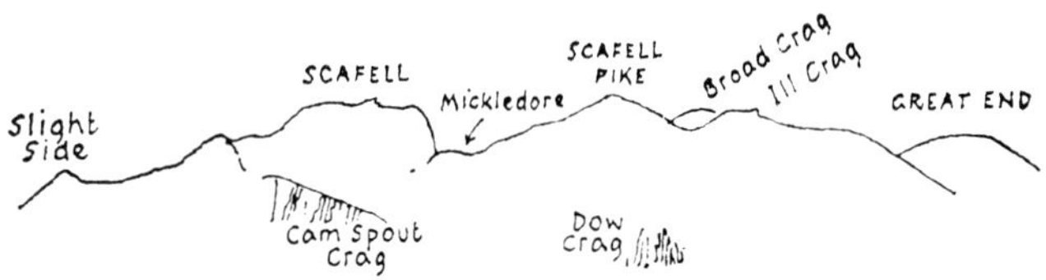

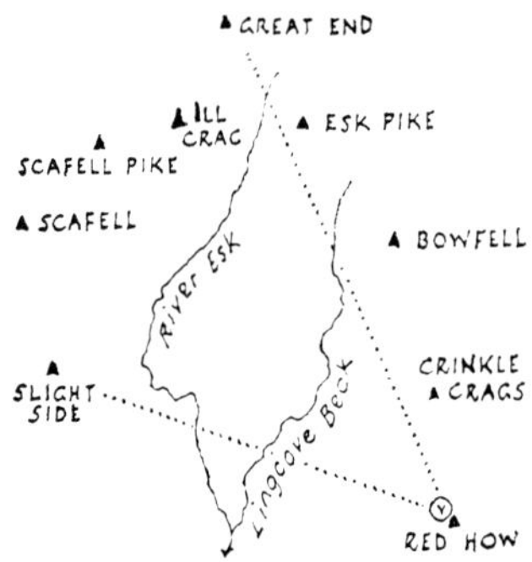

369 The Scafells, from Red How

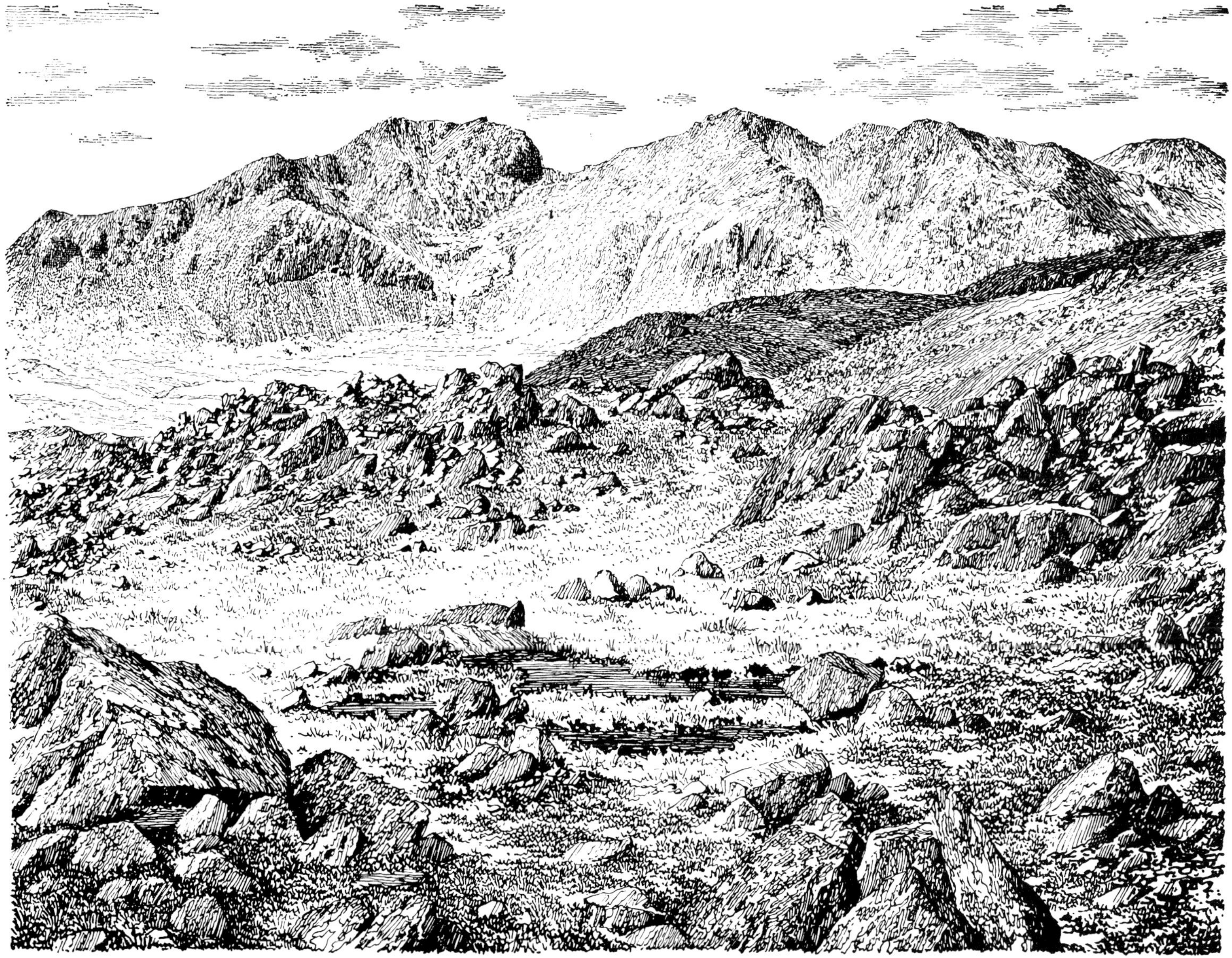

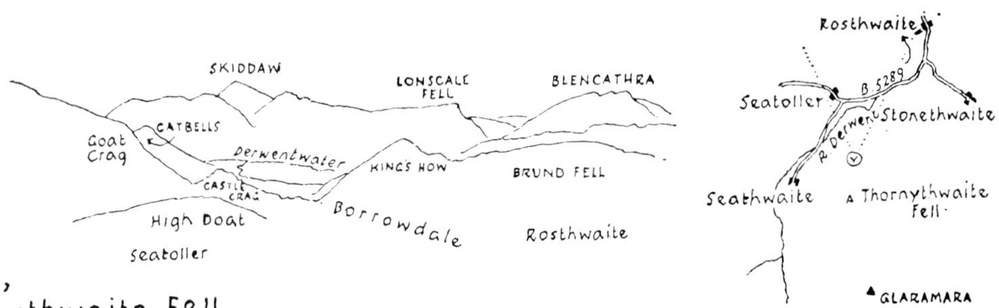

370 Borrowdale,
from Thornythwaite Fell

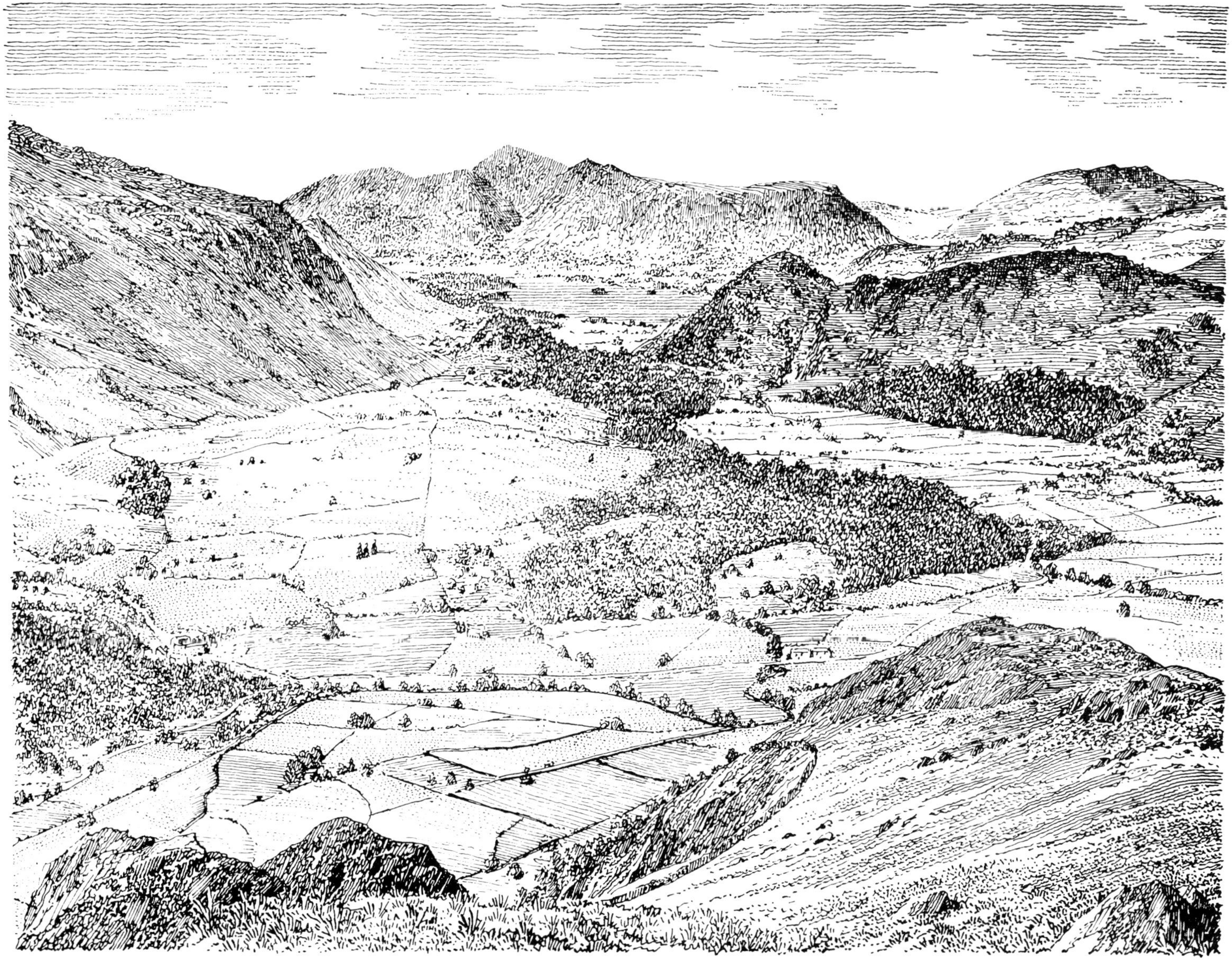

Dalegarth Force is not the highest waterfall in Lakeland nor the most spectacular but the approach to it upstream through the woodland of Stanley Gill attains a standard of beauty not found elsewhere and the fall itself is undoubtedly the most romantic and idyllic in situation and surroundings.

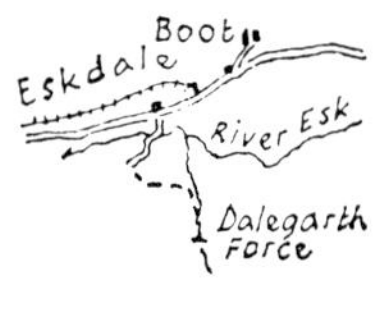

371 Dalegarth Force

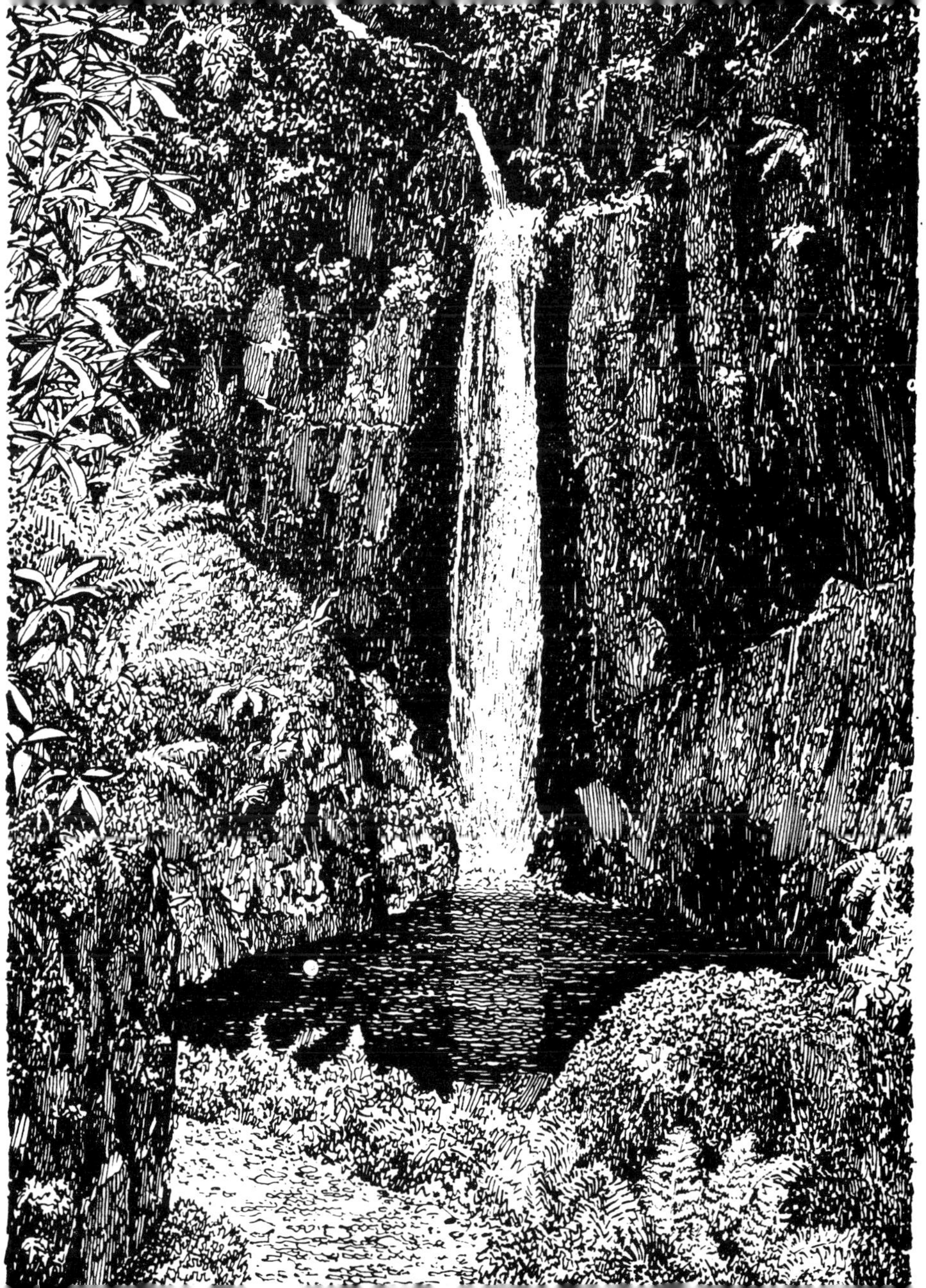

1: WETHERLAM
2: SWIRL HOW
3: PIKE O' BLISCO
4: CRINKLE CRAGS
5: BOWFELL
6: HARRISON STICKLE
7: PAVEY ARK

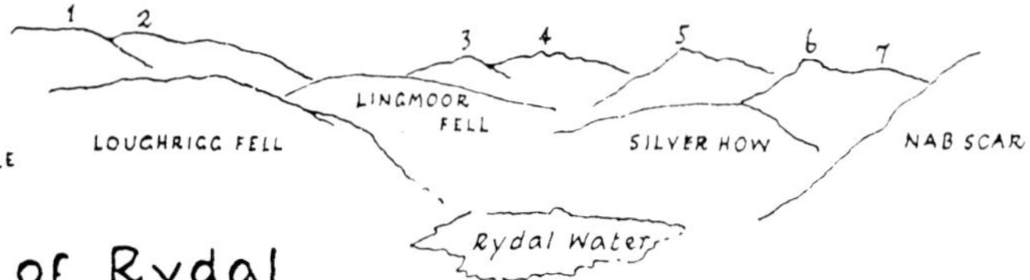

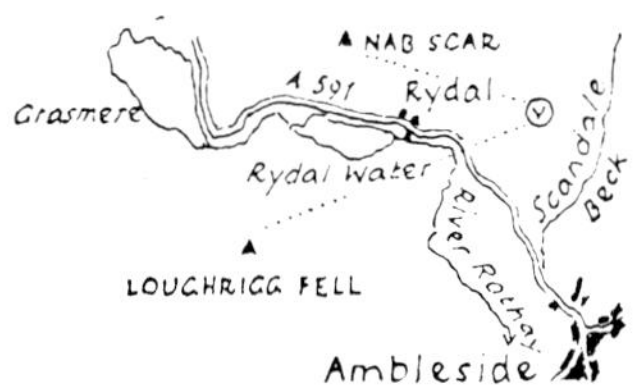

 The Vale of Rydal

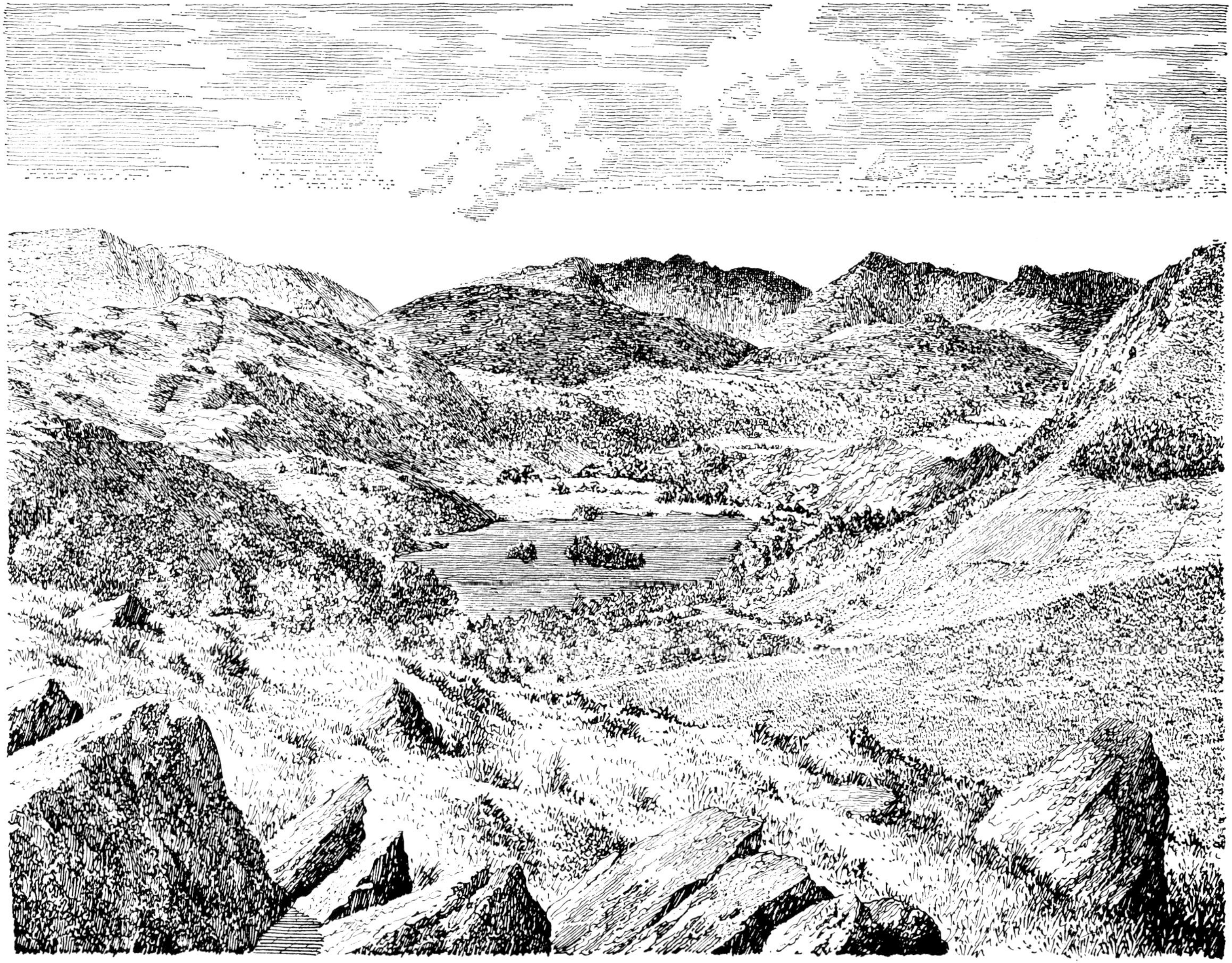

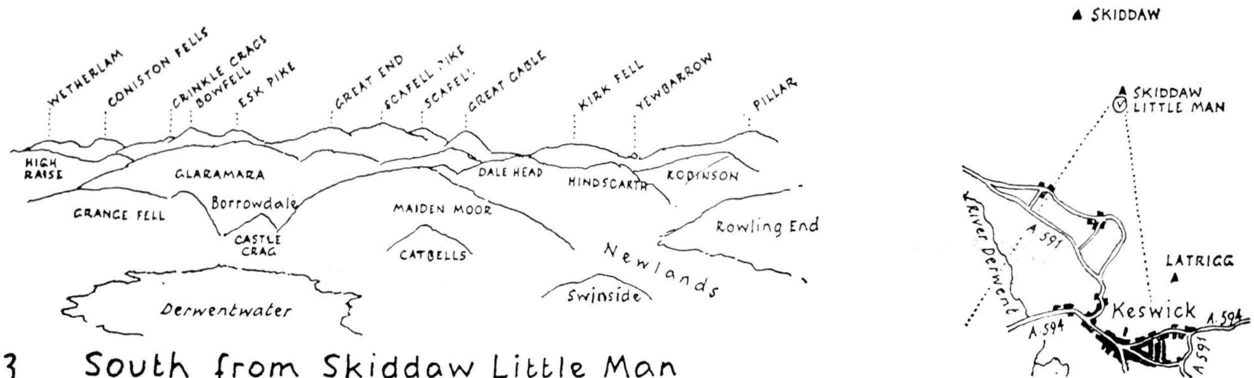

373 South from Skiddaw Little Man

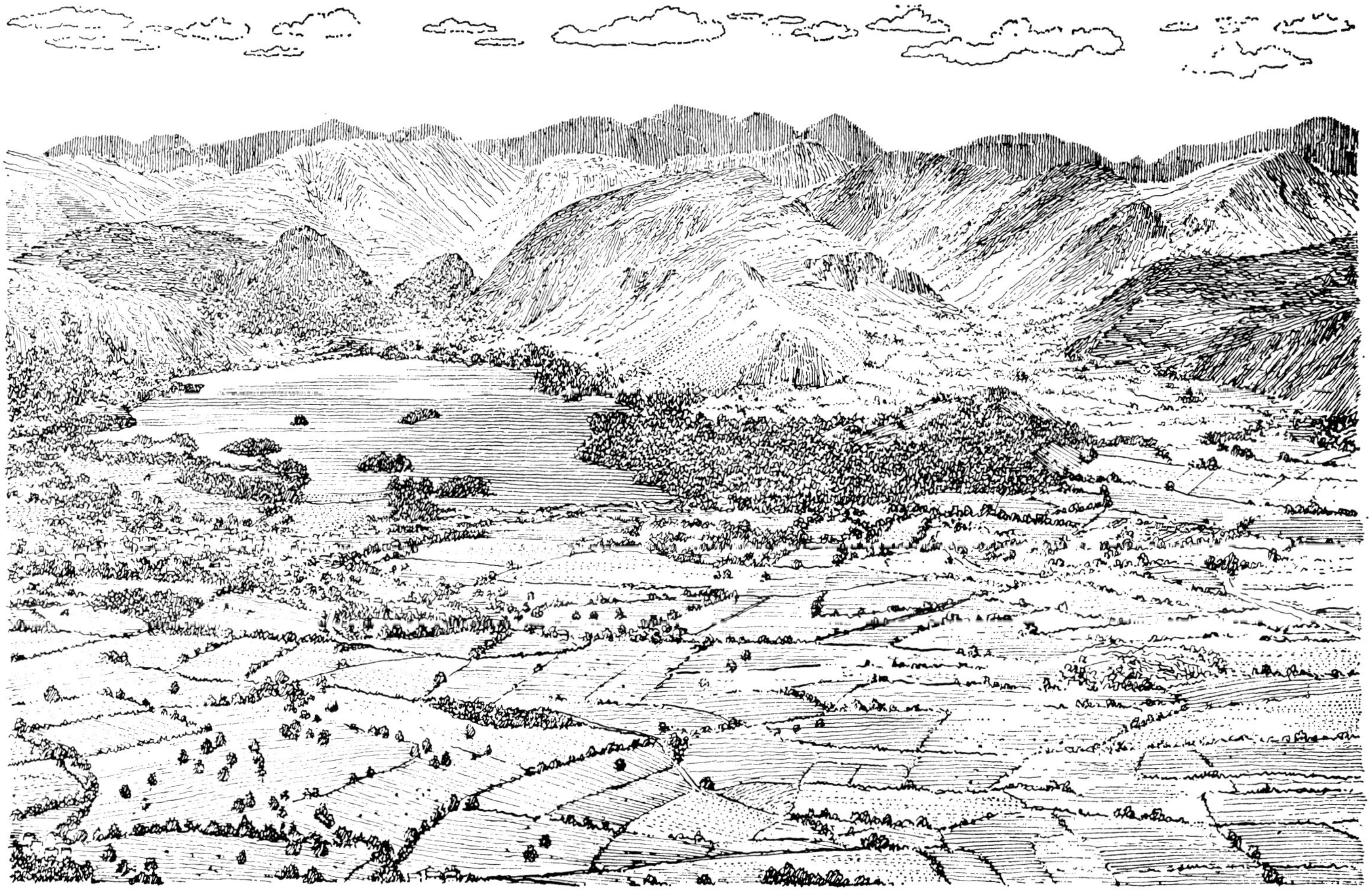

White Craggs has long opened its gates to passers by and offered its charming rock gardens for the pleasure of all. Serpentine paths wind up a steep fellside in a blaze of colour to a tiny shrine in the rocks where outdoor religious services are occasionally held.

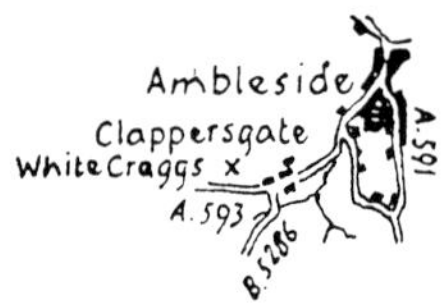

374 White Craggs, Clappersgate

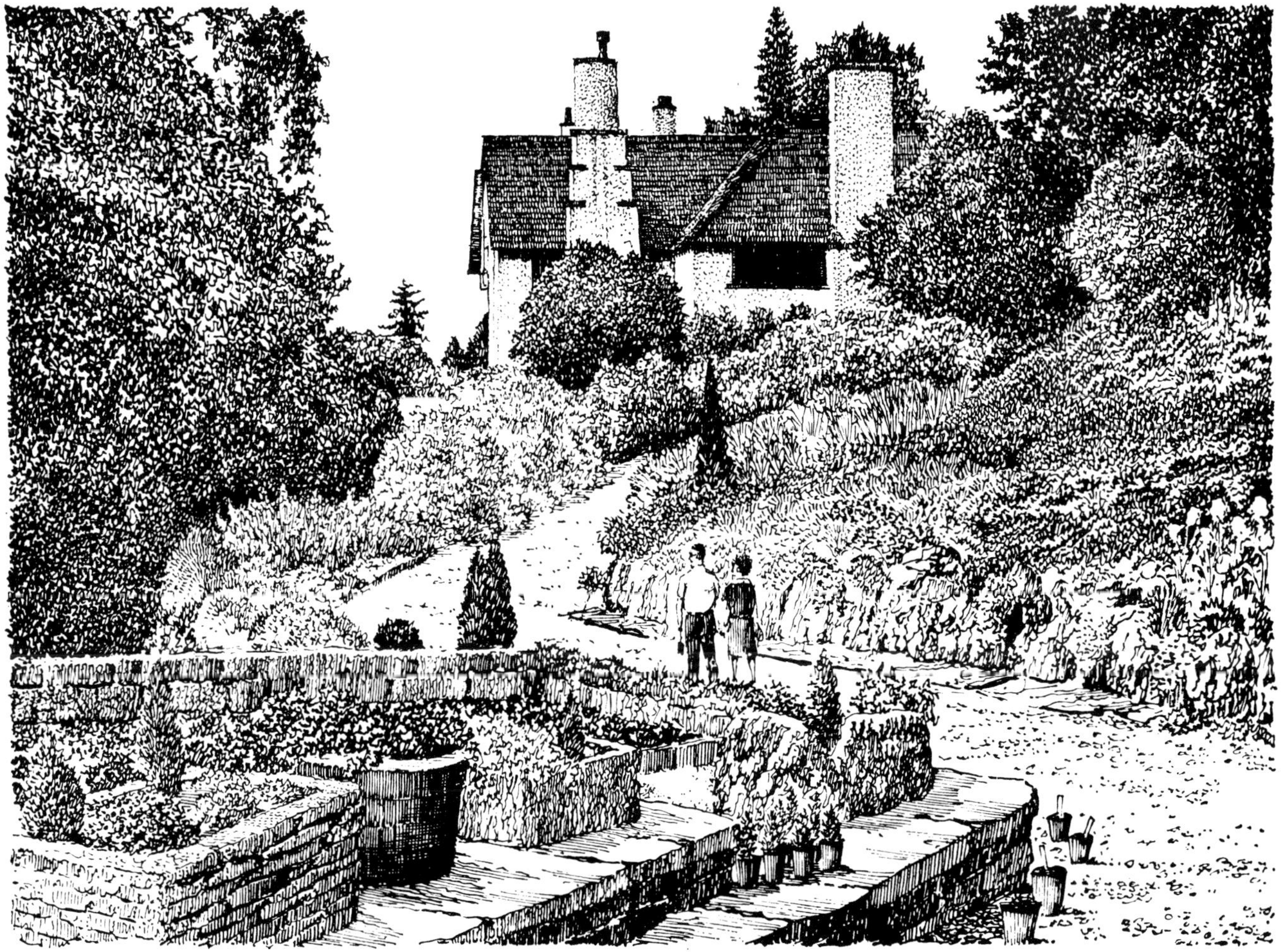

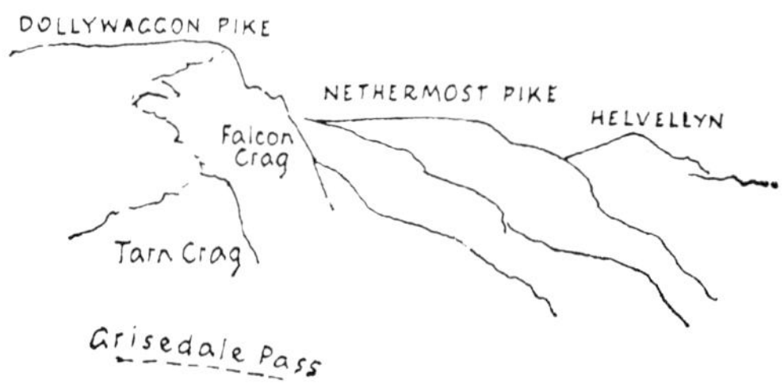

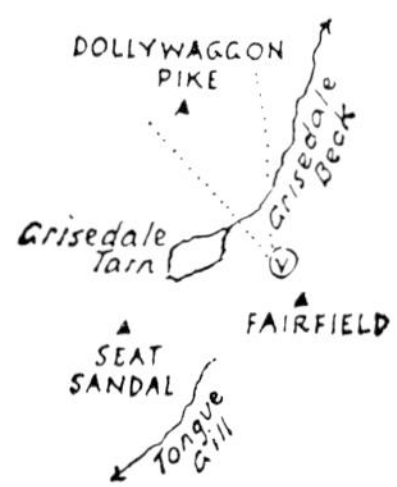

375 Grisedale Pass

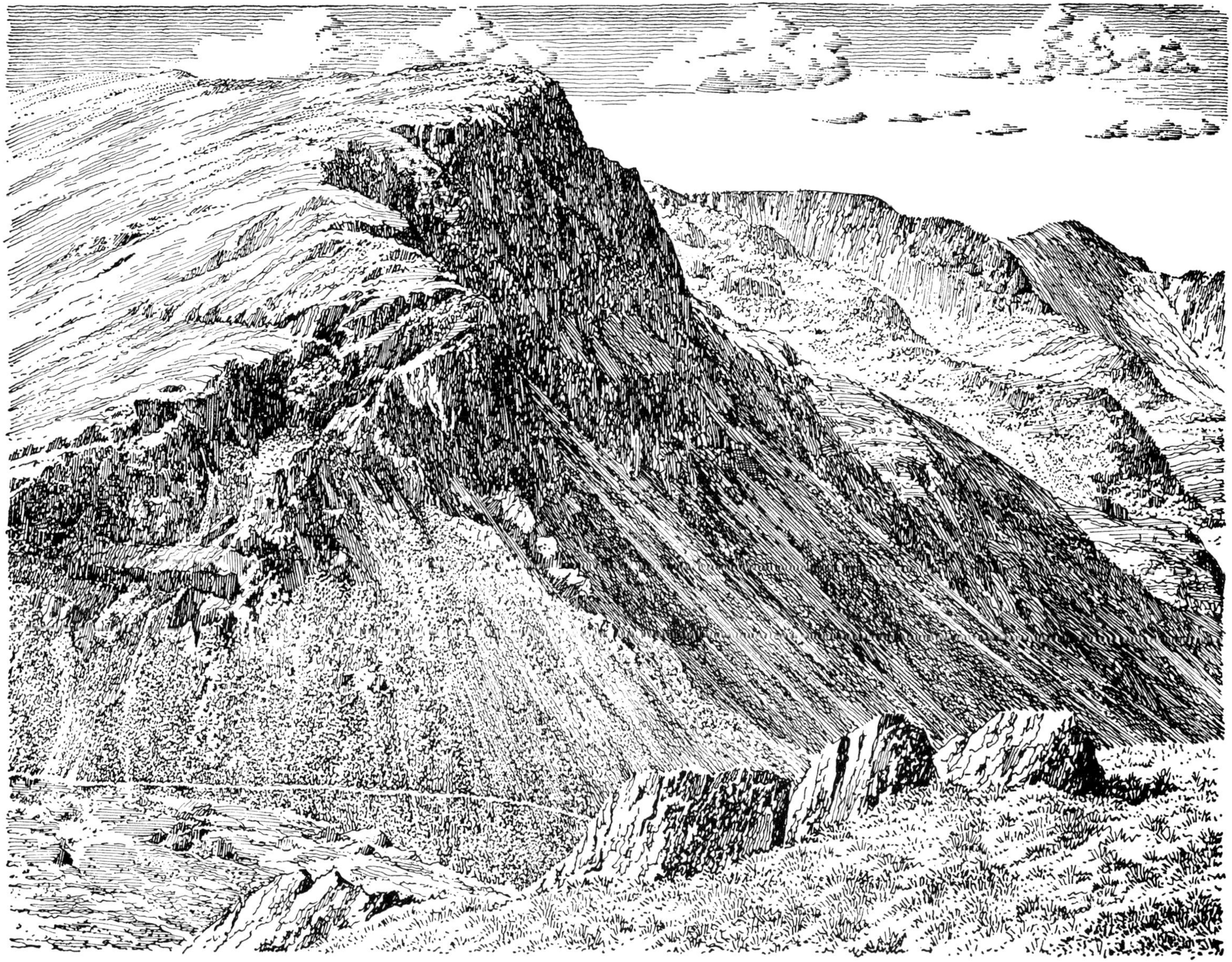

The little church of St. Kentigern, an old foundation, is typical of the places of worship serving small Lakeland communities. Humble, unpretentious, shyly secluded by trees, it fits unobtrusively into the quiet landscape of Mungrisdale.

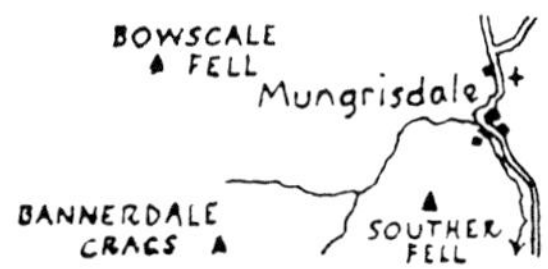

376 Mungrisdale Church

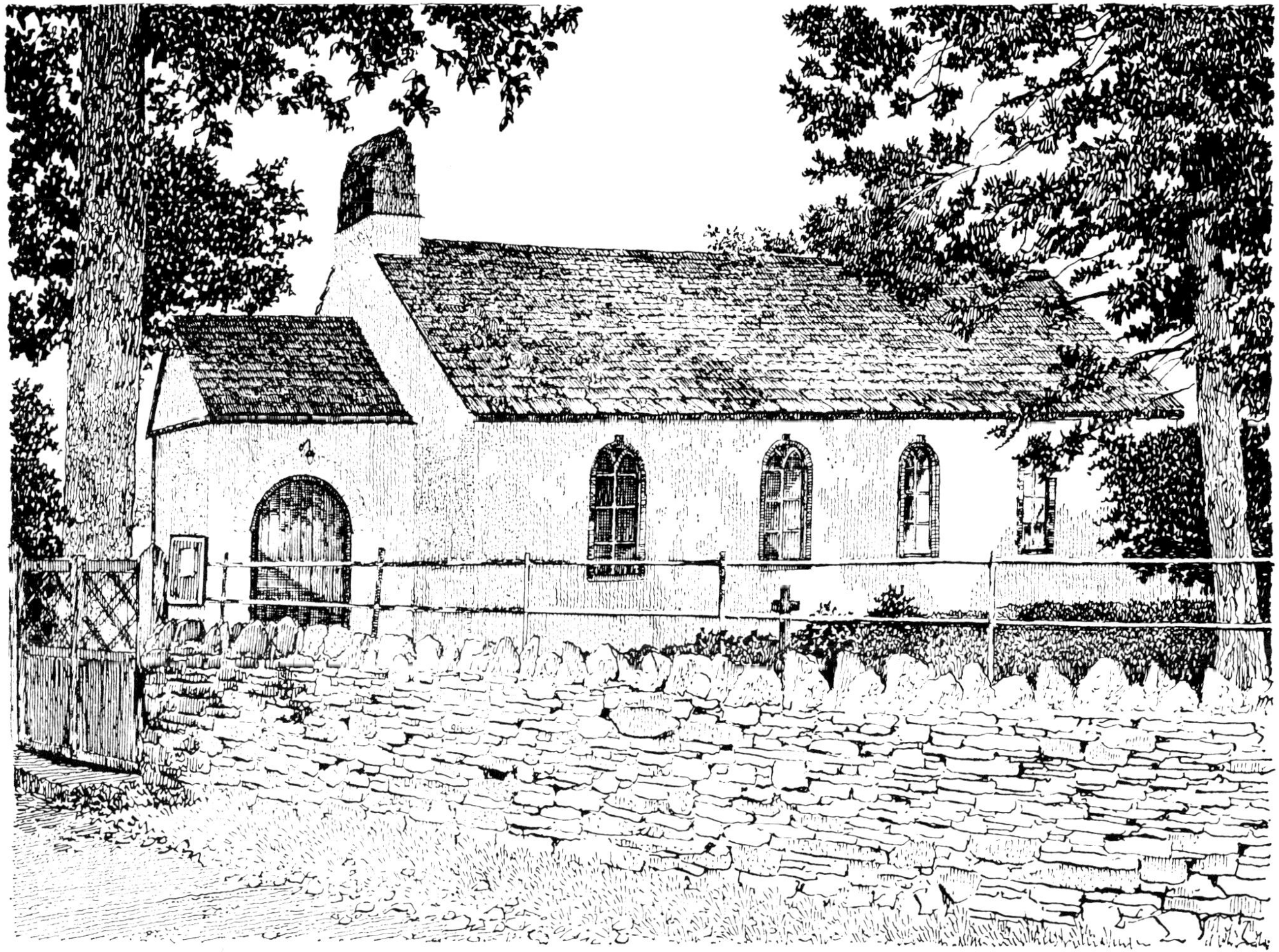

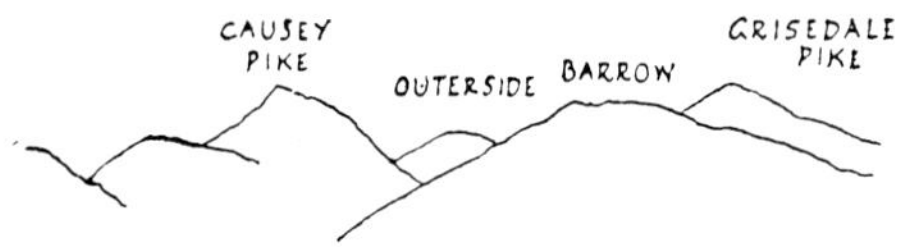

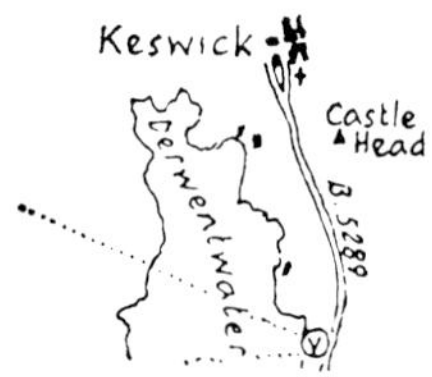

377 Calf Close Bay, Derwentwater

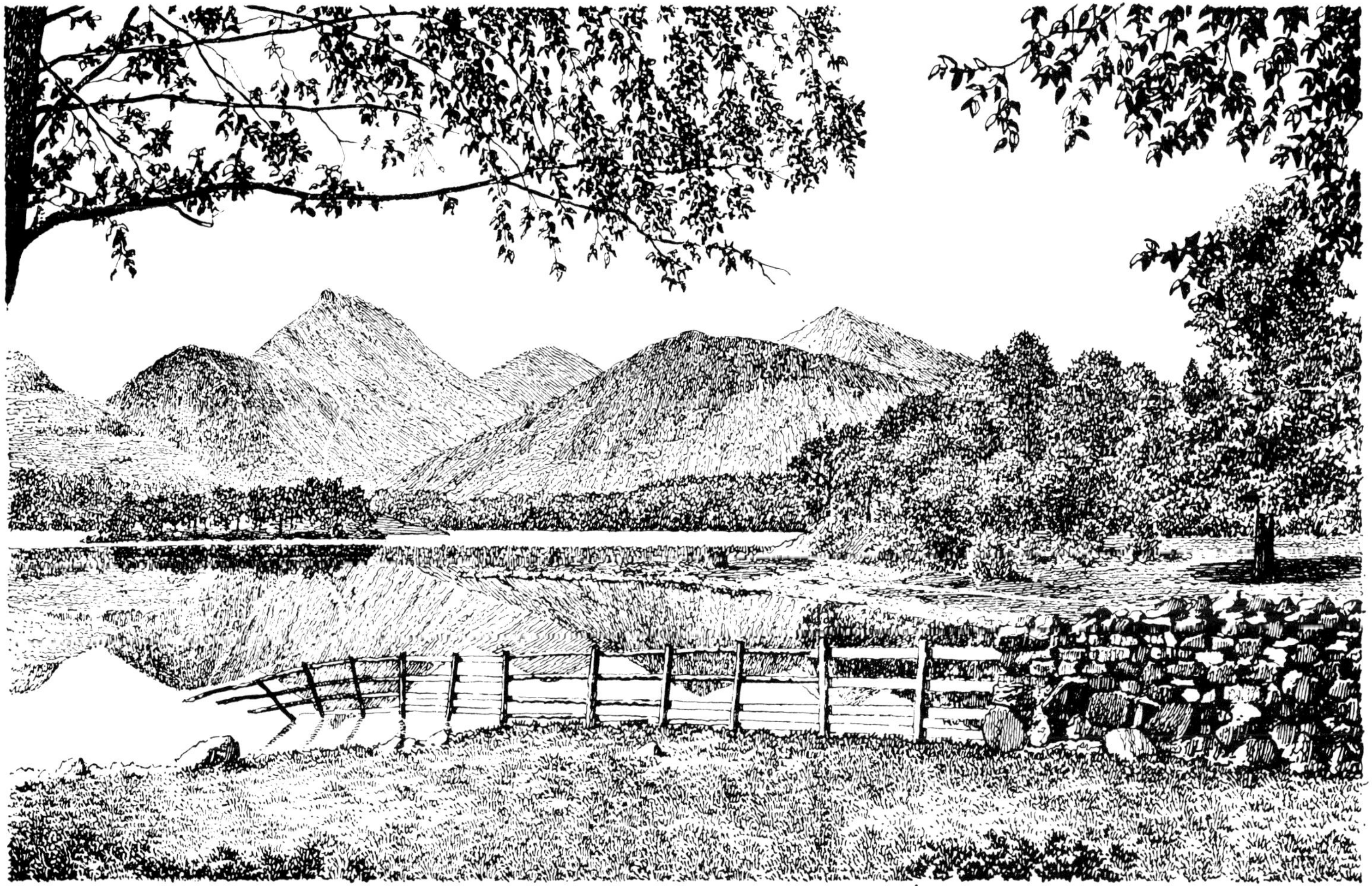

378 Red Screes

Red Screes is the popular name of the mountain dominating Kirkstone Pass, derived from the rivers of ruddy stones in its great eastern hollows. The Ordnance maps give more prominence to the insignificant feature of Kilnshaw Chimney, and strangers to the area may be forgiven for assuming this to be the name of the fell, as many do.

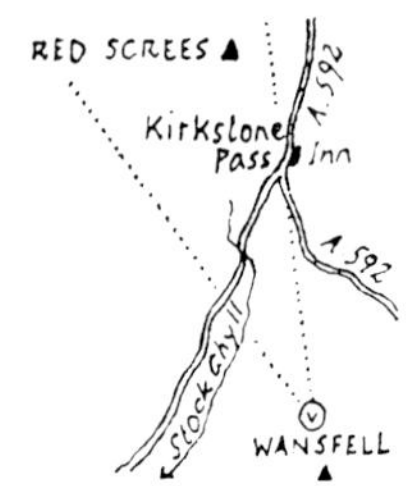

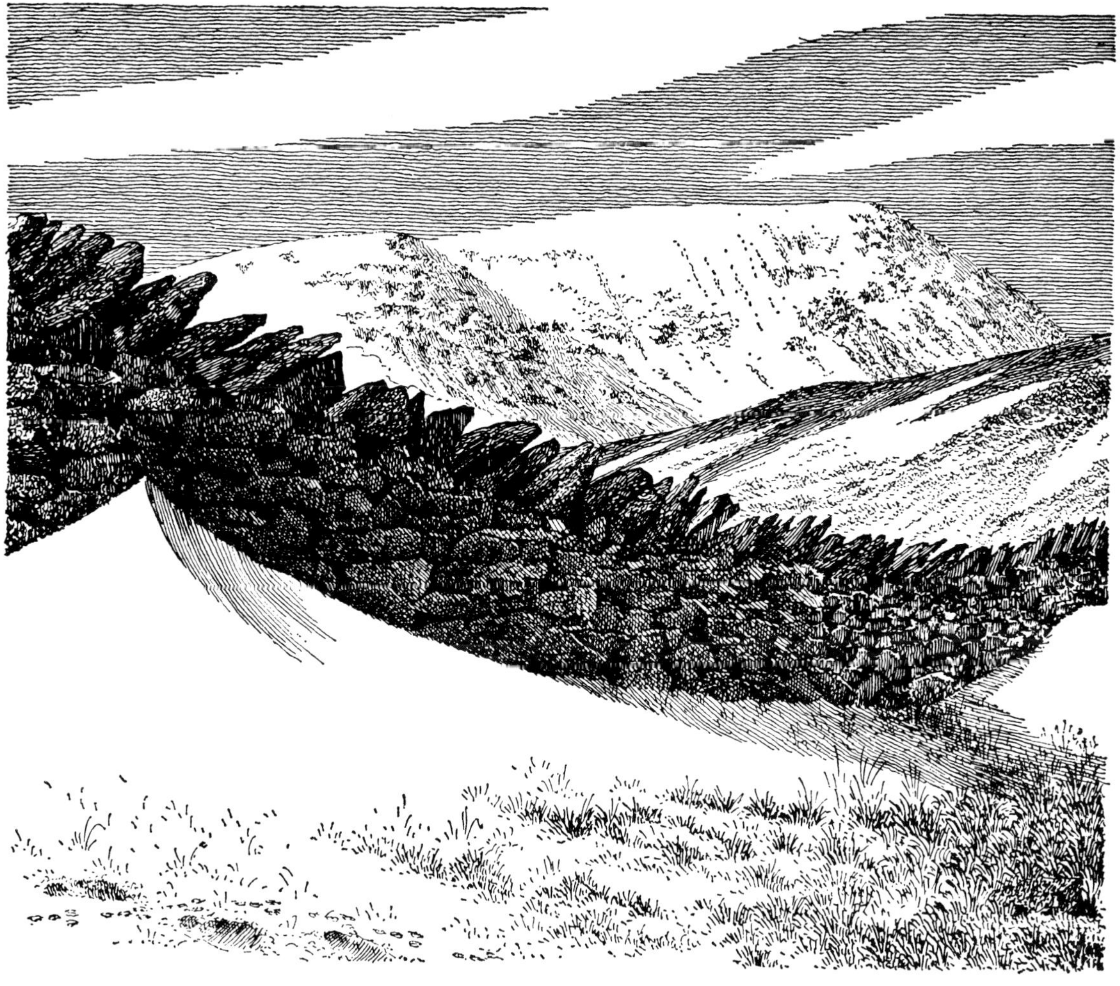

379 In Eskdale

Tommy Dobson's name has not lived on as has John Peel's yet his local reputation as a Master of Foxhounds was greater. Foxhunting was his life and fittingly his gravestone reflects his passion. It stands in the churchyard of St. Catherine's on the quiet banks of the River Esk, surprisingly out of the way and hidden from the sight of travellers along the valley.
Esk Bridge is half a mile distant, on the way to Dalegarth Force.

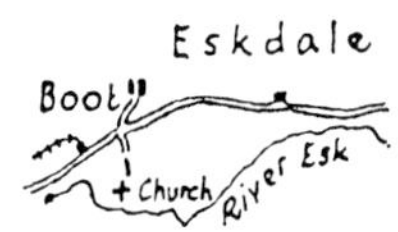

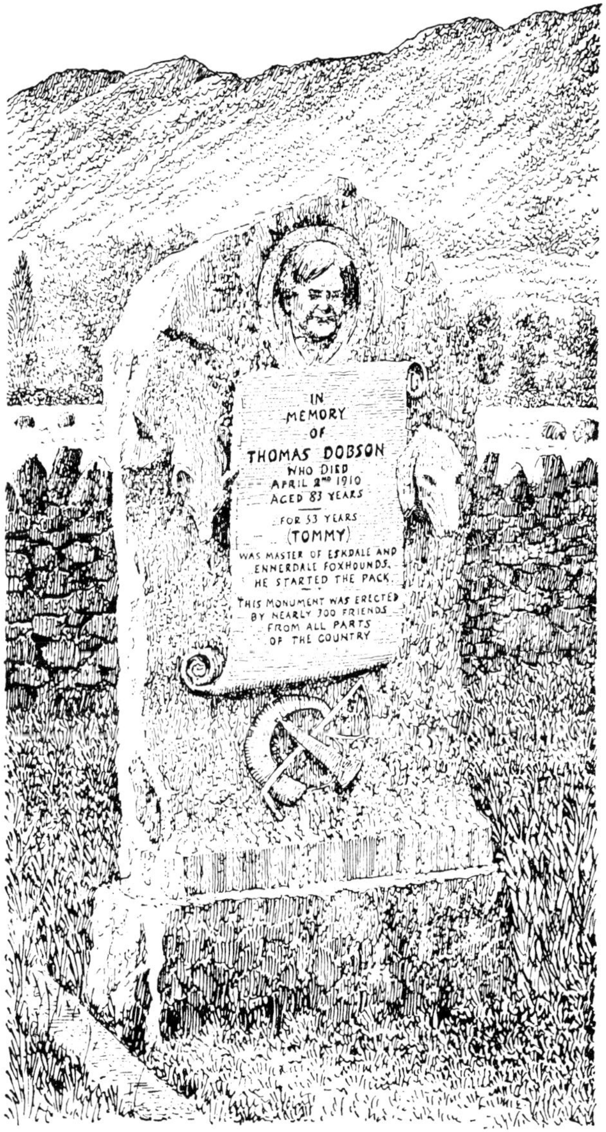
IN
MEMORY
OF
THOMAS DOBSON
WHO DIED
APRIL 2ND 1910
AGED 83 YEARS
FOR 53 YEARS
(TOMMY)
WAS MASTER OF ESKDALE AND
ENNERDALE FOXHOUNDS.
HE STARTED THE PACK.
THIS MONUMENT WAS ERECTED
BY NEARLY 300 FRIENDS
FROM ALL PARTS
OF THE COUNTRY

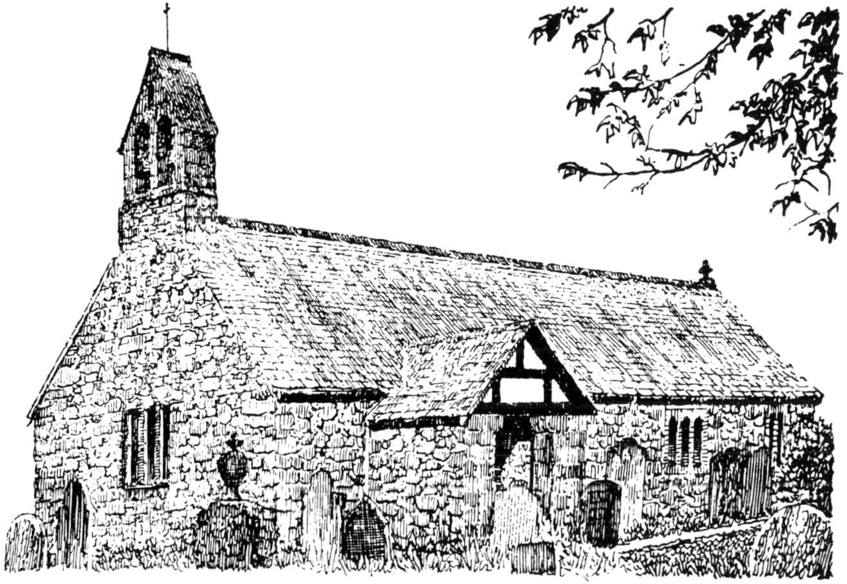

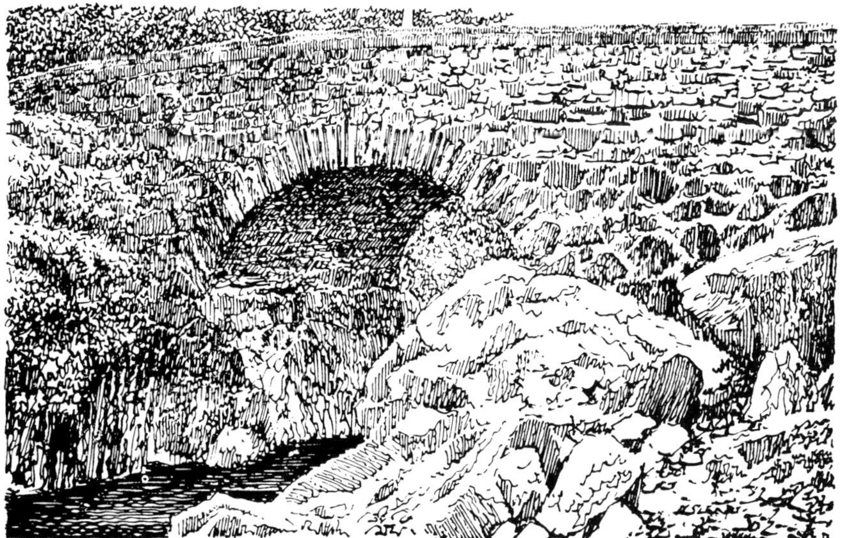

380 The Kirk Stone

The Kirk Stone, near the top of the wellknown pass to which it gives the name, is an unremarkable boulder overlooking the long descent to Patterdale, 80 yards over the wall on the west side. When approached from the north it assumes the shape of a church tower clearly seen on the skyline — hence the name.

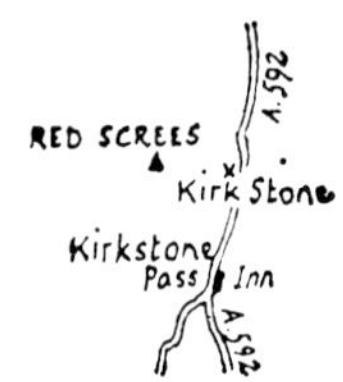

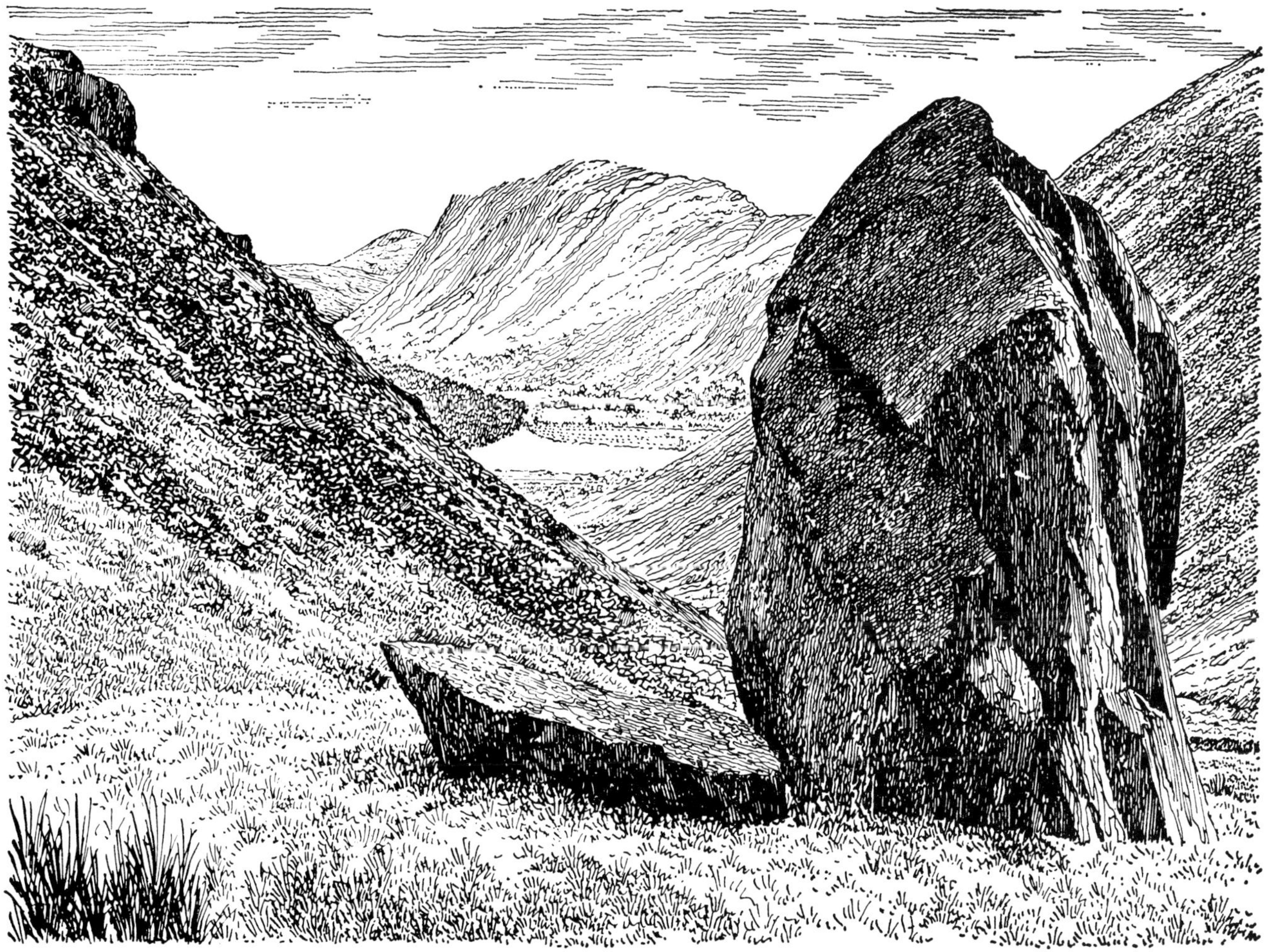

381 Pillar Rock

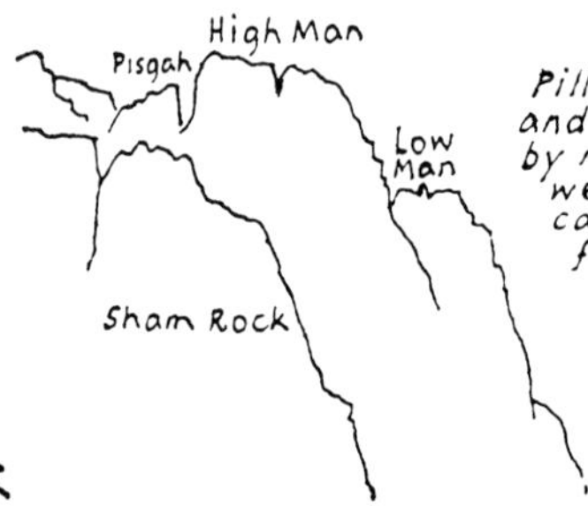

Pillar Rock is 500 feet in height and an awe-inspiring sculpturing by natural forces. It has been well likened to a shattered cathedral, and thrusts boldly from the fellside almost as though severed from it.

Long thought inaccessible, the Rock now has hundreds of climbing routes, but not a single one that is safe or easy for ordinary walkers, a fact fortunately starkly obvious.

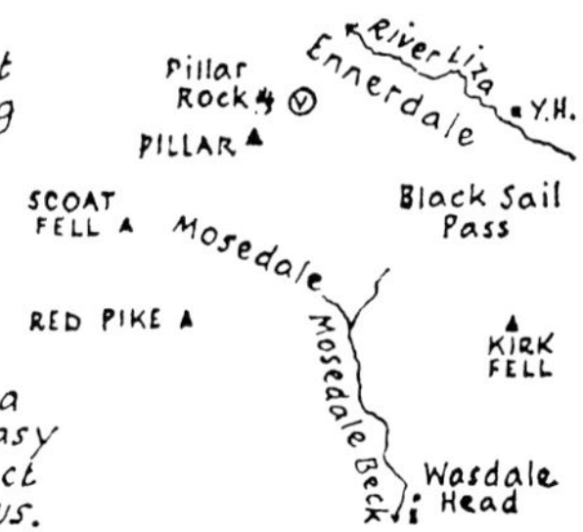

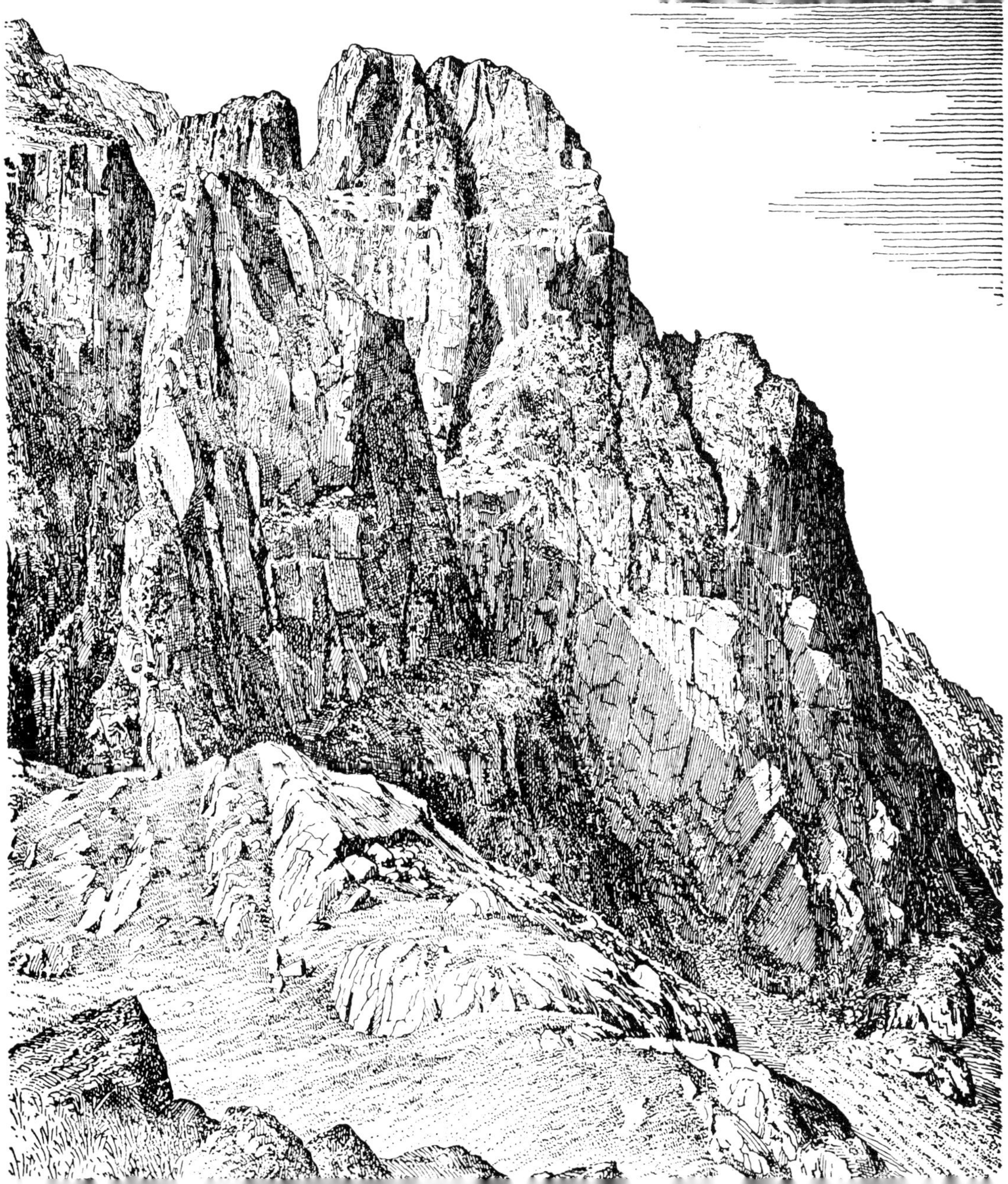

Great End is the massive northern headland of the Scafell range and is usually bypassed on the way to or from Scafell Pike, but its omission, in clear weather, deprives walkers of a highlight of the journey: the full-length view of Borrowdale seen from the rim of the cliffs, standing on the edge of space near the cairn pictured here.

382 The summit of Great End

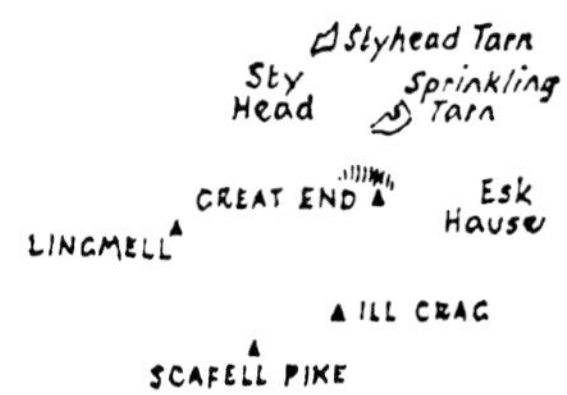

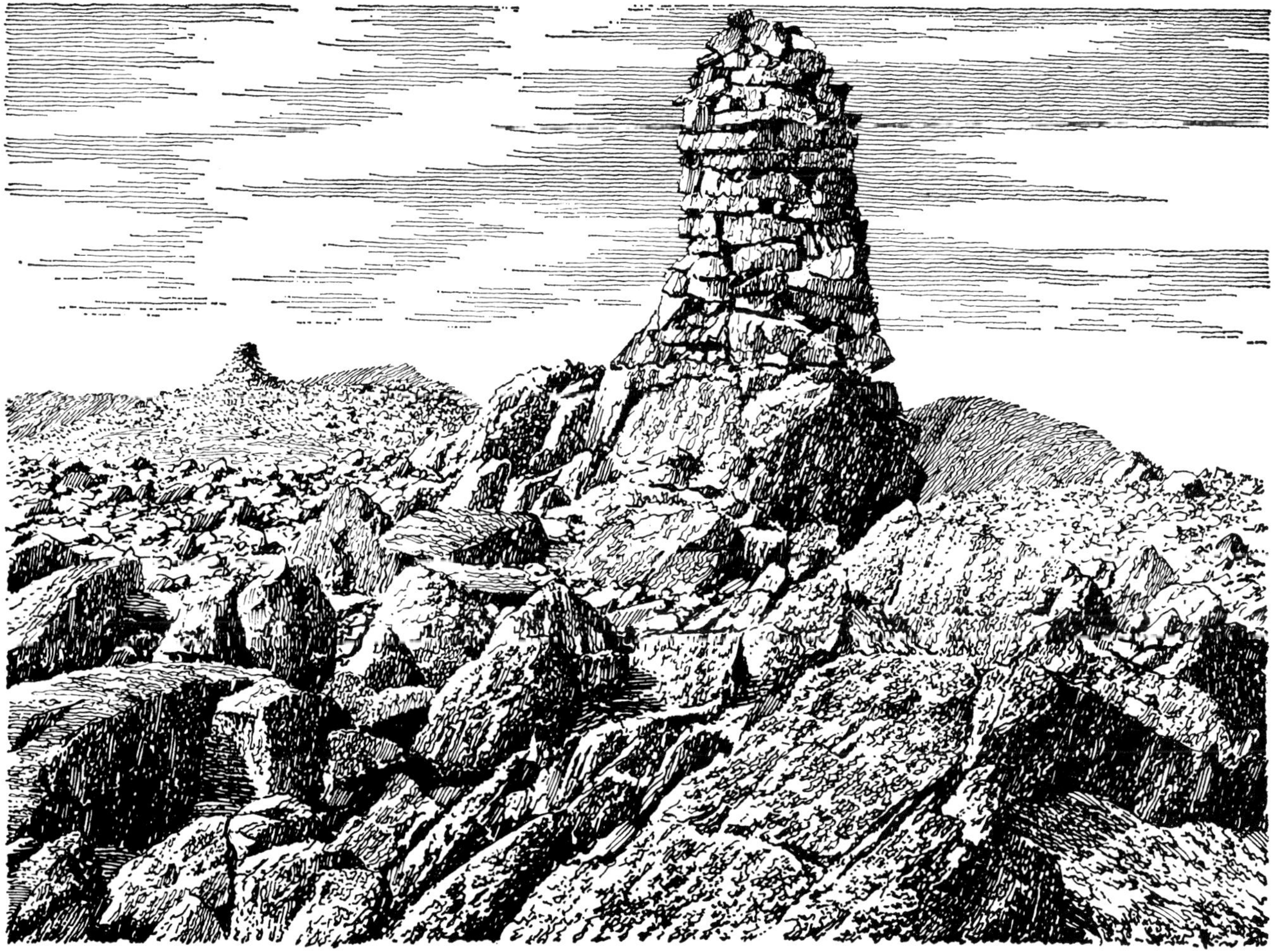

As a general rule the best views are obtained only by walking or climbing away from the main roads, but the motorist travelling north along the A.6 is privileged, at one point, by this lovely glimpse of Long Sleddale — without leaving the driving seat or even halting the car.

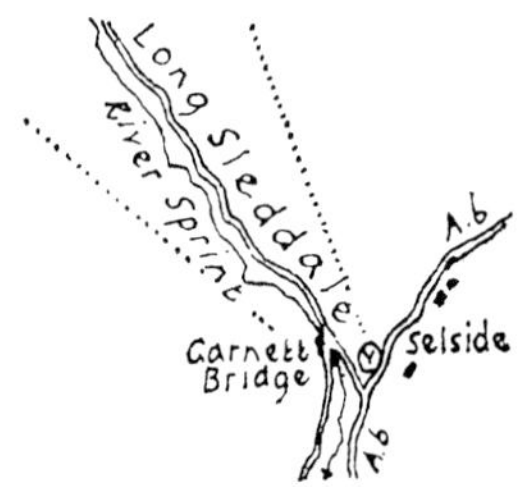

383 The foot of Long Sleddale

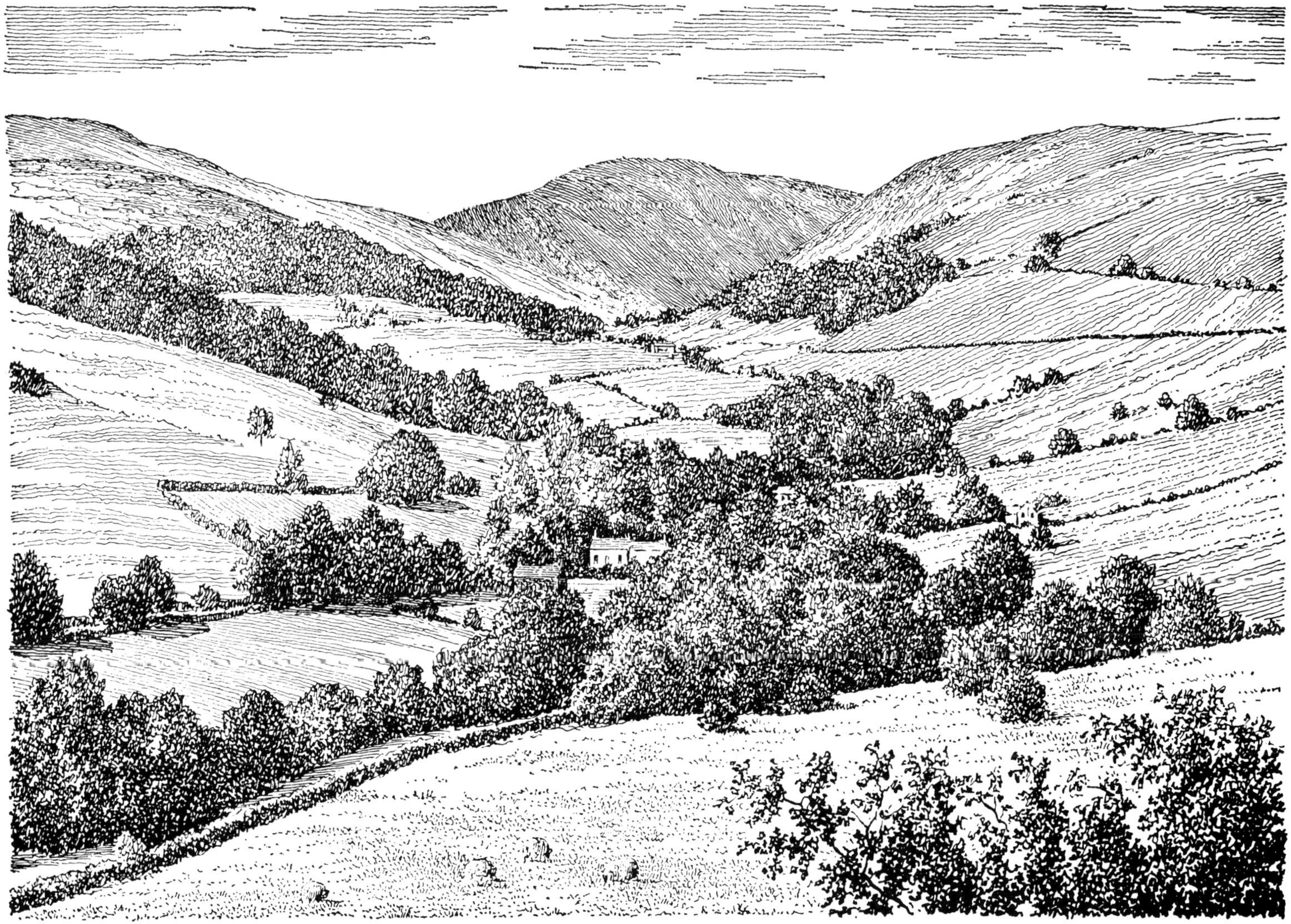

384 Grisedale Pike

It seems a little odd that Grisedale Pike should be so named when, as every visitor knows, the valley it dominates is Coledale, but there is in fact a subsidiary valley of Grisedale, almost unknown and rarely visited (except by foresters), of which the Pike is the precise culmination, not, as in the case of Coledale, rising to one side of it. Yes, the name is right. In the drawing, the Pike is seen towering at the head of a twin subsidiary valley, that of Sanderson Gill.

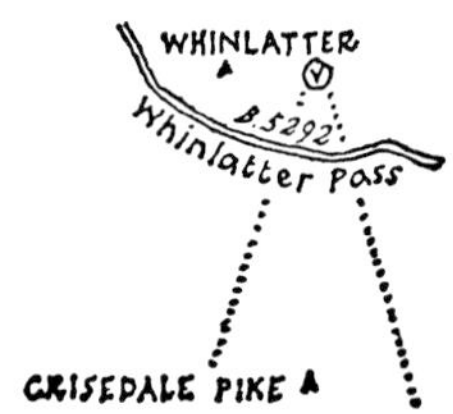

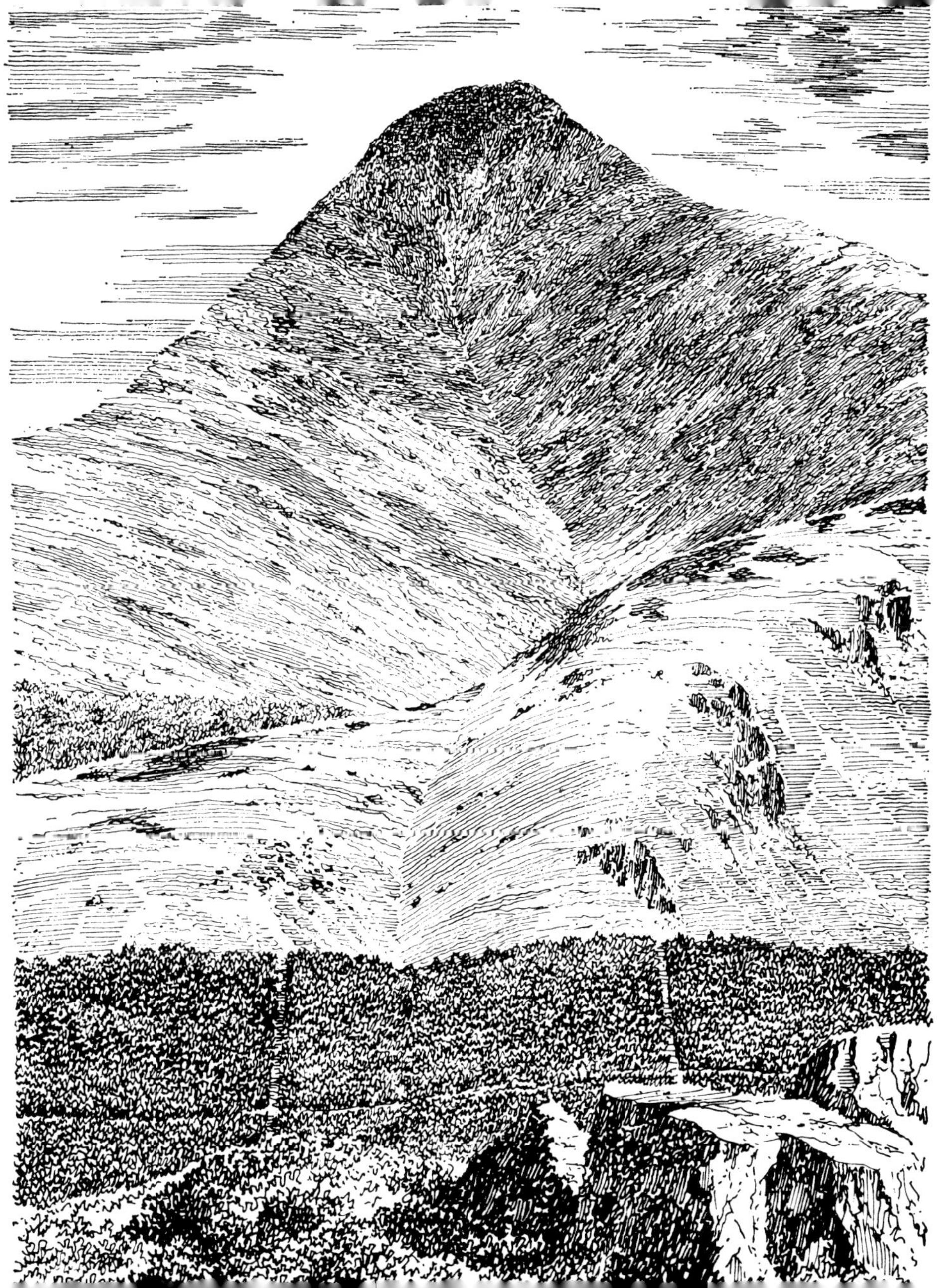

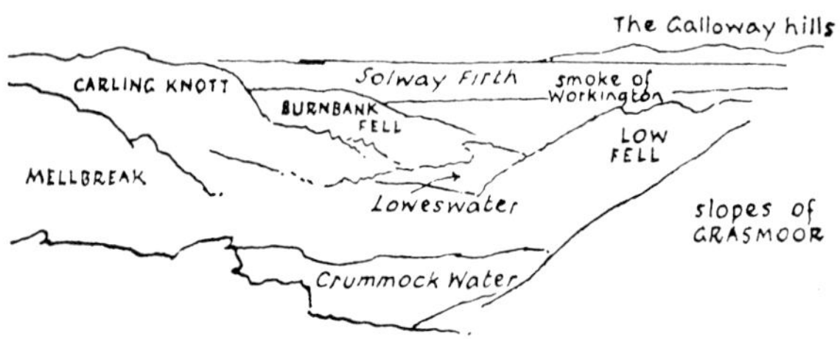

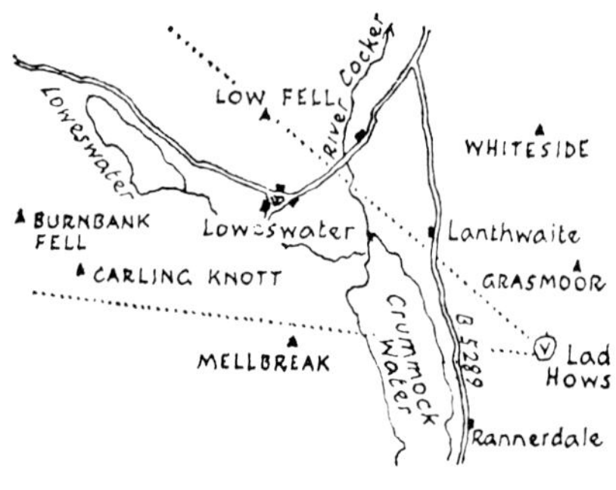

385 The Loweswater Valley

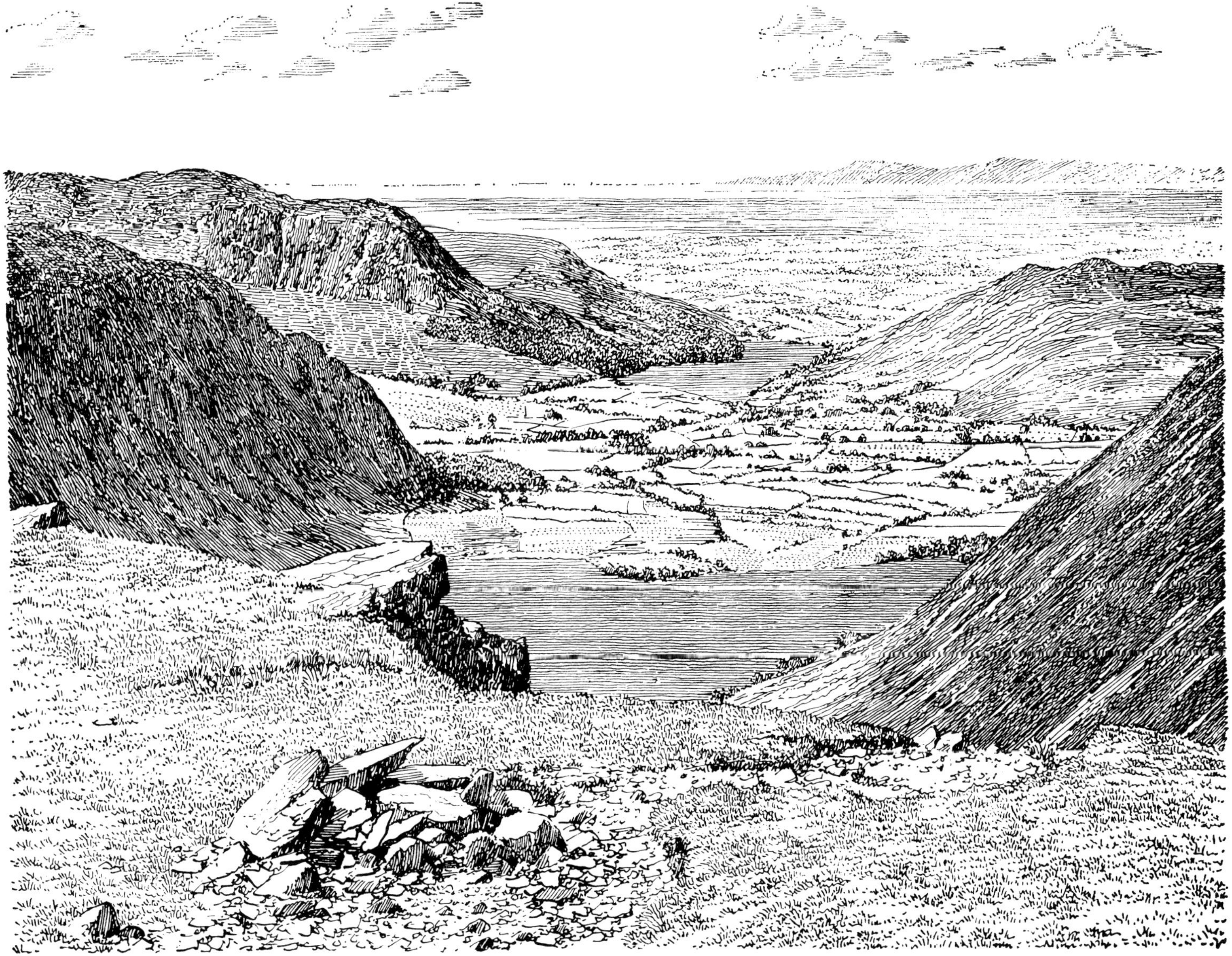

386 Ashness Bridge

Miles of camera film are used annually at Ashness Bridge, the arrangement of features here being in classic harmony. The bridge has been a revered shrine for a century of photographers and artists ; latterly it has attracted also the brave new generation : the vandals. Death to all such! Who, loving Ashness Bridge and seeing its wanton defacement, can argue against capital punishment?

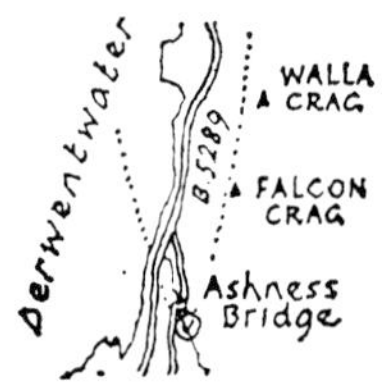

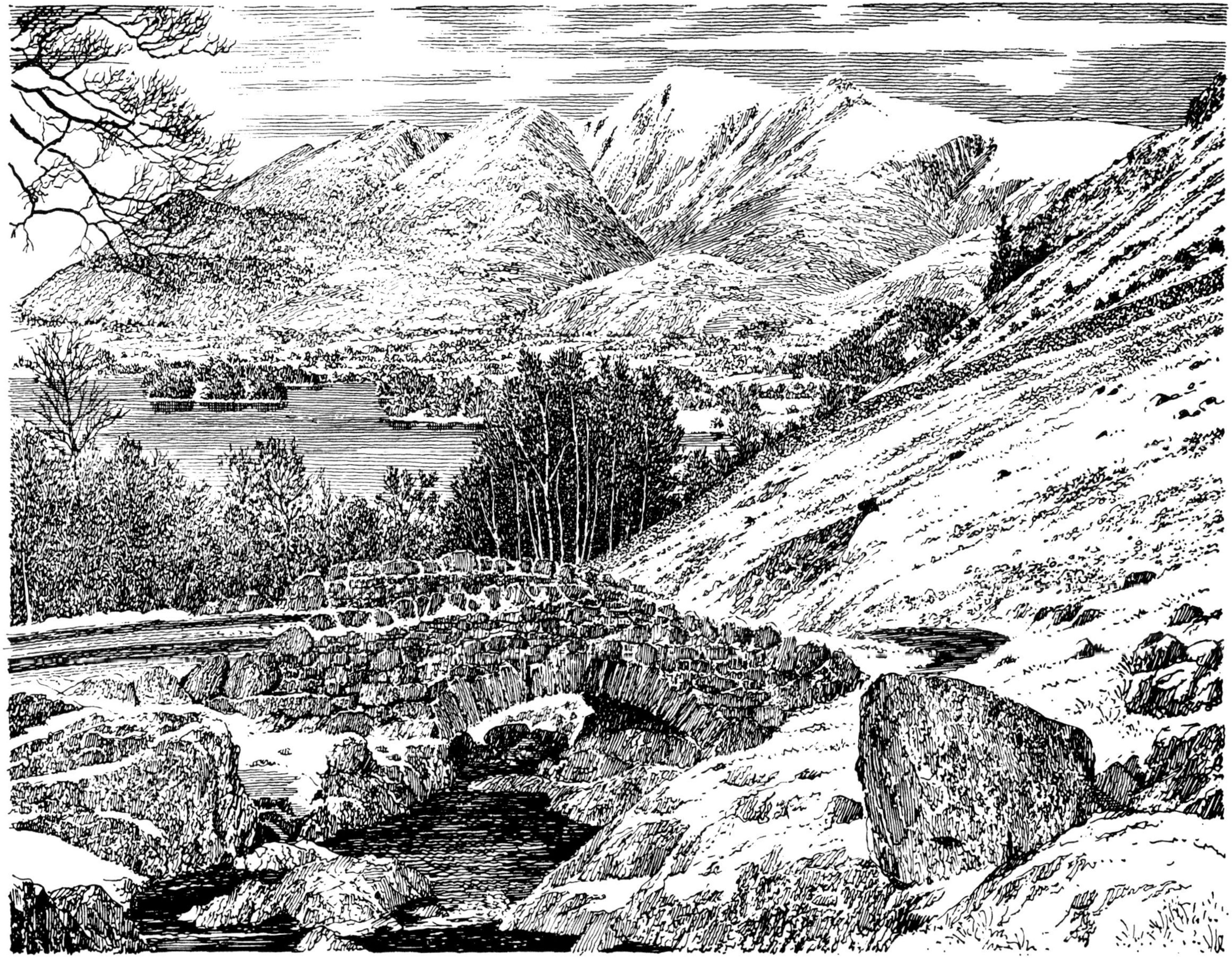

Who does not know the road to Seathwaite and who has not thrilled as the view of mountains opens up ahead on a bright morning? This is the supreme way to the supreme hills, and although many walkers now travel the road by car, its morning magic is reserved for those on eager foot.

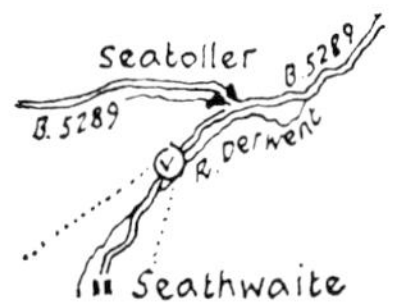

387 The road to Seathwaite

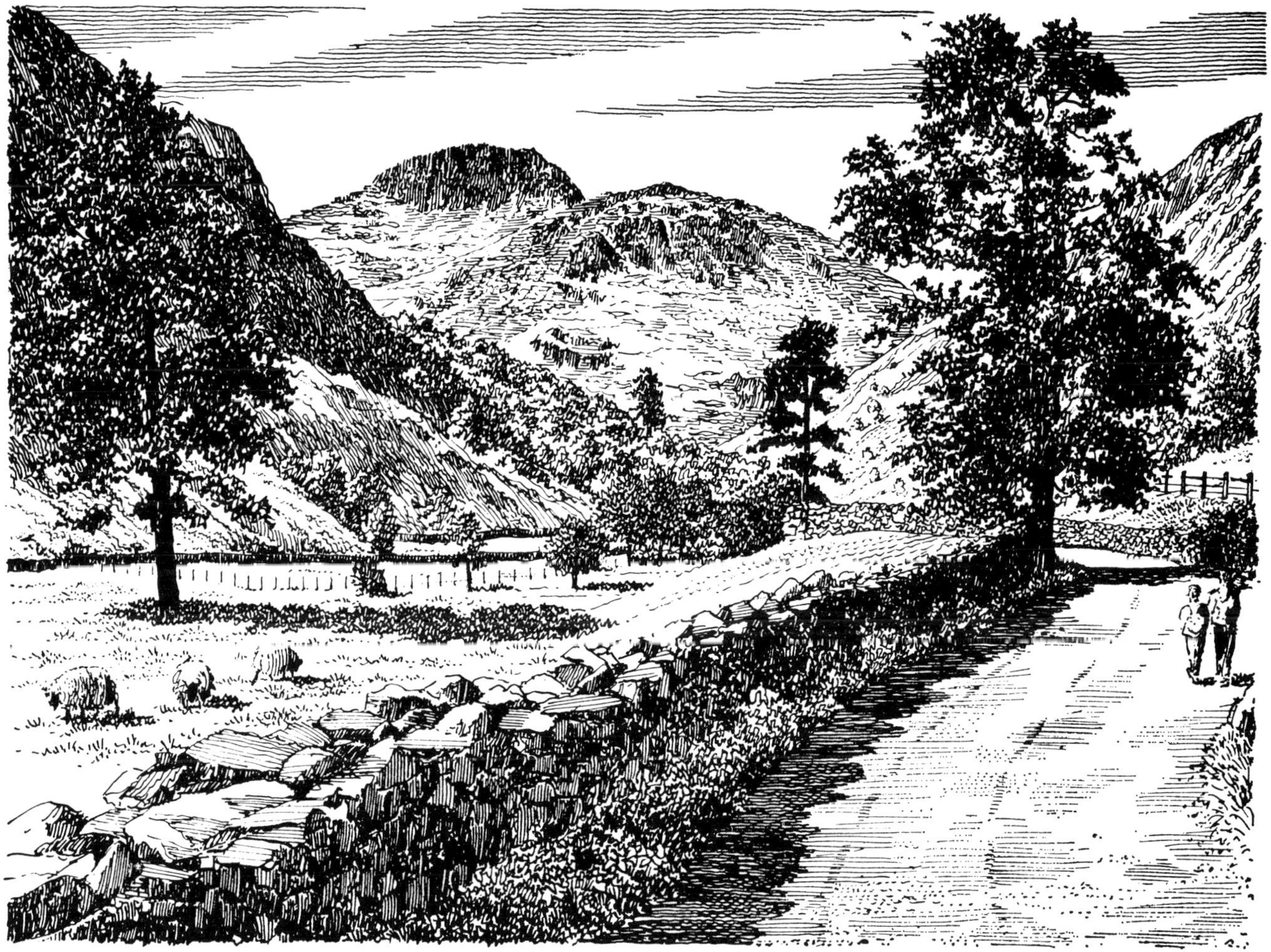

388 Great Gable, from Moses' Trod

Moses' Trod was originally a secret passage through the hills planned by a quarryman-cum-smuggler named Moses Rigg, who took by sled his contraband wares this way to avoid the exciseman and evade the law. His path is still a secret to many but once located it is revealed as an excellent high-level route skirting Great Gable on the way from Honister Quarry to Wasdale Head.

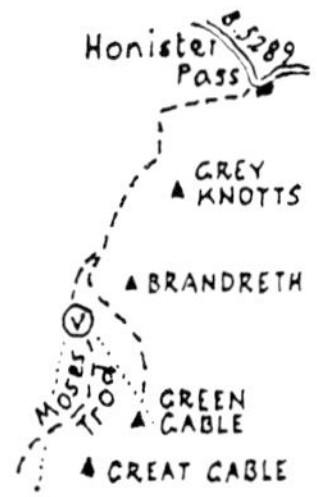

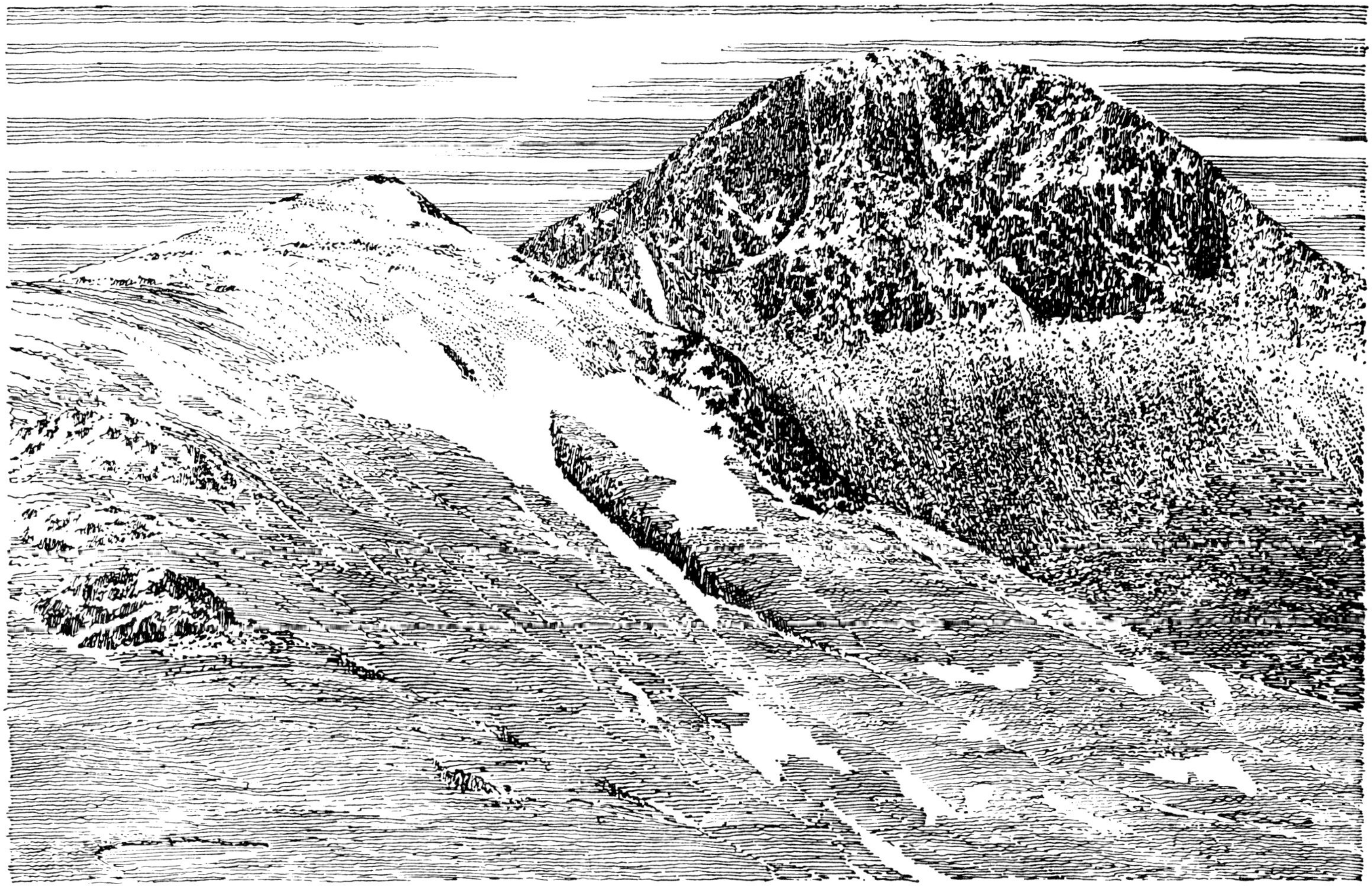

389 Crook

The road to the Lakes from the south is now a fast highway slashed through the countryside, but motorists who prefer a more leisurely approach along a quiet road with fragrant hedgerows may with advantage turn aside on the B.5284 and enjoy en route the charming rural scene presented by the neat white cottages and flowery gardens of the hamlet of Crook.

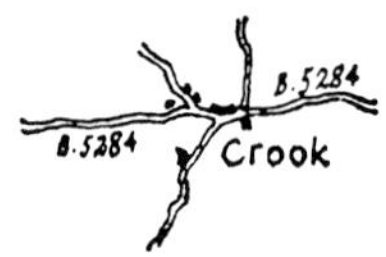

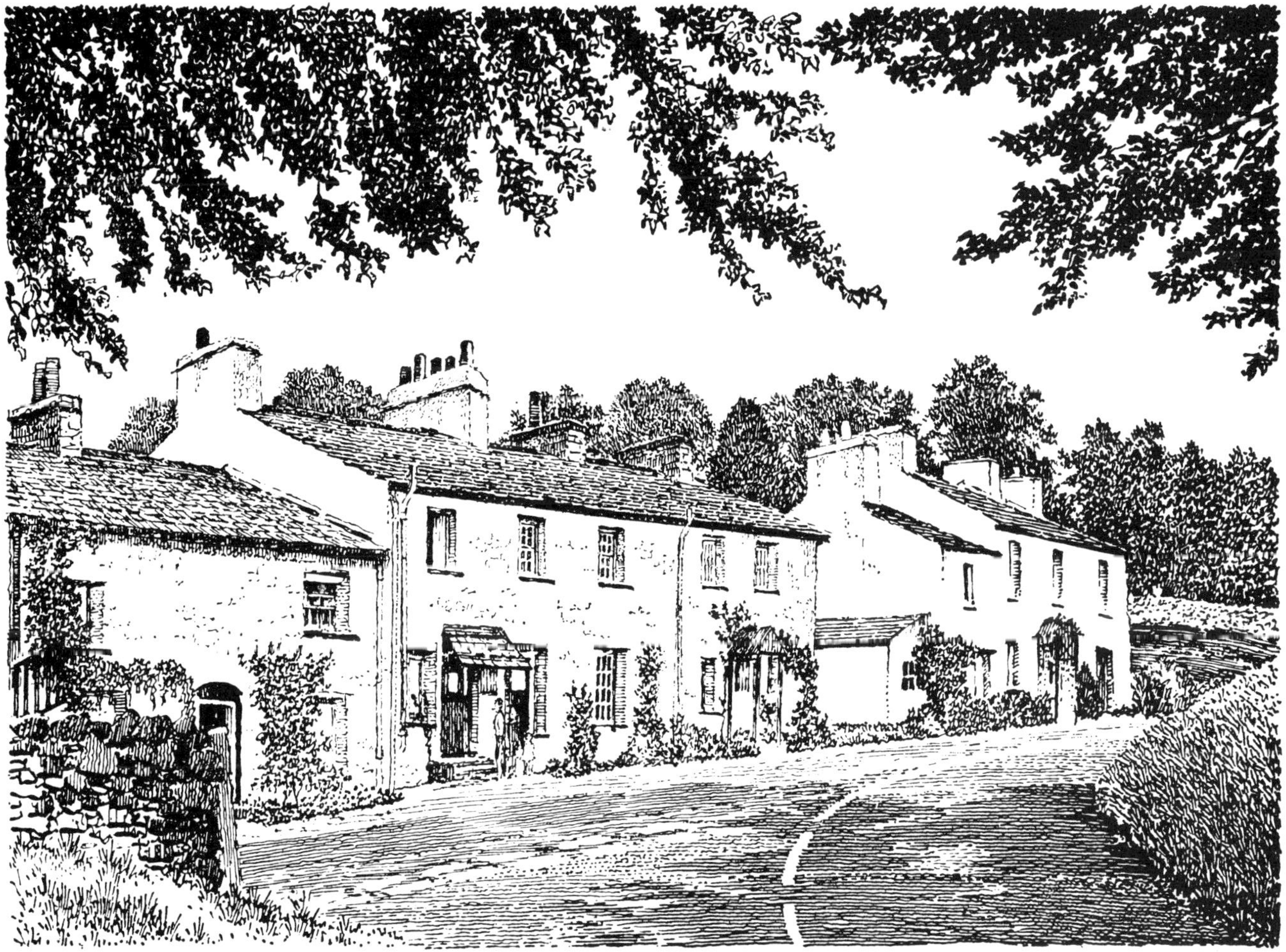

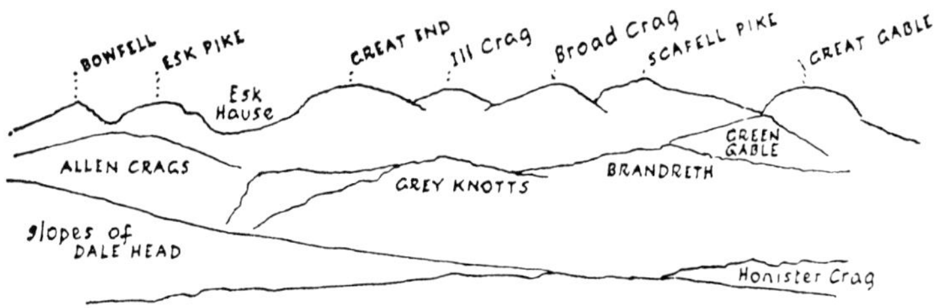

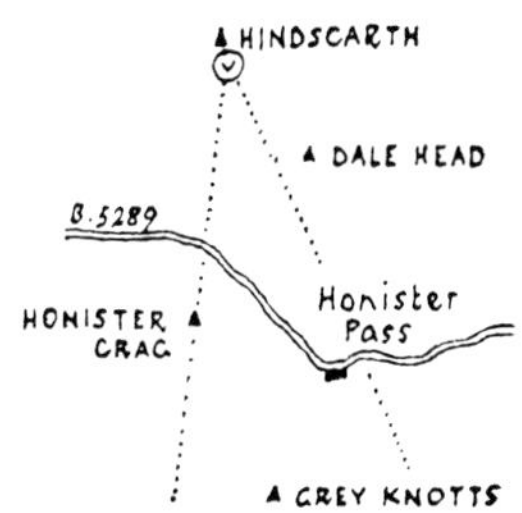

390 South from Hindscarth

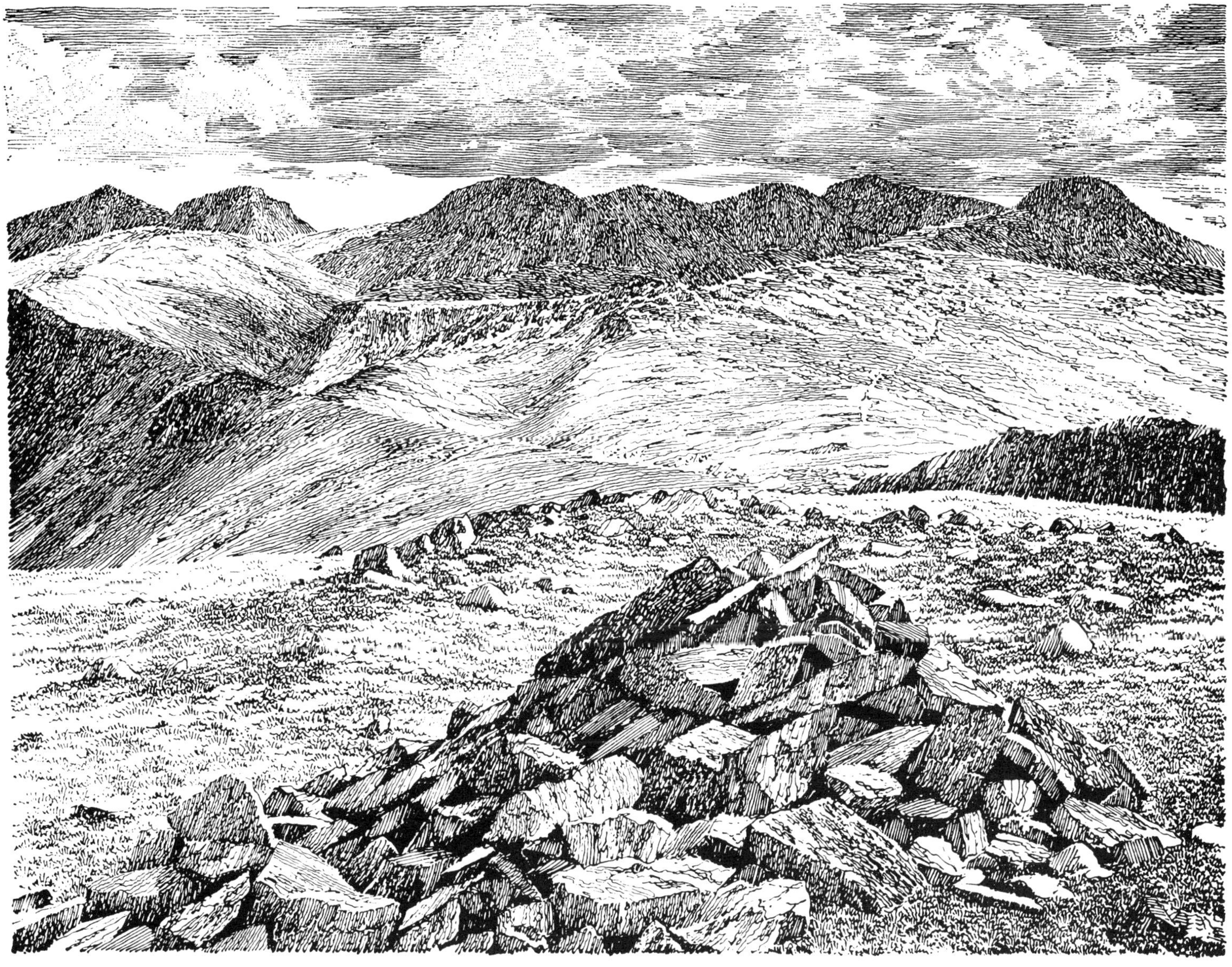

391 **Skiddaw,**
from Friar's Crag

Visitors to the Lakes are lovers of beauty yet most never see the district in its winter raiment, when the valleys are transformed by snow into a fairyland of glittering crystals and the fells seemingly add to their stature and stand gaunt and aloof in white mantles. This is a new beauty and not a lesser one.

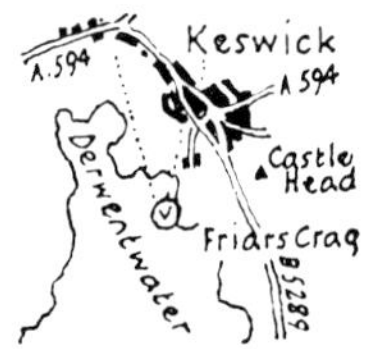

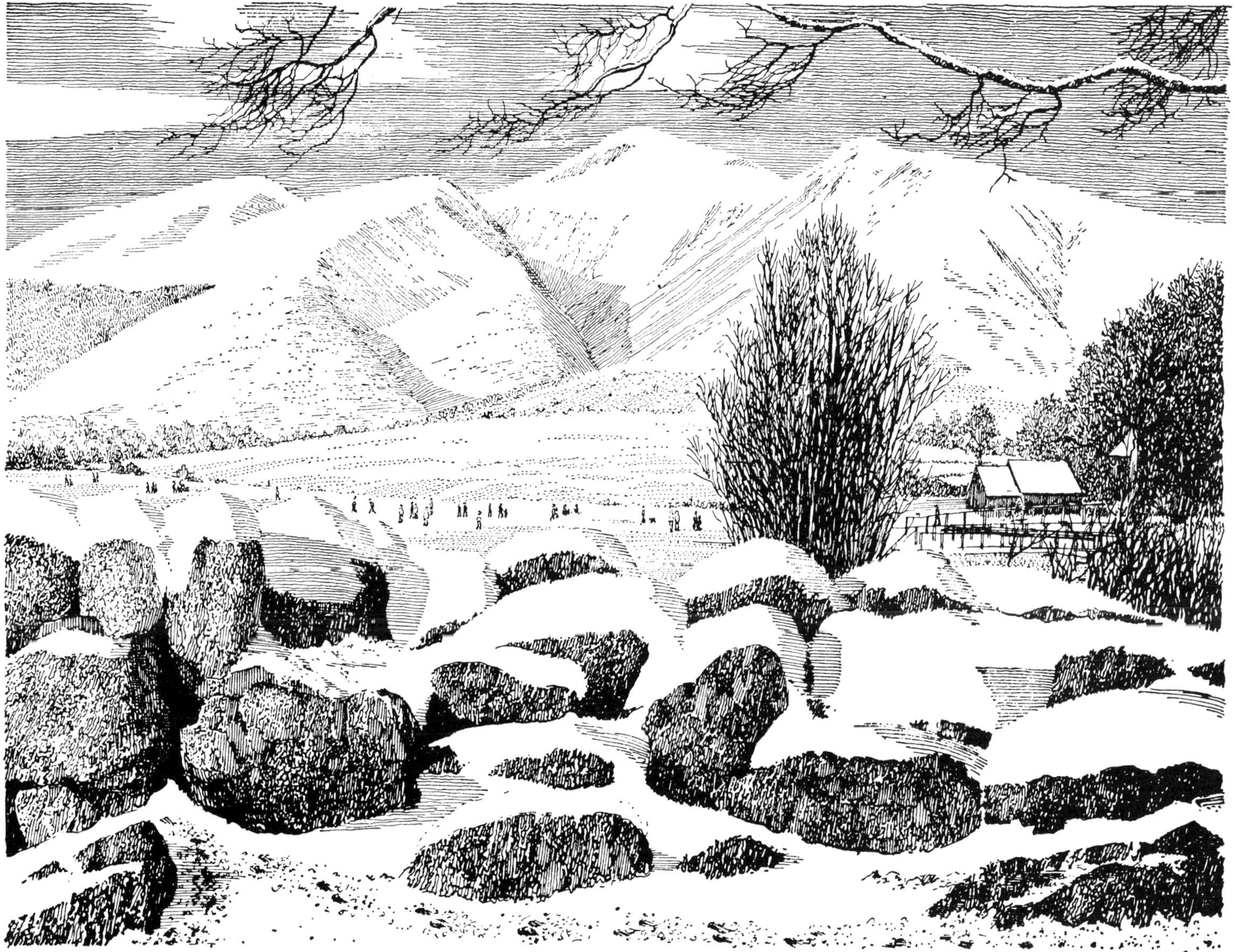

Some mountain features are common to all — the rocky buttresses, the rivers of scree, the fields of boulders — but the Great Slab of Flat Crags on Bowfell is unique: a half-acre of naked rock tilted at an easy angle, but (explorers beware!) cut away abruptly in vertical cliffs.

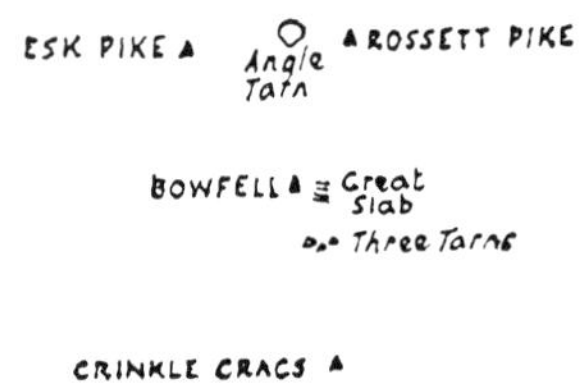

392 Great Slab, Bowfell

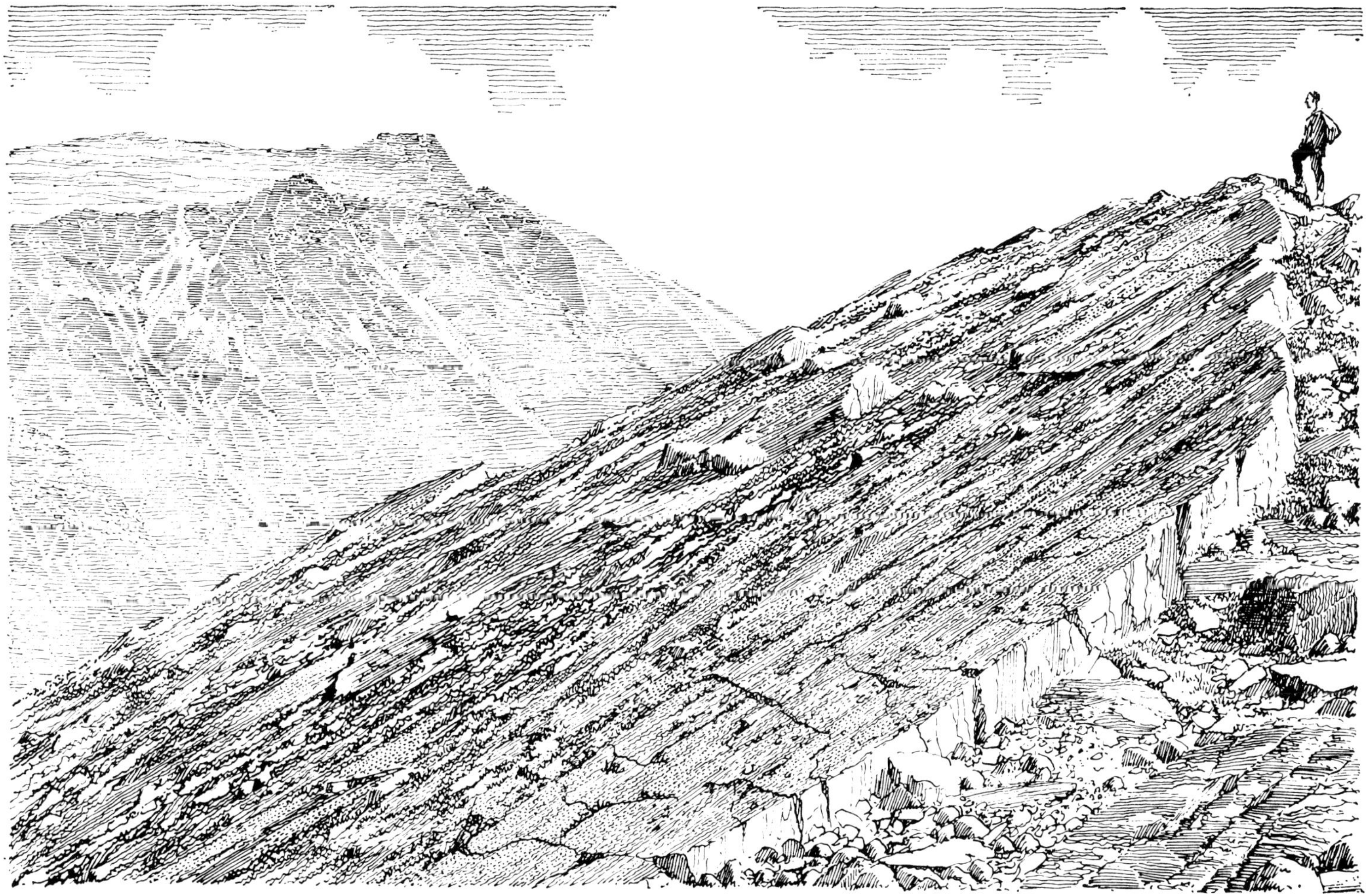

The eastern wall of the shy Swindale valley between Haweswater and Shap is formed by the long escarpment of Gouther Crag. There are rock-climbing routes here but no queues to do them : the remoteness of the valley ensures the crag's immunity from disturbance.

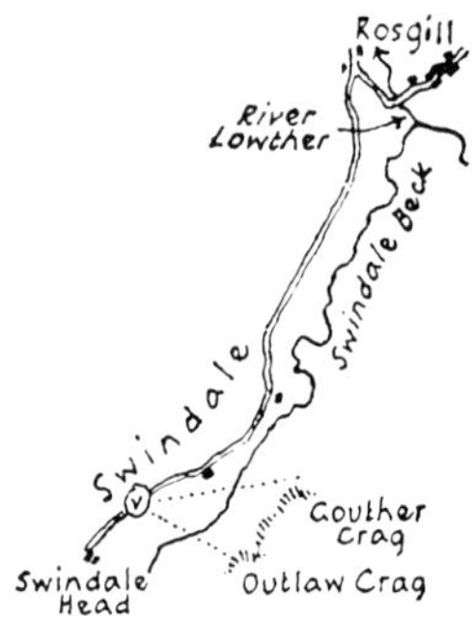

393 Gouther Crag, Swindale

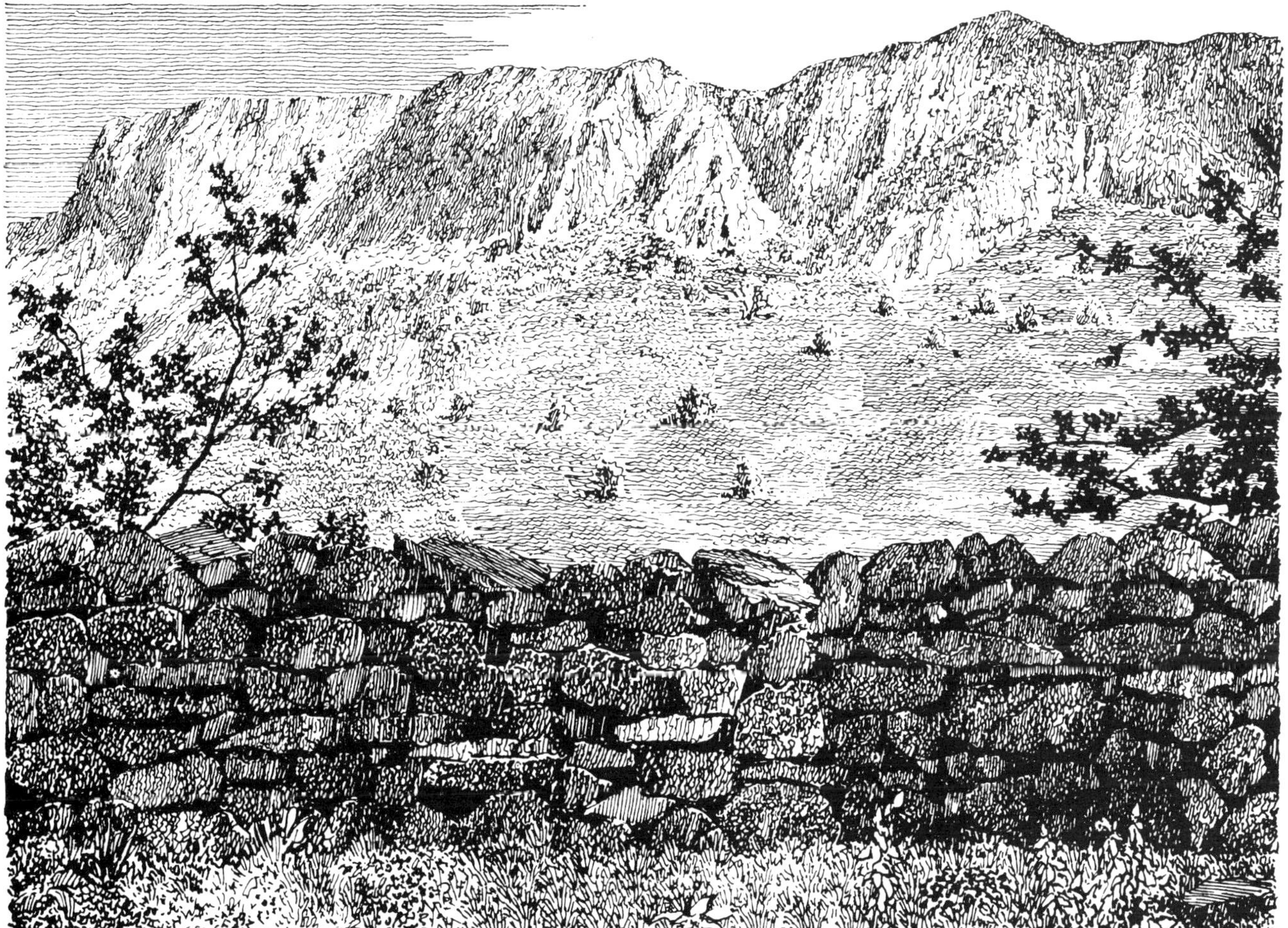

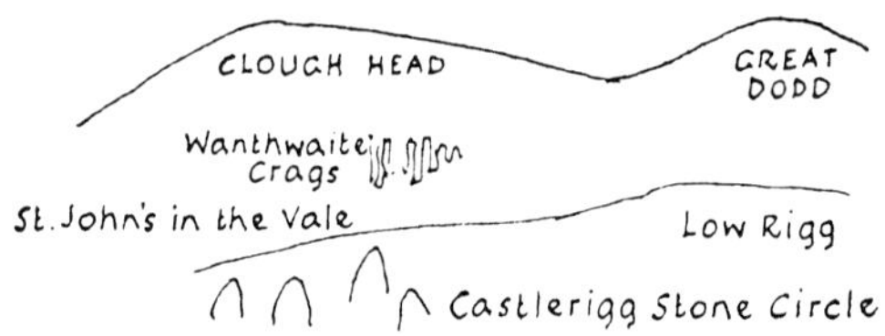

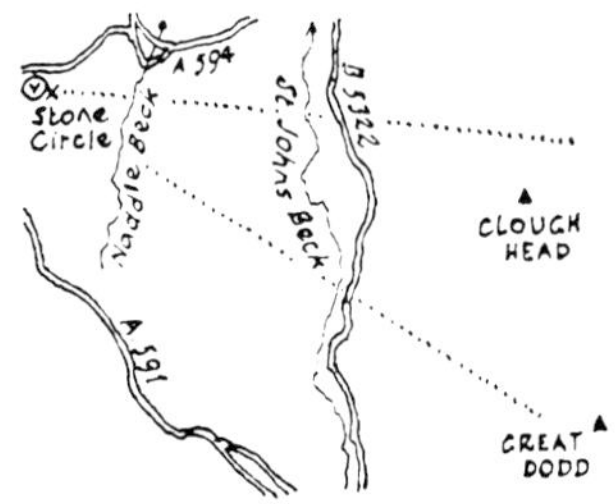

394 Clough Head and Great Dodd

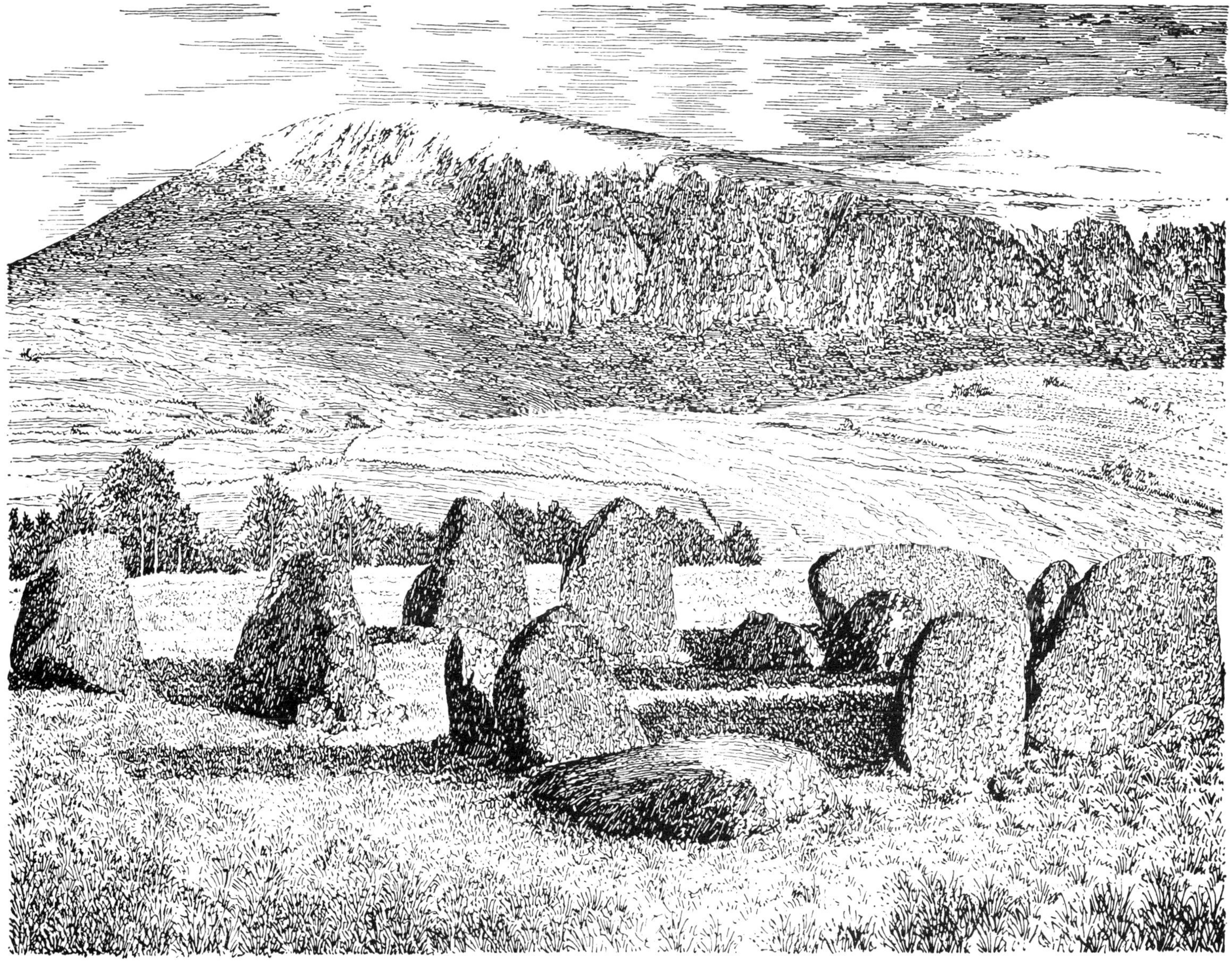

Innominate Tarn, a jewel in the crown of Haystacks, derives its name from the fact of not having one. It was formerly considered to be nameless, although old Ordnance maps indicate it as Loaf Tarn, a title happily forgotten and not good enough for so lovely a gem.

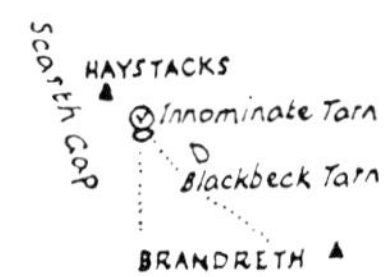

395 Innominate Tarn, Haystacks

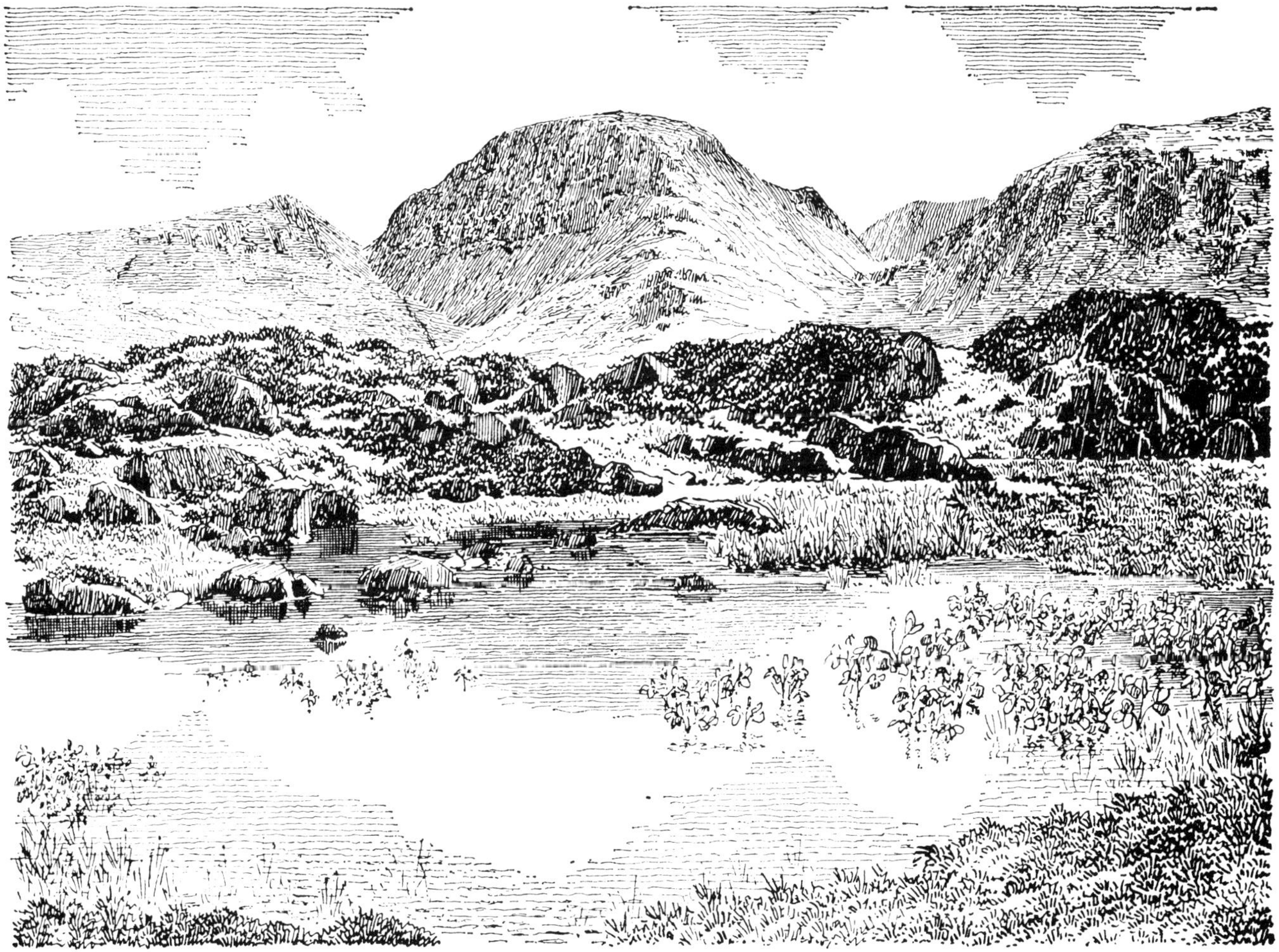

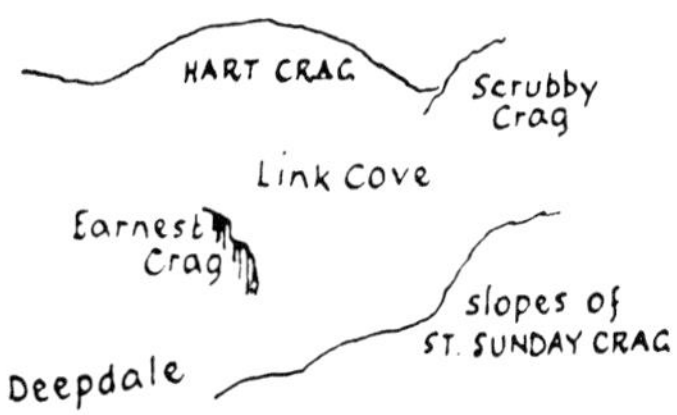
HART CRAG
Scrubby Crag
Link Cove
Earnest Crag
slopes of ST. SUNDAY CRAG
Deepdale

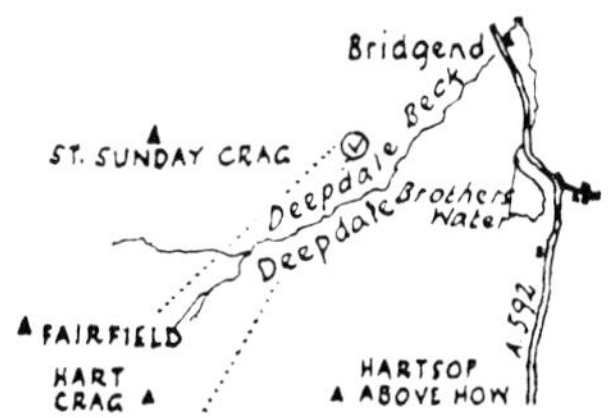
Bridgend
ST. SUNDAY CRAG
Deepdale Beck
Deepdale
Brothers Water
FAIRFIELD
HART CRAG
HARTSOP ABOVE HOW
A 592

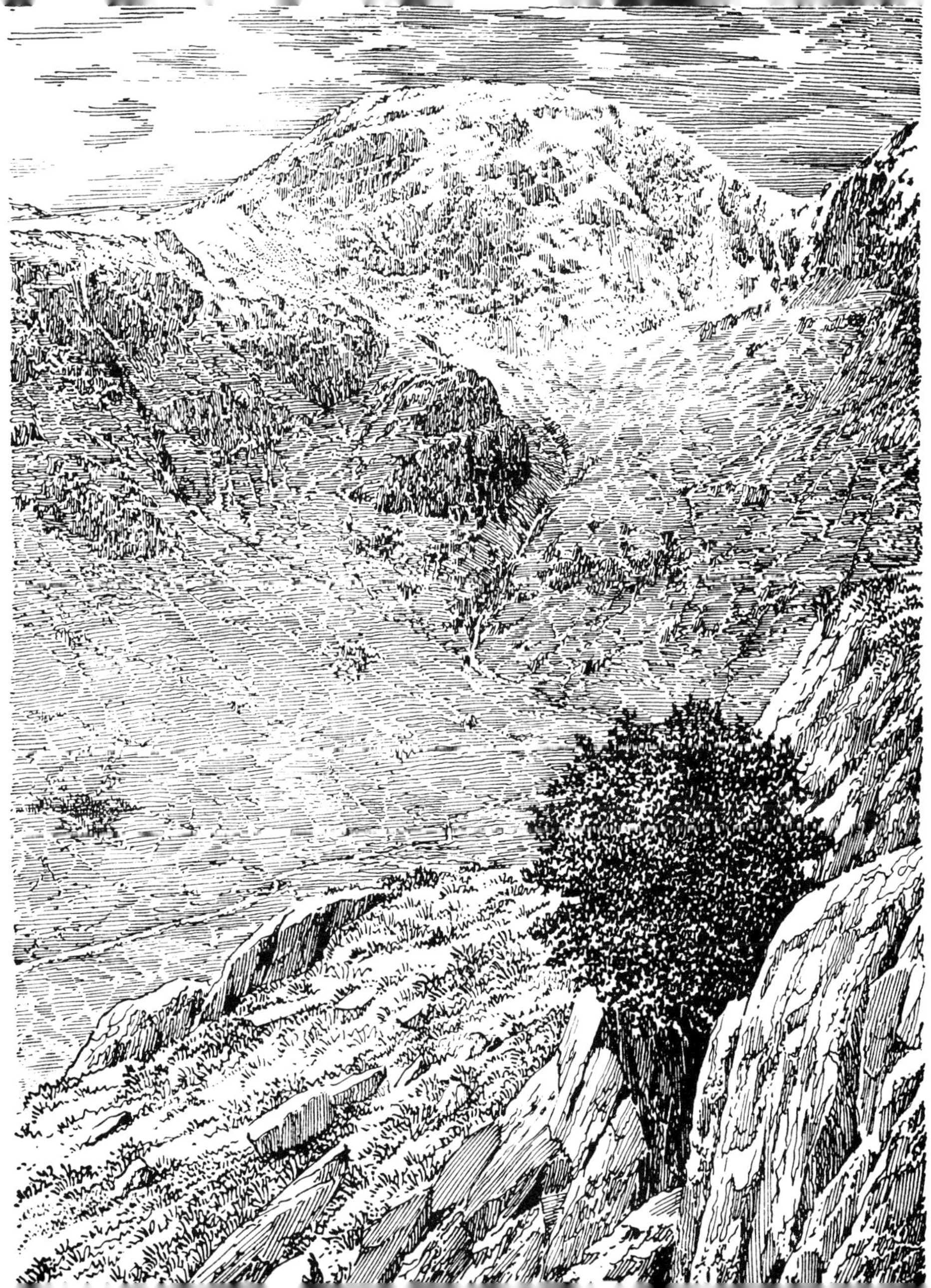

397 **Borrowdale,**
from Great End

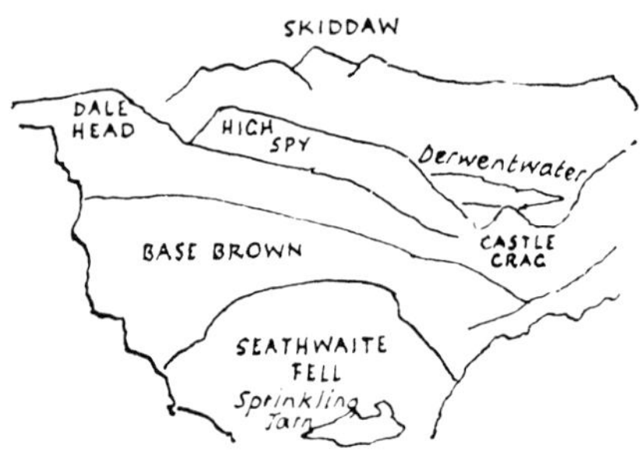

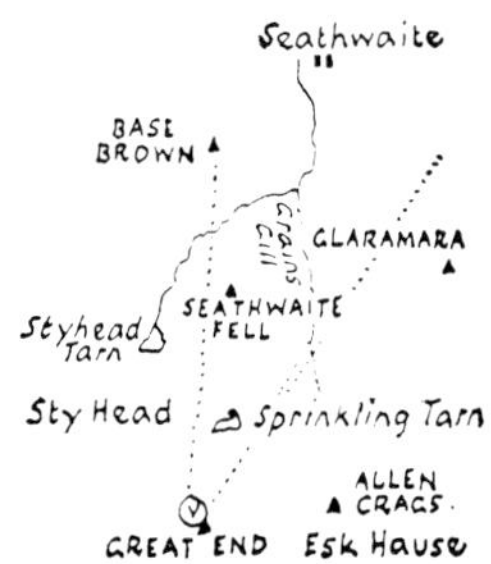

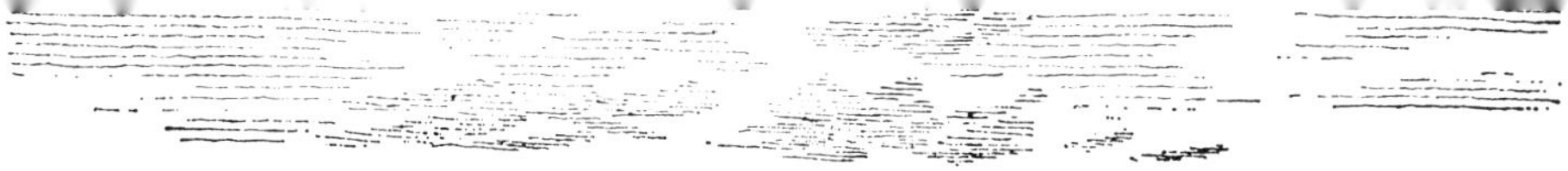

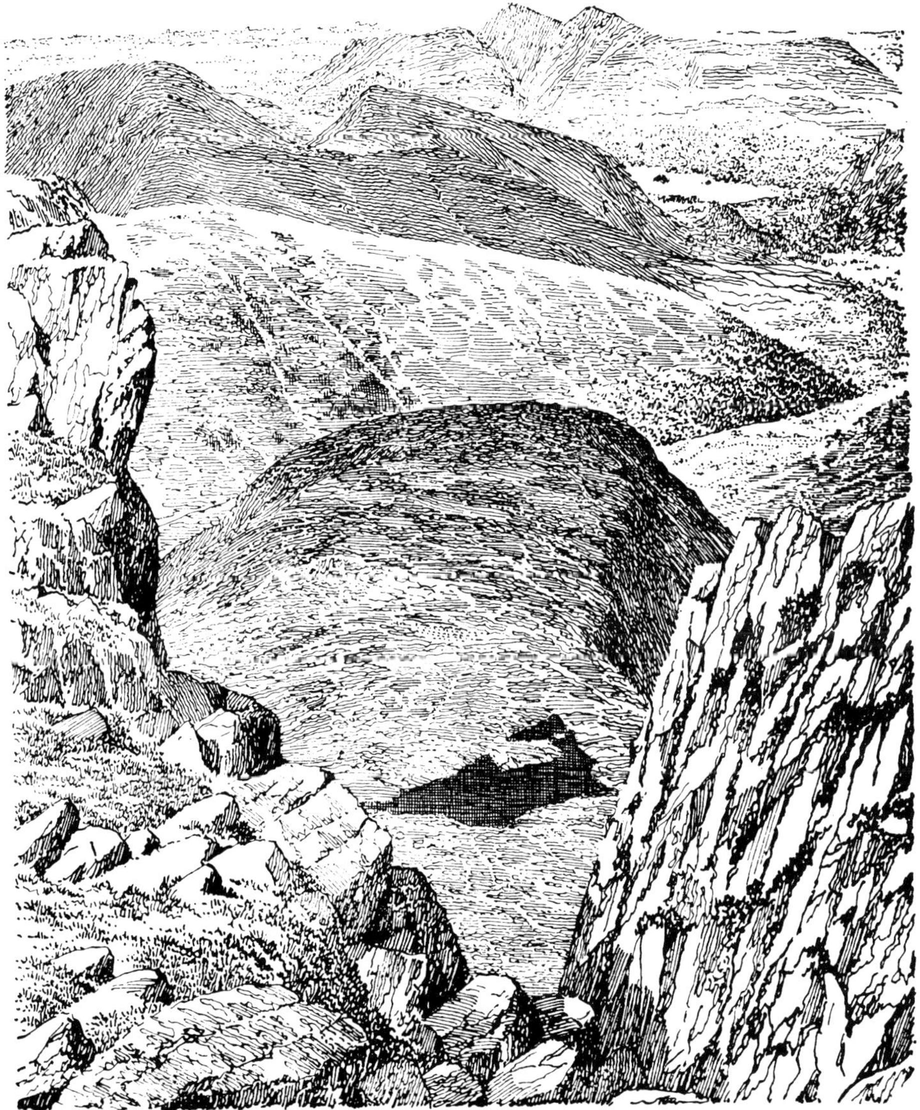

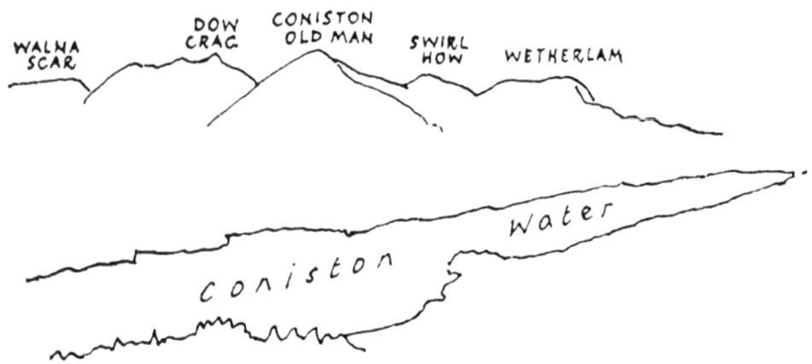

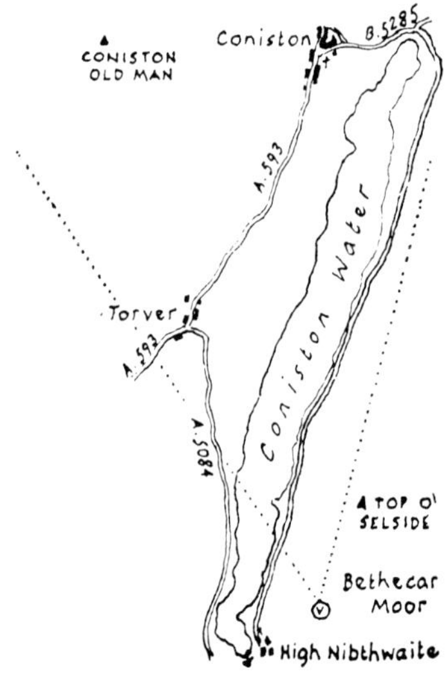

398 Coniston Water

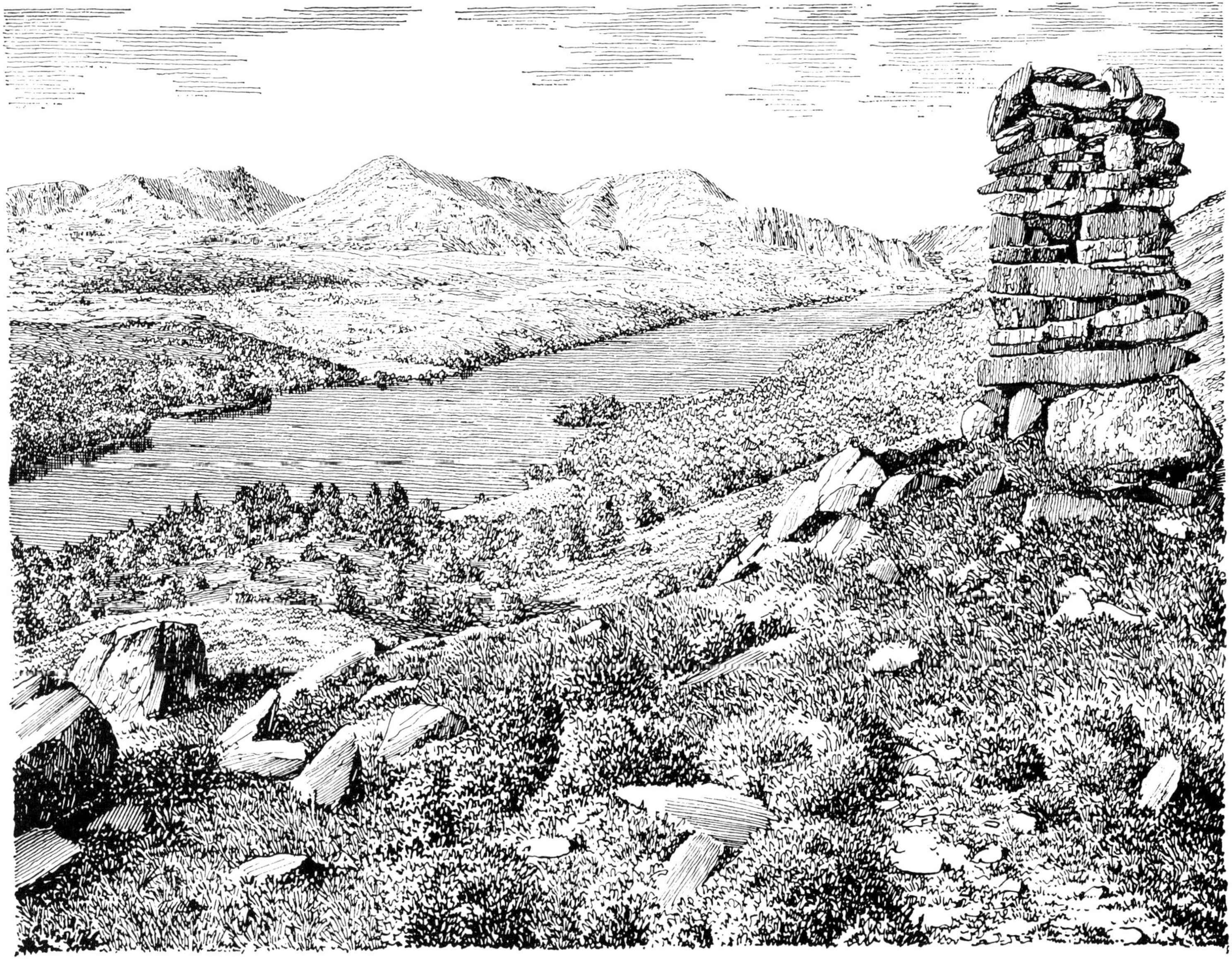

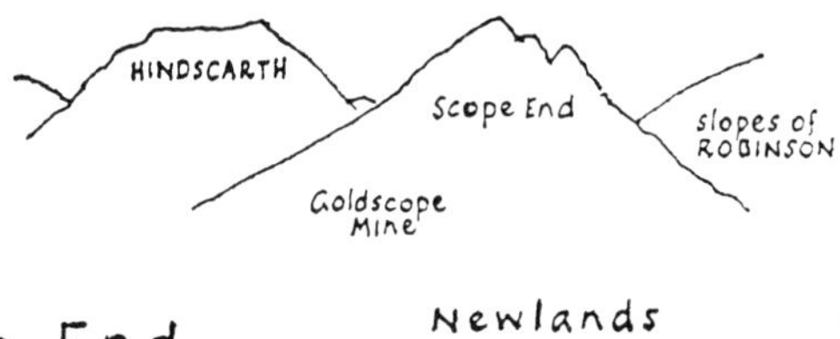

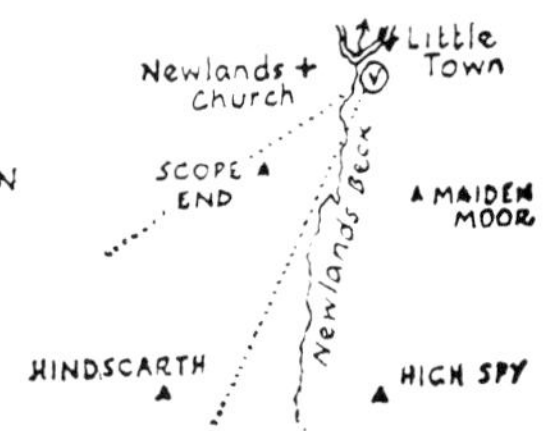

399 Hindscarth and Scope End

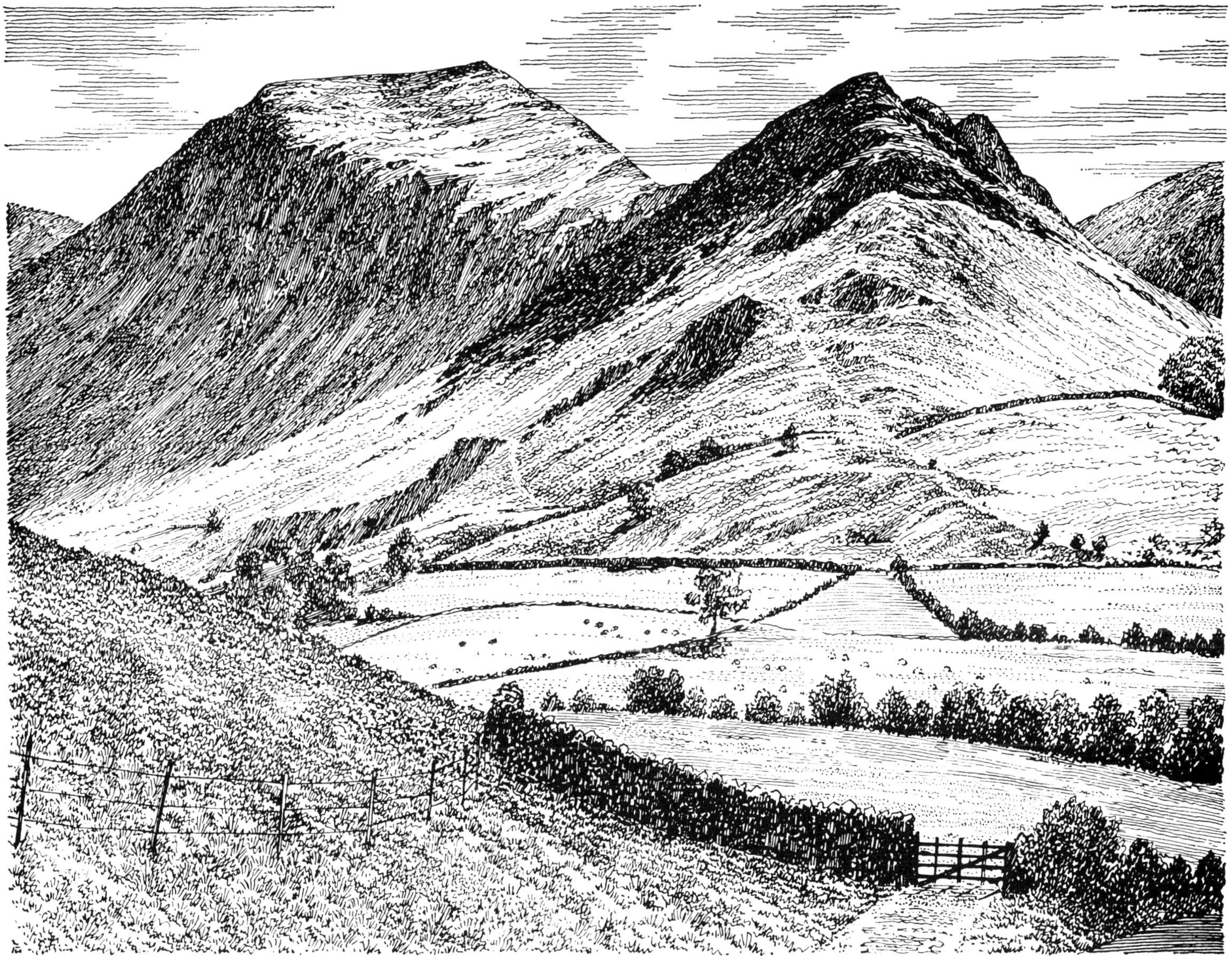

400 Wray Castle

Wray Castle is a familiar sight to those who sail the length of Windermere, its battlemented towers rising above the trees near the water's edge. This is no ancient pile but a 19th century structure built privately in the style of a feudal fortress (complete with sham ruins). It is today owned by the National Trust.

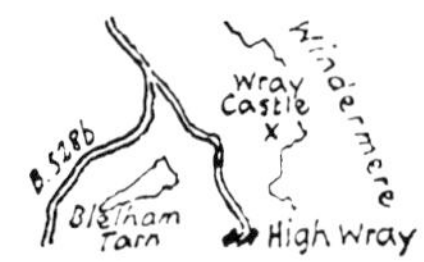

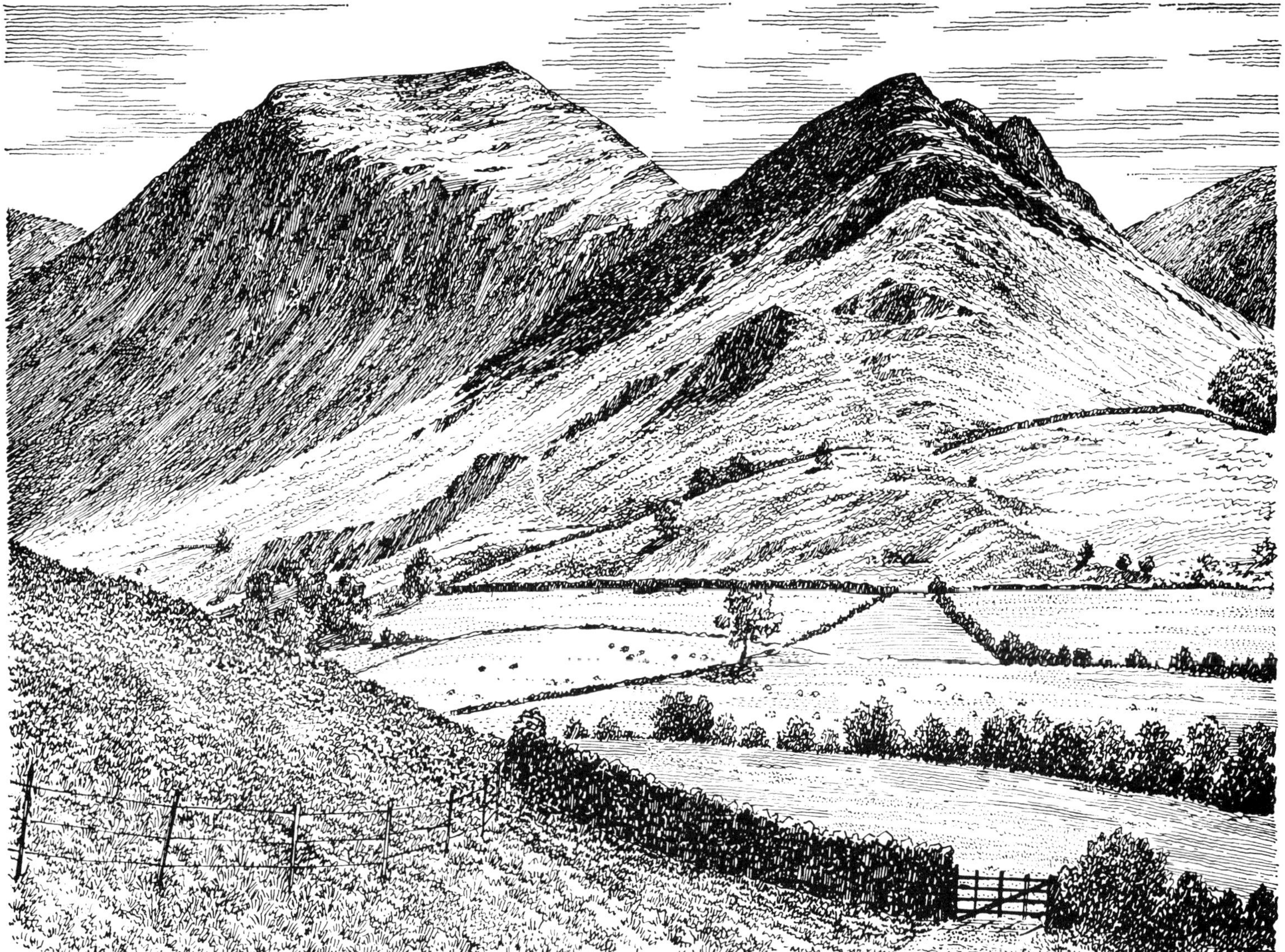

400 Wray Castle

Wray Castle is a familiar sight to those who sail the length of Windermere, its battlemented towers rising above the trees near the water's edge. This is no ancient pile but a 19th century structure built privately in the style of a feudal fortress (complete with sham ruins). It is today owned by the National Trust.

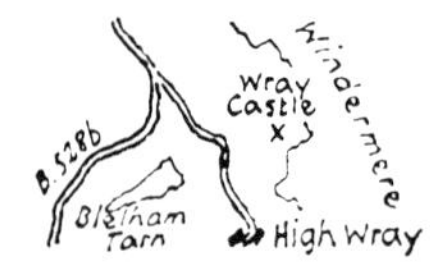

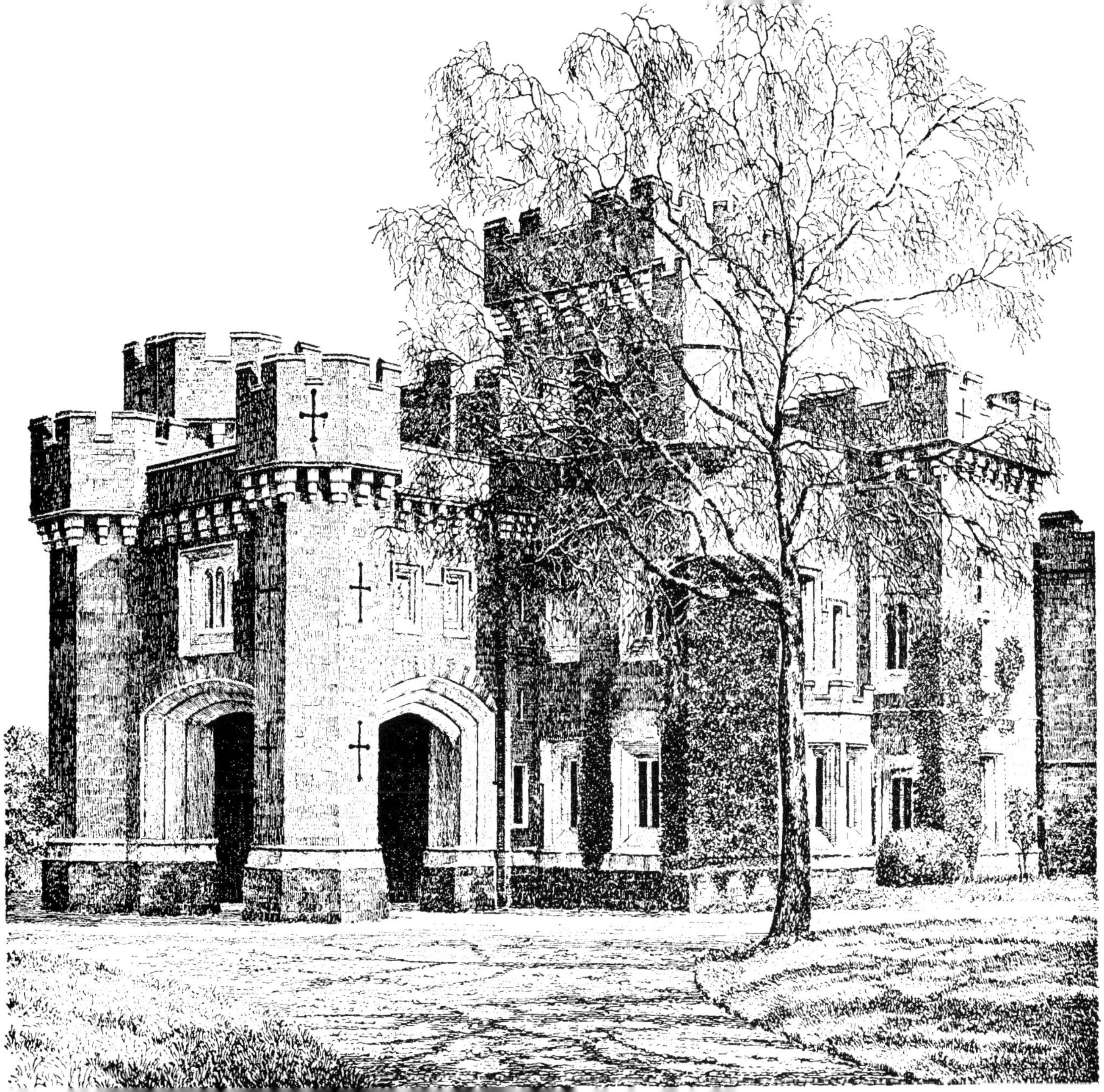